Current Trends in Management Consulting

Edited by

Anthony F. Buono
Bentley College

INFORMATION AGE
PUBLISHING

80 Mason Street
Greenwich, Connecticut 06830

CONTENTS

REFLECTIONS ON MANAGEMENT CONSULTING

INTRODUCTION

Anthony F. Buono

Management consulting has undergone an exponential explosion over the past decade. Most observers readily agree that the industry has experienced tremendous growth—despite the fact that the exact nature of the consulting industry is neither well understood nor well defined. Indeed, one of the difficulties in pinpointing the size, parameters and influence of the management consulting industry lies in lingering disagreements on how to exactly define it—from relatively narrow definitions that include a handful of influential strategy firms (e.g., McKinsey) to the growth and expansion of professional services companies, to the inclusion of "one-man bands" and boutique operations, to much broader views that encompass a full range of outsourcing initiatives particularly in ERP (enterprise resource planning) and technology installation, integration and convergence efforts (cf. Dunford & Clark, 2001; Greiner, 2001; Wooldridge, 1997). Yet, while the way in which management consulting is defined may shape our perception of its parameters and influence, a brief glimpse at the corporate landscape suggests that consultants are literally everywhere.

Complexity and uncertainty in today's fast-paced business world have prompted a growing number of organizations—profit and not-for-profit alike—to seek guidance in their concomitant change efforts. Increased globalization and deregulation, an organizational penchant for reengineering and downsizing, an attempt to reemphasize and build on core competencies, the rise of information technology and the convergence of existing technological systems, and a general competition for ideas and talent have all contributed to a world wide consulting boom (Wooldridge, 1997). As a result, external and internal consultants and change agents have become increasingly visible in most, if not all, organizational initiatives. While some forecasts raise dire assessments about consultants and consulting, even questioning whether traditional management consulting has a future (Greiner, 2001), others are much more positive. From a base of approximately $3 billion per year in 1980, for example, some analysts predict that industry revenues will soar past the $100 billion mark during the early 2000s (Kennedy Research Group, 1998).

Individual consultants and consulting firms are becoming increasingly involved in not only providing organizational clients with advice and new ideas but, in an escalating number of instances, working to implement those ideas and solutions as well. In essence, the boundary between dispensing advice and managing systems is becoming increasingly blurred. Despite these changes and realities, however, management consulting is often criticized for its mystery and ambiguity. Much of the attention on the consulting world was triggered by the publication of *The Witch Doctors* (Micklethwait & Wooldridge, 1996), a penetrating condemnation of the industry that was also captured in a widely read *Economist* supplement. Describing the management consultancy business as a "tale of mystery and imagination," it was suggested that along with the myriad advice given by consultants, a "little witchcraft" seems to be typically thrown in as well (Wooldridge, 1997). Similar critiques have focused on the "unseemly secrets and rites" that characterize the large consulting firms (e.g., Pinault, 2000), the businesses that are literally ruined by following consulting advice (O'Shea & Madigan, 1997), the "shadowy," con-game dimensions of (Ashford, 1998) and "cookie-cutter" approaches to consulting (Pringle, 1998), and even cartoon-based lampoons on the consulting profession (e.g., Adams, 1996). These assessments are a far cry from the bulk of research and writing on consulting that had largely been prescriptive in nature, focusing on an array of recommendations and self-help strategies on how to improve one's consulting efforts—including ways to achieve everything from "flawless" to "high-impact" consulting (cf. Biech, 1998; Block, 1999; Schaffer, 1997). Somewhat between these two extremes lies an emerging focus on professional services firms themselves, including their management, marketing and general operations (e.g., Dunford, 2000; Greenwood & Lachman, 1996; Maister, 1993, 1997).

RESEARCH IN MANAGEMENT CONSULTING

The basic objective of this research series is to capture the concomitant growth and development of research and theory building on management consulting. Our intent is to further the links and dialogue between applied scholars and scholarly practitioners in the consulting field, capturing innovative empirical and conceptual research and field experience as well as critiques and criticisms of the field, and disseminating the resulting insight to a broad range of practitioners, academicians and organizational executives. Targeted articles will focus on a wide range of topics, encompassing research on: the consulting industry itself, including the management, marketing and expansion of professional services firms; critical examinations of current trends in the consulting field; conceptualization and evaluation of intervention techniques and strategies; and reflections on consulting experiences and practices. The series will include interdisciplinary and international perspectives on these different topics as well as perspectives from both internal and external consultants and change agents. Future volumes will focus on knowledge and value development in consulting, consulting in an interorganizational context (mergers, acquisitions, partnerships and alliances), the management of professional services firms, and related aspects of consulting and the consulting industry.

CURRENT TRENDS IN MANAGEMENT CONSULTING

Volume One in this series focuses on current trends in the management consulting industry. It is divided into three sections: (1) a look at some of the broad changes taking place in the management consulting industry, (2) an examination of recent trends and techniques in the practice of management consulting, and (3) reflections on the current state of affairs in the industry.

The Management Consulting Industry

The first section in this volume focuses on the Management Consulting Industry, with three chapters that examine some of the myriad changes taking place in the industry—from the rapid increase in networks across small- and medium-sized consulting firms to the nuances associated with the ways in which professional expertise is delivered to clients and the ways in which consulting firms amass and disseminate information.

According to Kari Lilja and Flemming Poulfelt, management consulting, especially within small- and medium-sized firms, is increasingly being delivered via a network of relationships. The article identifies three operating modes—creativity, experience and procedure-based practices—that differ along a number of dimensions, including type of work system, client relationships, management effort, and external network relationships. By conceptualizing these different operating modes, Lilja and Poulfelt create several propositions about the various ways in which different types of network relations across consulting operations are formed and implemented. Researchers should find the framework and propositions useful as a baseline for guiding field-based studies and for making sense of the ways in which consulting-related capabilities are mobilized to meet the needs of different aspects of organizational and client systems.

While professional services represent a growing and critical type of consulting, there has been a paucity of research on *how* such professional expertise is delivered to the client. Kate Walsh considers ways in which consultants use a relational approach to provide their expertise. Although relational approaches—in contrast to more traditional, expert-based approaches—to service delivery are typically linked to gender dynamics, Walsh found that a relational approach to consulting was successfully employed by both women and men within the context of their organization's structure and reward system. As the foundation for her analysis, Walsh characterizes a relational approach by four specific traits: (1) empowering vs. advising the client, (2) learning from the client vs. taking information away from a project, (3) being dependent on vs. independent from the client, and (4) asking questions and listening vs. telling information. Walsh concludes that the use of this type of relational approach enabled the professionals in her study to skillfully determine the best way to meet their clients' needs.

In the final chapter in this section, Matt Semadeni draws on knowledge arbitrage theory to suggest that consultants, as knowledge brokers, perform the dual roles of knowledge arbitrageur (which focuses on knowledge diffusion) and knowledge arbiter (which focuses on knowledge adjudication). According to Semadeni, the tensions between these roles provide insight into the knowledge creation and diffusion process, including the potential loss of competitive knowledge by clients as consultants "liberate" this knowledge to apply it to other clients, knowledge isomorphism and homogeneity leading to "cookie-cutter" solutions to organizational problems, knowledge cross-pollination of industry-specific data, and the accrual of power by consulting firms as knowledge brokers. As further explored in a later chapter by Bertrand Venard, this knowledge arbitrage process creates an environment that is fertile ground for the planting of management fad and fashion seeds by consultants as knowledge arbitrageurs. Given the pressures associated with the time-to-market rush for new management concepts and ideas, consultants—as management "fashion setters"—often find themselves in a literal race to get their ideas (fashions) out to market before their competitors (see Abrahamson, 1996). As Semadeni argues, those fashion setters who delay in advocating and disseminating new concepts risk being labeled as "laggards," having their contribution marginalized, and being left behind in a dynamic, ever-changing industry.

Tools and Techniques in Management Consulting

The second section of the volume contains four chapters that focus on current trends and techniques in consulting, examining the growing focus on emotional intelligence and executive coaching, the changing nature of project management-oriented consulting, the use of an integrated, socio-economic approach to organizational diagnosis and analysis, and the use of linking research as a tool to enhance customer satisfaction.

The first chapter by Aaron Nurick examines the considerable popularity of "emotional intelligence" (EQ) in both academic and business environments. As EQ has also captured the imagination of the general culture, the concept (which deals with such non-cognitive factors such as empathy, adaptability and related interpersonal skills) has given rise to numerous opportunities for consultants to work with organizations and their managers to develop innovative approaches, interventions and programs (e.g., executive coaching). Nurick reviews the theoretical development of emotional intelligence as a concept and provides an intervention model based on the application of Reuven Bar-On's (1997) Emotional Quotient Inventory (EQ-i) as a diagnostic instrument. The resulting process model focuses on how to work with EQ data to develop targeted interventions that are meaningful for the client, avoiding the pitfalls of quick-fix fads associated with selling products that promise immediate success.

In the next chapter, Hans Thamhain suggests that while most business leaders would readily agree that project management provides an important tool set for implementing a broad array of ventures, there is also a growing sense of frustration that these efforts create value in some situations while leading to disappointment or even outright disaster in others. The chapter explores the multitude of forces that is driving today's project management environment, and the ramifications these trends have for consulting interventions. Thamhain's analysis and prescriptions develop criteria for effective project management consulting, which link the tools and systems approach of project management with a change management orientation. His recommendations include the need to align project system improvements with company goals, the need for clearly defined objectives, directions and implementation plans, the importance of custom-designed interventions, the critical role played by involvement and participation strategies, and, in general, the need to engage the organization in a systematic evaluation of its specific competencies and improvement opportunities.

The next contribution is by a team of researchers from France's Socio-Economic Institute of Organizations (ISEOR). Henri Savall, Veronique Zardet, Marc Bonnet and Rickie Moore present a system wide, integrated framework that reflects the ISEOR approach to organizational analysis and intervention. Briefly tracing the development and evolution of ISEOR, Savall and his colleagues discuss their socioeconomic approach to management (SEAM), an approach that focuses on the multifaceted nature of organizational dysfunctions and the hidden costs associated with such problems. By combining the academic tradition of directed research with the consulting tradition of intervention and organizational improvement,

Savall and associates provide a useful framework for conceptualizing and guiding large-scale consulting projects.

This section concludes with an examination of linking research, and the emphasis on the relationship between employee and customer satisfaction. As Kyle Lundby, Kristofer Fenalson, and Shon Magnan argue, linking research has become increasingly valued, especially by consultants, because it provides insights into cause and effect relationships within and outside organizations. While the most popular linking models differ slightly in detail, Lundby and his associates note that they all share a common emphasis on the relationship between employee and customer satisfaction. Consequently, many organizations now pursue employee satisfaction as a sort of "Holy Grail" in the belief that this focus is the clearest path to customer satisfaction. The authors, however, believe that, while important, employee satisfaction is only one of many paths to customer satisfaction. Using structural equation modeling, Lundby, et al compare nested models containing several employee variables (satisfaction, empowerment, workgroup functioning, and supervision) and customer satisfaction. Based on their finding that models which incorporate a broader range of organizational variables that directly and indirectly influence customer satisfaction (through employee satisfaction) are more robust, they suggest that management consultants engaged in their own linking research should emphasize employee satisfaction within the context of other potential factors and relationships.

Reflections on Management Consulting

The final section in the volume contains three chapters that probe the current state of the field, looking at the ramifications of different ways of conceptualizing change and change-related processes, how consulting knowledge and insight are typically transformed into management fads and fashions, and the extent to which business school curricula are meeting the changing needs of the management consulting industry.

The challenges of organizational change were made visible in a powerful way during the corporate downsizing activities of the 1980s. These and other experiences, such as the frequent failures of reengineering, acquisitions, and alliances, have helped to identify key factors impacting the effectiveness of planned change. Yet, as Kenneth Kerber argues, while change management has emerged as a popular approach for mitigating the well-known negative impact of change on productivity, even well managed change continues to result, more often than not, in significant reductions in productivity. Kerber suggests that an approach to addressing the productivity loss associated with planned change may be to increase the effectiveness of continuous organizational change initiatives. Drawing on experiences with various change initiatives at 3Com Corporation, the chapter proposes ways in which support for continuous change ("guided changing") might be embedded in an organization's culture.

The next chapter by Bertrand Venard examines how consultants contribute to the spread and practice of management fads and fashions—an increasingly common aspect of contemporary business life. Drawing on his experience as a Senior Management Consultant in two large consulting firms, Venard thoughtfully examines the initial creation of such fads and fashions, tracing their development, expansion and ultimate decline when they are replaced with the next management fad. His analysis draws out the broader ramifications of this knowledge development process, with implications for both consultants and their clients. Venard's analysis points to the need for a higher level of consultant-client involvement in the consulting process (e.g., in data gathering and analysis) with joint control of the consultancy process itself, spreading the resulting knowledge among key employees throughout the client organization, and client input for the selection of the team of consultants who have developed knowledge about the client and its environment. He also calls for consultants to be true agents of change, bringing objectivity and legitimacy to the consulting assignment and a focus on problem solving and the knowledge creation process rather than the creation of management fashion and fads.

Finally, Susan Adams and Alberto Zanzi explore the extent to which business school curricula are geared toward enhancing student consulting skills and capabilities in a way that meets the changing needs of organizations in the Information Age. Based on their categorization of career stages for consultants, their analysis sheds light (1) on the developmental needs of aspiring and current consultants, and (2) how academic institutions can play a bigger role in developing consultants for the Information Age. Looking at the needs of a host of consultant types—which range from raw recruits to accidental entrants and expert contributors to junior and managing consultants—Adams and Zanzi conclude that B-schools are falling short of meeting the concomitant challenges the Information Age poses for the consulting industry. Their findings indicate that there is a decided lack of consensus on content, format, and placement within curriculum for consulting-oriented course work, and student need for industry knowledge, fieldwork, and an understanding of internal consulting is underserviced by current course offerings. As Adams and Zanzi conclude, B-schools need to enhance both the availability and content of course offerings if they are to adequately prepare the burgeoning market of aspiring and practicing consultants for the demands of the Information Age.

As this brief overview has hopefully captured, the first volume in this series provides ample insight into and differing perspectives on the multifaceted world of management consulting. Thanks are due to all the authors for their thoughtful work, good-natured colleagueship, and willingness to contribute their thoughts and insights about the consulting field. This volume would not have been possible without their efforts.

REFERENCES

Abrahamson, E. (1996). Management fashion. *Academy of Management Review, 21*(1), 254–285.

Adams, S. (1996). *The Dilbert principle.* New York: Harper Business.

Ashford, M. (1998). *Con tricks: The shadowy world of management consultancy and how to make it work for you.* London: Simon & Schuster.

Bar-On, R. (1997). *Bar-On Emotional Quotient Inventory technical manual.* Toronto: Multi-Health Systems.

Biech, R. (1998). *The business of consulting: The basics and beyond.* San Francisco: Pfeiffer & Co.

Block, P. (1999). *Flawless consulting: A guide to getting your expertise used.* San Francisco: Jossey-Bass.

Dunford, R. (2000). *Key challenges in the search for the effective management of knowledge in management consulting firms.* Paper presented at the Academy of Management, Toronto, Canada.

Dunford, R., & Clark, T. (2001). *The developing critique of management consulting: The critics, the criticisms and the implications.* Symposium presented at the Academy of Management, Washington, DC.

Greenwood, R., & Lachman, R. (1996). Change as an underlying theme in professional services firms: An introduction. *Organization Studies, 17,* 563–572.

Greiner, L. (2001). *Does consulting have a future?* Keynote address, International Conference on Knowledge and Value Development in Management Consulting, Lyon, France.

Kennedy Research Group. (1998, January 7). Kennedy Research predicts $114 billion consulting market by 2000. *Kennedy Research Group,* Fitzwilliam, NH.

Maister, D.H. (1997). *True professionalism: The courage to care about your people, your clients, and your career.* New York: Free Press.

Maister, D.H. (1993). *Managing the professional services firm.* New York: Free Press.

Micklethwait, J., & Wooldridge, A. (1996). *The witch doctors: Making sense of management gurus.* New York: Times Books.

O'Shea, J., & Madigan, C. (1997). *Dangerous company: The consulting powerhouses and the businesses they save and ruin.* New York: Random House.

Pinault, L. (2000). *Consulting demons: Inside the unscrupulous world of global corporate consulting.* New York: Harper Business.

Pringle, E.G. (1998). Do proprietary tools lead to cookie cutter consulting? *Journal of Management Consulting, 10*(1), 3–7.

Schaffer, R.H. (1997). *High-impact consulting.* San Francisco: Jossey-Bass.

Wooldridge, A. (1997, March 22). Management consultancy: The advice business. *The Economist,* Supplement, pp. 1–22.

PART I

THE MANAGEMENT CONSULTING INDUSTRY

CHAPTER 1

THE ANATOMY OF NETWORK BUILDING IN MANAGEMENT CONSULTING FIRMS[1]

Kari Lilja and Flemming Poulfelt

INTRODUCTION

The management consulting business has undergone significant change over the last ten years. The demand for management consulting services has increased (Byrne, 1994; *Economist*, 1997; Kyrö, 1999; Talouselämä, 4/1999), international management consulting firms have established offices in the capitals and business centers of most European countries, and many of the medium-sized management consulting firms have been acquired by or merged with larger international firms. These dynamics have changed the competitive scene in the management consulting business, especially in smaller European countries (Erhvervsfremmestyrelsen, 1999; Tienari, 1999). Andersen Consulting, which has recently become an independent entity as Accenture, for example, advertised the presence of 260 management consultants in its Copenhagen office and 250 in its Helsinki office by the end of 1999. These offices can draw on the support of more than 50,000 experts working within the entire corporation, providing wide-scale support for a range of assignments that would be difficult, if not impossible, for more ethnocentric, small- and medium-sized consulting firms.

In response to such competitive pressures, a growing number of small- and medium-sized management consulting firms are forming collaborative networks, enabling them to create social and inter-organizational relationships that substitute collaboration across inter-firm competencies for internal organizational growth (Kanter, 1994). Yet, despite the potential of such collaborative endeavors, it has proven difficult to combine the person-based client relationships, capabilities and personalities of experienced consultants with the economic framework of joint partnership or even looser types of social and organizational networks (Ram, 1999).

The literature on network relations between management consulting firms is largely normative in nature (e.g., Sabath, 1992) or based on questionnaires with low validity (e.g., Berry & Oakley, 1994). Building on this work, our research is based on in-depth fieldwork, combining a series of dialogues with practicing management consultants, participation in training sessions for management consultants, attendance at conferences on management consulting, and participant-observer roles on the boards of management consulting firms. We have also had access to the case studies on representative assignment projects of management consultants for the Certified Management Consultant (CMC) title. These observations, which are based on more than ten years of experience, have gradually been complemented with more than 100 focused interviews with key management consultants, predominantly in Denmark and Finland. Overall, the data provide an overview of the operations of thirty small- and medium-sized management consulting firms. In addition, we have collected and analyzed numerous documentary materials, including relevant trade publications and professional association literature (e.g., *Management Consultant International*, Institute of Management Consultancy), brochures of consulting firms, and internal strategy documents.

DYNAMICS OF NETWORK BUILDING IN MANAGEMENT CONSULTING FIRMS

Our observations on network relations can be divided into two basic categories. The first illustrates the difficulties inherent in collaboration and network building, emphasizing such dynamics as "wait-and-see" attitudes, frustration around collaborative endeavors, suspicion, jealousy, and failures in joint action. The breakup of consulting firms is a fairly common phenomenon and the mismatch of chemistries among self-conscious consultants is well known. In strategic alliances, cross-firm coordination of frameworks, tools and styles is often missing, and it takes a long time from initial joint product development initiatives to a steady stream of assignments. There are, indeed, many traps in collaboration among independent experts (Empson & Morris, 1997; Ram, 1999; Sabath, 1992). In fact, it is becoming increasingly obvious that "abortive tracks" (Greenwood & Hinings, 1988) are more common than collaborative competence development and successful common assignments in such endeavors.

The second category contains observations on successes in network building. These observations have been complemented with secondary sources on network relations between management consultants and consulting firms (Alvesson, 1993; Empson & Morris, 1997; Ram, 1999; Sturdy, 1997; Viitanen, 1993). This perspective provides a new angle for making sense of the quest for network relations. One of the major problems of such assessments, however, is that the descriptive content about these networks fails to provide sufficient conceptual tools to analyze and understand the requisite collaborative expert action needed across consultants from different firms. Similarly, the general social and inter-organizational network frameworks (e.g., Miles & Snow, 1986, 1992; Powell, 1990; Scott, 1991) are not sufficiently sensitive to these issues, falling well short of capturing the substantive content of the work system in management consulting.

In order to tackle this issue, we found Maister's (1993) conceptual framework of three types of practice in professional service firms to be a good analytical starting point. Maister uses metaphors—"Brains," "Grey Hair" and "Procedure"—that are characterized along different dimensions. Creativity, for example, is the dominant characteristic of the "Brains" mode. "Grey Hair," in contrast, reflects the accumulation of professional experience, and "Procedure" denotes efficiency in operations, which is the major reason for a client deciding to buy a service offered. Since internal differentiation in work systems and client relations has been recognized in the literature on professions (Abbott, 1998, 1991) and on professional service firms (Löwendahl, 1997; Winch & Schneider, 1993), we suggest that by conceptually expanding Maister's operating modes his metaphoric ideal types can be translated into analytical tools (e.g., Tsoukas, 1991) that are more sensitive to the distinctiveness of management consulting firms.

Maister (1993) also suggests that professional service firms can move from one operating mode to another during their life cycle. Our view is that these types of operating modes and their life cycle-based changes reflect important dynamics in the operation of small- and medium-sized management consulting firms. An underlying assumption is that while operating modes are ontologically more fundamental than network relations, in many instances operating modes and network relations will be strongly interrelated. Thus, it is our thesis that *understanding the different operating modes of management consulting firms will help uncover the typical ways in which network relations are used to enhance the capabilities of small- and medium-sized management consulting firms.*

Our approach is based on three deductive steps. First, it is necessary to *elaborate conceptually the variety in operating modes.* This step can be accomplished by introducing descriptive categories that characterize a firm's internal systems, such as the prime purpose of the firm, the way it is managed, and various sub-processes of its work system (e.g., the nature of its knowledge base, types of assignments, how the knowledge base is marketed). The conceptual distinctions that elaborate the typical features of the operating modes at the sub-process level provide a language that facilitates a more robust description of the relations between operating modes and network types.

The second step is to *provide a systematic overview the different network types described in the literature on management consulting firms.* Finally, it is necessary to *formulate propositions on the patterning of ideal typical operating modes and network types.* This process can be done deductively by building on the conceptual distinctions and reasoning drawn from our fieldwork. The size of the sample, unfortunately, does not allow us to make generalizations from the available cases and interviews. Moreover, our fieldwork experience further suggests that nomothetic ideals of the nature of scientific knowledge do not reflect the day-to-day reality of small- and medium-sized consulting firms. Situational opportunism is widespread in choosing service concepts, and the consistency of their operations over time is very dependent on individuals.

OPERATING MODES IN MANAGEMENT CONSULTING PRACTICES

Our three operating modes—creativity, experience and efficiency—differ on several dimensions. First, there appears to be great variety among practitioners in their emphasis on profit versus content of work as to the type of intellectual challenge they are seeking. Second, the operating modes clearly require different management inputs and styles. Third, the three sub-processes in the work system—development of the knowledge base, its marketing and assignment delivery—have very different characteristics in the three operating modes (see Table 1). This section outlines some of the differences in operating modes with respect to the sub-processes in the work system. The dominant purpose and the type of managerial input are only taken as contextual influences for the work systems. By distinguishing these differences it becomes possible to uncover potentials and obstacles for collaborative expert action.

Table 1.   Operating Modes in Management Consultant Practice

	Efficiency	Experience	Creativity
Prime purpose	Profits	Competence building and business development	Intellectual challenges and increased reputation
Knowledge base	Turning established knowledge into action programs	Updating framework based knowledge and expanding experiences	Renewing knowledge by combining best practices with leading research
Marketing	Strong investment in specialized marketing	Marketing based on the reputation of assignments	Marketing based on the personality and reputation of exceptional knowledge base/consultants
Assignment delivery	Executing standardized procedures	Customized implementation of concepts and experiences	Solving unstructured problems with highly skilled clients
Managerial content in the work system	Strong management control of the work system	Semi autonomous work system with management back up	Work system driven by need to generate new knowledge

As a comparison point, the internal heterogeneity of the restaurant business is very similar to the management consulting business (Maister, 1993, 28). We encounter chefs who are constantly experimenting with new types of cuisine and find satisfaction in their work from exploratory cycles. Breaking new ground makes them also interesting from the perspective of the wider community of practitioners and well-informed customers. At the other end of the spectrum, we have fast-food outlets such as McDonald's where standardization of the work and management processes have resulted in predictable quality, profits and worldwide expansion but far less fame among the culinarists.

In the management consulting industry, the variety characterized above can be traced in the nature of knowledge obtained and offered as expert service. We suggest that the variety in knowledge base can be captured by the distinction between (1) programmed knowledge, (2) partially-programmed knowledge, and (3) unprogrammed knowledge. These differences reflect and expand well-known conceptual dichotomies, such as routine and genuine decisions and behavior, closed and open social systems, and exploitative and exploratory modes of organizational learning (cf. Lilja, Penn, & Tainio, 1993; March, 1991b). The main elaboration is related to the category of partially-programmed knowledge. Our observation is that partially-programmed knowledge is the most typical form of knowledge base in management consulting firms. Thus, understanding this form is critical in explaining why consulting firms succeed (or fail), in essence how they are able to stay in business.

The Efficiency Mode

As reflected in Table 1, the *efficiency mode* is based on *programmed knowledge*. This type of knowledge is generally available and is built on causal relationships or teleological regularity. It can be stated in the form of "if, then" statements. In most cases, relationships are only probabilities, but for practical reasons, this establishes a plausibility that is tested by experience. Programmed knowledge is similar to what Whitley (1988) refers to as "principles."

In a consulting firm, programmed knowledge is the systematization of operative practices into product-like services and tools. As a consulting product, it can take many forms: books, detailed manuals, training courses, videos, software or standardized questionnaire studies linked with data bases for comparative profiles of results for feedback sessions or benchmark assignments. In most cases, specificity to individual client organizations is low. As knowledge is standardized, it is highly transferable among various actors in the consulting firm. The target segment of clients is typically managers in charge of operational routines. Drawing on Abbott's (1988) model of professional work—which contains the interrelated activities of diagnosis, inference and treatment—the client could be said to be in a position to do the diagnosis and select the proper treatment. The client, however, prefers to buy the treatment procedure from the market of standardized professional services.

The Experience Mode

The *experience mode* is based on *partially-programmed knowledge*. This type of knowledge rests on rather generic concepts and frameworks that are known to specific managerial communities, such as experts in specific functional areas. The frameworks and models provide a joint language and jargon for communication. They specify cognitive maps and means-end relations. This knowledge type, however, differs from the programmed type of knowledge in three ways. First, the objects of knowledge are rather wide and complex action systems, such as functional areas in business management or cross-functional organizational development processes. Second, the frameworks comprise several levels of abstraction. This means that their application in specific situations requires considerable experience and ability to improvise. Third, the consulting service does not imply a "one best way" approach. Instead, it consists of optional modules of knowledge and repertoires of analytical tools that are activated by contingencies relevant to the client. This hierarchical and modular form of the knowledge base makes it possible to customize the service to meet the needs of the individual client. These processes take place by getting acquainted with the problem, experience, and knowledge of a client before entering into the consulting process. Thus, the diagnostic competence and inferences related both to diagnosis and treatment rest heavily on the jurisdiction of the consultant.

The Creativity Mode

The *creativity mode* is based on a conception of *unprogrammed knowledge*. It consists initially in the intuition of and guesses by highly informed consultants about action elements that might create a new best practice. Thus, instead of being part of an available knowledge structure, unprogrammed knowledge refers to collective knowledge generating, experimenting and learning processes, similar to new scientific inventions that shape a field of knowledge. Overlaps between the experience and formal knowledge of participants and the ability to place available experiences in new conceptual contexts are necessary conditions for such cumulative processes. It is also necessary to mediate between conflicting views and action trajectories in a constructive way. Such processes can lead to conceptions of new causality patterns that typically require the removal of cognitive and contextual constraints and the reshaping of action system components. In this case, no single actor has the diagnosis and actionable knowledge (Argyris, 1993) in his or her jurisdiction.

Comparisons

The deepest level in the work system is the actual *undertaking and delivery of assignments*. A firm's cash flow is generated through its consulting assignments and the relevance of its knowledge base is being tested. For the efficiency mode, attractiveness in the marketplace is related to the capacity of saving time and transferring skills to the client (e.g., by undertaking recruitment and training assignments) or providing procedures that would have been too expensive for a client to develop and operate (e.g., market share assessments, surveys of consumer satisfaction of comparable products). The dominant characteristic of the assignment delivery—efficiency—is achieved by the constantly repeating execution of the same standardized action program. The competitive strength comes from exploiting the existing knowledge base.

The distinguishing feature of the experience mode is the large overlapping experience of the consultant with managers in the client organization. March (1991b) refers to this aspect of a consultant's contribution as the pooling of experience. An additional input comes from the generic, conceptual repertoire of the consultant's knowledge base. Partially-programmed knowledge is typically copied and adapted from frameworks developed by leading international consulting firms or prominent academics (Payne & Lumsden, 1987). Investments in knowledge development, however, are typically considerable in the experience mode because of the competition with large international consulting firms. Thus, investments cannot be recovered from the first assignment only. High fees would hinder the selling of the prototype service from which no references can be given to the client. Therefore, repeating the same type of assignment is essential for both cash flow and for developing the knowledge base—new contingencies can be turned, case by case, into blueprints.

The creativity mode is reflected by a prominent person in academia who has moved into management consulting, or alternates between academia and consulting. The initial investment in the knowledge base through an academic career enables that person to launch new ideas and concepts that, over time, become enriched with the new best practices that are confronted during assignments.

The differences in types of knowledge base, the nature of assignments, and work styles also create different requirements and opportunities for *marketing*. The product form, the ability to duplicate and transfer programmed types of knowledge, is an incentive for investing in marketing as a separate and specialized function in a consulting firm. Part of the task of keeping in contact with clients can also be delegated to back office staff. In contrast, unprogrammed types of knowledge have no conceptual shape before the interdisciplinary search through complementary experiences are initiated. Thus, the client can only evaluate the past performance and reputation of the highly innovative expert when a service assignment is negotiated. In fact, the often long lasting and informal discussions of an assignment are part of the process of defining the parameters of the final assignment design. CEOs or general mangers who share similar assessments of future trends with the consultant will initiate such negotiations. In terms of marketing partially-programmed knowledge, the reputation of individual practitioners is also essential because their experience and depth of knowledge guarantee the possibility of customizing the service according to client needs. Based on previous assignments, the client can more easily evaluate the service offers of the partially-programmed knowledge type compared with the unprogrammed type.

The management input in the three types varies as well. In the efficiency mode, the management content of operations is high. This is due to the need to pay attention to the recruitment of new consultants, support the transfer of competence of the standardized action program, increase the efficiency of the procedure in question, and control the quality of the service. In the experience mode, management input is subsumed under the influence of personal examples shown by the partners and senior consultants in their expert practices. In the creativity mode, in contrast, the relevance of preconceived managerial routines is minimal. Each assignment is dominated by the idea of "making history" in a cosmopolitan expert community.

As this comparative discussion suggests, the various characteristics of sub-processes in the work system and the diverse needs for managing consulting practices within the operating modes give reason to explore the different agendas for creating network relations as part of the consulting practice.

THE LANDSCAPE OF CONSULTING NETWORKS

A management consulting practice is typically embedded simultaneously in a wide span of network types. From disparate surveys on management consulting firms, we can infer that network linkages among management consulting firms have increased rapidly, both nationally and across borders. One estimate is that more than 50% of consulting firms cooperate in some kind of network setting (Forening, 1991, 1994). To make sense of the web of potential network relations, four types have been identified: the *information sharing club, relational contracting, strategic alliance,* and the *intra-firm network of consultant teams*. These types represent qualitatively different types of mobilization of expertise and forms of collective action (Berry & Oakley, 1994, pp. 15–16; Payne & Poulfelt, 1992; Poulfelt, Payne, & Frow, 1994; Sabath, 1992) (see Table 2).

Information sharing clubs are networks in which the relations among members are based on personal relationships instead of the firm level. These relationships include sharing of experiences, informal cooperation, and joint training activities. In many cases, the primary purpose of this type of a social network is to give "mental support" to "lonely riders." Due to their often haphazard mode of emergence, accumulation of joint knowledge base tends to be limited because of divergent operating modes among the participants. In order to reduce internal competition and increase external complementary capabilities, selection to such information clubs favors practitioners of varied service profiles. Due to their interpersonal nature, their visibility in the marketplace is low. Participants undergo a continuous motivational struggle in having to strike a balance

Table 2.   Network Types in Management Consulting Practice

	Information Sharing Clubs	Relational Contracting	Strategic Alliances	Intra-firm Network of Consultant Teams
Prime purpose	Ticket to grapevine	Extending expert capacity	Increasing market visibility and expert credibility	Creating broad-based service offerings
Knowledge base	Sharing of insight	Assignment based knowledge	Building and/or sharing complementary knowledge bases	Integrating complementary knowledge bases
Marketing	Club-related referrals	Contractor-based	Firm-based, embedded in the alliance	Team-based, under the company umbrella
Assignment delivery	None	Assignment specific	Attempts to develop assignments	Cross-team joint assignments
Managerial content in the work system	Allocation of time	Assignment linked coordination	Partner-based risk taking in joint knowledge development	Partner-based support for intra-team competence development

between billable hours and the time allocated to network activities. Therefore, commitment to this type of network is often low and varies over time. This type of network is primarily national, but it has become typical in Europe to advertise cross-national network connections although they are often only of symbolic value.

The second type of network linkage is *relational contracting.* In this network, individual practitioners have established closer business relations concerning cross referrals and undertaking joint assignments. This network is typically based on long-term personal relations among the involved experts. The prime purpose of the contractor is to be able to serve clients by extending the resources of the firms without involving unnecessary, fixed costs. Most of the time spent in these networks concerns delivery of the task. Joint knowledge development is therefore primarily related to specific assignments. Ties based on relational contracting are not formally marketed and therefore not visible in the marketplace from the client perspective.

The third category, *strategic alliances,* includes networks of firms on a more formalized basis. In these cases, the firms have declared (1) to work together in the market under specified financial conditions and (2) to perform specific activities on an exclusive basis. These agreements can also include either undertaking minority stakes in different firms or setting up joint organizations to carry out specific tasks, such as product development or specific types of assignments. The basic idea in most alliance types of networks has been to increase the visibility and credibility of expertise in the market. A strategic alliance is especially beneficial to firms that have not accumulated sufficient resources. By engaging in an alliance, they can launch joint product development teams, relieved from the immediate pressures associated with clients and amassing billable hours. Examples of networks with such binding relations can be found on both national and international level. In the international arena, many of the joint ventures and strategic alliances have been used as mechanisms for internationalizing nationally-based consulting firms (Poulfelt et al., 1994). Examples in this category of strategic moves are the international membership of the consulting arms of the major accountancy firms. However, the idea of strategic alliance within the consulting business may be more conceptual than real. In fact, many loose networks have been promoted as strategic alliances to make them appear more exotic in the marketplace though they only are based on promises for cross-referrals of assignments.

The final category comprises *intra-firm networks of consultant teams* that are able to provide a wide scale of services through independent sub-firms (e.g., Viitanen, 1993). This network type is of a two-tier structure. On one level is the corporate umbrella, consisting of corporate image, marketing and public relations activities, financing of operations and support staff as well as resource allocations to knowledge and competence development. The other level consists of individual teams responsible for creating the business and financial results. At the same time, the senior partners are instrumental in feeding in cross-team consulting assignments. In their billing, the financially independent sub-firms must cater to the need to finance the costs of the corporate umbrella. This can occur through management fees, royalties for using consulting products, and other types of internal invoicing. In intra-firm networks, the senior partners function as project coordinators with the vision to integrate specialized competence areas and consulting services into a unified consulting framework. Thus, intra-firm networks come very close to the concept of "the one-firm firm." This concept implies that there is an intentional drive to create and maintain a unified company culture (Maister, 1985). The intra-firm network approach, however, differs from the one-firm firm concept by not hiring junior consultants to be developed internally. Growth in new knowledge areas happens by adding new teams of experts who have already earned their reputation in the market.

COMPLEMENTING OPERATING MODES WITH NETWORK TYPES

The four distinct types of networks are relatively stable social and inter-organizational forms that have emerged to solve the problems of scale and scope in business operations. In concrete cases, it is not uncommon that a consulting firm is engaged in all four of these network types. We suggest that, for analytical purposes, it is useful to produce propositions of the ways in which the ideal typical operating modes of consulting firms are or can be complemented with network types. Such propositions can be deducted from the inherent logic of the operating modes.

One facilitating condition for this approach is that elaborating the typical practices at the level of the internal work systems or sub-processes of consulting firms have turned the operating modes from metaphoric images to analytical concepts. Another limitation is that our analysis disregards a variety of contingencies. First, individual consulting firms do not always restrict their business offerings to a single operating mode. Maister (1993), for example, takes this into account by elaborating the life-cycle model of the professional service firm. This dynamic implies that in medium-sized consulting firms there can be traces of several operating modes functioning simultaneously. In our fieldwork, we have encountered several firms that are good examples of this situation. Second, personalities can always make a difference as to the type of network connections. Despite these reservations, it is useful to develop propositions of the ways in which operating modes induce consulting firms to develop network relations.

Proposition 1.   In the efficiency mode, there is only a weak incentive to be linked in networks. Participation in an information sharing club is a low commitment option and may add value to the operations by giving insights into competitors and markets. Firms in the efficiency mode enter into strategic alliances when their services complement each other or they can share marketing efforts and back office services.

The key to practice in the efficiency mode is connected with the ability to develop available knowledge into a procedure. The knowledge base internalized in the consulting firm does not serve as a stimulus for external contacts because of its generic nature. The efficiency of the procedure is secured by in-house staff training, a practice that requires considerable management efforts, including the monitoring the implementation of the procedure. For this reason, it is difficult to link outsiders via relational contracting for assignment deliveries. When the visibility of the service has been achieved in the market, the main concern shifts to control of ownership of the operations and copyright of the standardized products. This focus is an important part of the business concept because of the significant potential for repeating business, licensing and royalties. Profits in this type of a service firm come from volume.

It is typical that the founders of efficiency-based consulting firms are like entrepreneurs who get their satisfaction in the innovation phase of the procedure concept. If they do not like working as hands-on managers in the mature phase of the operations, they may enter into a strategic alliance that will relieve their energy for developing new procedure-based services. Such strategic alliances can lead to a holding company structure covering several firms operating in the efficiency mode. Profit and ownership motives, as well as the need for hands-on management, give a strong flavor to the social, cultural and organizational context of firms in the efficiency mode. For these reasons, further supported by our field observations, there appear to be weak positive linkages toward information sharing clubs and strategic alliances for efficiency-based practices.

Proposition 2. In the creativity mode, there is a great incentive to be engaged in relational contracting due to the uniqueness of each assignment. Information sharing clubs constitute a social infrastructure for relational contracting. Participation to such clubs is considered to be an investment in the future.

The most preferred network types in the creativity mode stem from the way in which assignments are developed. Consultants who have built a reputation in the creativity mode are contacted due to their visibility, exceptional intellectual capacity and leadership. The clients are not seeking solutions per se but am interchange of ideas for diagnoses. As the diagnoses unfold, new types of expertise are called upon. One of the reasons for contacting a consultant with a reputation in the creativity mode is the expectation that she or he has access to a portfolio of experts and will be able to ensure their cooperation. Such connections can be nurtured in exclusive information sharing clubs. The missing parts of an assignment design can be customized according to customer needs and the necessary overlaps in knowledge and experience with the client organization can be secured through network relations. Such a combination of relational contracting and resort to information sharing clubs as a pool of contacts allows the flexibility needed in the creativity mode without having to bear overhead costs. Thus, in this mode, there is less incentive to turn assignment specific network relations into strategic alliances or intra-firm networks of consultant teams. However, there are cases where this has happened. Influential consultants, sticking to the creativity mode themselves, have also had sufficient managerial talent to link experienced consultants working in the experience mode under the same company umbrella. In Europe, Eric

Rhenman and Richard Normann are examples of such combinations of intellectual and managerial capabilities.

> **Proposition 3.** Consulting firms reproducing the experience mode, especially those with more than one senior partner, tend to internalize relational contracting, strategic alliances and/or an intra-firm network of teams.

With respect to the relevance of network ties, the *experience mode* differs from the other two modes. To fully appreciate the nature of this difference, the impact of time must be taken into account. Thus, it is useful to take a look at the idealized view of the life cycle of a partially-programmed management consulting service. In small- and medium-sized firms, the framework part of their services is very dependent on fads and the layering of reforms in client organizations (Abrahamson, 1996). At the early phases of internal knowledge accumulation projects, consulting firms must extensively scan potential consulting concepts and their markets, the path-dependence to earlier services in the firm, and the credibility of the firm within a new service area. To make sense of these scanning efforts, information sharing clubs are needed. They contain rumors of competitor plans and indications of how responsive clients are toward new managerial fads (Kieser, 1997). To get the prototype to the market, senior consultants contact some of their most loyal or cutting-edge clients. This phase is done alone, as quickly and as unnoticed as possible, to reap the first mover advantages and to be ready to start the marketing of the partially-programmed service. After having completed the prototype development, the next managerial target is to move down the learning curve. This action puts demand on a focused flow of incoming assignments. The relative strength of the firms in the experience mode is not only dependent on the "modernity" of the frameworks, but also on the industry-specific experience of the consultants. By confronting assignment after assignment and different local conditions in the implementation of a service concept, the customization of the concept becomes increasingly elaborate. When the markets have rated the consulting firms as to the quality and credibility of their new services, the phase for volume business starts.

As imitators come to the market and generate sufficient credibility, however, fees are lowered. One response is to increase the rate of junior consultant involvement. As a way of consolidating their competitive positions, consulting firms are eager to look for matched pairs to form strategic alliances or to link external consulting capacity through relational contracting. The hierarchical and modular form of parts of the knowledge base allows inclusion of externally developed modules and analyses into marketing efforts as well as into the semi-standardized delivery of assignments. Complementary service profiles boost the marketing and relational contracting, relieving pressures associated with over-contracting and work overload, which are typical during peaks of demand.

One of the difficulties in managing consulting firms in the experience mode is that they simultaneously operate "products" that are at different phases of their life cycles. Paying attention to the search for new service areas often conflict with the need to allocate time to prototype development or negotiating an alliance with a firm having services that have also reached the partially-programmed stage. A further critical decision is when to exit from providing a specific service. Offering a service that is still in demand, but which is turning into disrepute among leading-edge customers, easily labels the entire consulting firm as a laggard. This may contradict its efforts to reposition the competence pool of the firm into a new service area that is claiming stronger jurisdiction at the diagnosis and inference moments in the consulting practice. One way to handle such exit decisions has been to offer a management-buy-out option to consultants who are responsible for the service at an end-game stage. The service in question is then often continued, but as a separate juridical entity. This practice has led to strategic alliances with firms based in different operating modes, as seen for instance, in the combination of experience- and efficiency-based modes.

The experience mode in management consulting can also be the platform for the formation of intra-firm networks of consultant teams. This network type is a hybrid form, because the network aspect of operating serves as the constitutive principle of the firm. Such development is based on exceptional capabilities of experienced consultants and is by no means restricted only to those who have earned their credentials in the experience mode. As mentioned earlier, there are examples of academicians who have mainly acted in the creativity mode but have been able to turn that knowledge base into partially-programmed consulting services.

Due to superior capabilities, the demand for the services of certain senior consultants can easily exceed their capacity. If they are able to take a long-term approach, they can start to nurture the cooperation of other consulting teams and become "rainmakers" to borrow Starbuck's (1993) terminology. In a Finnish case, the reputation of the founding partners of a consulting firm attracted established consultants and teams of consultants to join the firm one by one, ultimately turning the original firm into an umbrella firm (Viitanen, 1993). Combined resources facilitated cross-team and cross-functional service development and marketing efforts, which were inconceivable for small teams. The broad-based competence stock also allowed sensitive diagnosing of the client's real, underlying problem, instead of selling the only partially-programmed service available.

Table 3 provides a qualitative illustration of the interconnections contained in our propositions. The overall patterning of operating modes and network types contains clear clusters. The characteristics of the work system in the experience mode provide the largest variety of reasons *and* resources for entering into a variety of network relations. In our sample of consulting firms, companies based on the experience mode were more often than others capable of integrating consulting services from other consulting firms into a strategic alliance type of network as well as the concept of an intra-firm network of consultant teams. The creativity and efficiency modes, in contrast, provide fewer opportunities for consultants to create networks due to the niche approach in their client interface and the deep specialization, either in the knowledge base or in the implementation of procedures for executing specific assignments.

Table 3.   Proposed Patterns of Network Relations by Operating Mode

	Efficiency	*Experience*	*Creativity*
Information Sharing Club	+	++	++
Relational Contracting		+++	+++
Strategic Alliance	+	+++	+
Intra-firm Network of Consultant Teams		++	+

Legend: Plusses indicate the strength of the tendency toward a specific type of network relationship according to the propositions

CONCLUSIONS

We have attempted to develop a conceptual framework that elaborates on Maister's (1993) types of practices in professional service firms, extending it to include different network relationships between small- and medium-sized management consulting firms. The analytical sediments of the framework—the operating modes, network types and emergent interrelationships—are based on deductive reasoning and grounded in fieldwork and interviews with management consultants. The empirical research has sensitized us to look at the ways in which network relations are linked to the subprocesses of the work systems, including the need for variations in management input within the different operating modes and opportunities for network ties.

The observation that there are stable patterns of operating modes and network relations are of interest because small- and medium-sized management consulting firms are continuously struggling for survival. Yet, while the different network types do contribute to the reputation of consulting firms, it is clear that in their marketing efforts consulting firms often overemphasize the impact of existing and potential network relations to client assignments. Our fieldwork does, however, contain examples in which consulting firms had transformed their competence profile through network relations—for instance through strategic alliances during the course of their life cycles—to contain more than one operating mode. In some hybrid cases, the network mode of operating and expanding became the constituting principle of the management consulting firm in question. In some cases, this also allowed for the combination of different operating modes under the same corporate umbrella, but channeling assignments through different sub-firms.

When evaluating the epistemic status of the suggested framework and propositions, we stress the fact that the operating modes are strong abstractions and must be treated as ideal types. The primary purpose of the propositions is not that they should be tested in large samples of firms using quantitative measures. They are meant to serve as a baseline for empirical observations in fieldwork contexts, helping sensitize the fieldworker to obvious anomalies. As Yin (1984) has suggested, such cases have revelatory power if the researchers are able to reveal the mechanisms that produce the observed anomalies.

Despite the opportunities for growth through forming networks, small- and medium-sized consulting firms are quite different from the large, multinational management consulting companies. The latter are compelled to use hierarchic forms of management and complex managerial systems as integrative mechanisms. Such integrative mechanisms are also complemented by social networks that link offices in different countries, service areas and experts possessing knowledge in specific industries and specific types of companies. Internal training programs also create cohorts of consultants. Information technology is widely used as an integrative mechanism, facilitating collective work processes among consultants, between consultants and clients, and management of the consulting capacity. A different type of conceptual framework is needed to capture this type of work organization, management system and its offering to clients (e.g., Cooper et al., 1996, pp. 629–635). In such a comprehensive system, it is no longer possible to distinguish different operating modes and network types. For small- and medium-sized firms, however, this framework promises to deepen our understanding of both operational and network-based dynamics and possibilities.

NOTE

1.   An earlier version of this article appeared in the *Finnish Journal of Business Economics, 50*(1) (2001).

REFERENCES

Abbott, A. (1991). The Future of professions: Occupation and expertise in the age of organization. In P.S. Tolbert & R.S. Barley (Eds.), *Research in the sociology of organizations* (Vol. 8, pp. 17–42). Greenwich, CT: JAI Press.

Abbott, A. (1988). *The system of professions.* Chicago: Chicago University Press.

Abrahamson, E. (1996). Management fashion. *Academy of Management Review, 21,* 254–285.

Alvesson, M. (1993). Organizations as rhetoric: Knowledge-intensive firms and the struggle with ambiguity. *Journal of Management Studies, 30*(6), 997–1015.

Alvesson, M. (1994). Talking in organizations: Managing identity and impressions in an advertising agency. *Organization Studies, 15*(4), 535–563.

Argyris, C. (1993). *Knowledge for action.* San Francisco: Jossey-Bass.

Berry, A., & Oakley, K. (1994). Consultancies: Agents of organizational development, Part II. *Leadership & Organization Development Journal, 15*(1), 13–21.

Byrne, J.A. (1994, July 25). The craze for consultants. *Business Week,* pp. 60–66.

Cooper, D.J., Hinings, B., Greenwood, R., & Brown, J.L. (1996). Sedimentation and transformation in organizational change: The case of Canadian law firms. *Organization Studies, 17*(4), 623–647.

Economist. (1997). Management consultancy: The advice business. *The Economist,* Supplement, March 22, pp. 1–22.

Empson, L., & Morris, T. (1997, April). *When knowledge is power: Knowledge transfer and mergers and acquisitions between professional services firms.* Paper presented at the "Modes of Organising" Conference at University of Warwick, UK.

Erhvervsfremmestyrelsen. (1999). *Managementkonsulenter—kortlægning af en branche i vækst.* København: EFS.

Foreningen af ManagementKonsulenter (1991). *Profil af Management-konsulentbranchen i Danmark anno.* København: FMK.

Foreningen af ManagementKonsulenter. (1994). *Managementkonsulent-branchen i Danmark 1994—som konsulenterne brugerne ser den.* København: FMK.

Greenwood, R., & Hinings, C.R. (1988). Organization design types, tracks and the dynamics of strategic change. *Organization Studies, 9*(3), 293–316.

Hinings, C.R., Brown, J.L., & Greenwood, R. (1991). Change in autonomous professional organization. *Journal of Management Studies, 28*(4), 375–393.

Kanter, R. M. (1994). Collaborative advantage: the art of alliances. *Harvard Business Review, 72*(4), 96–108.

Kieser, A. (1997). Myth and rhetoric in management fashion. *Organization, 4*(1), 49–74.

Kyrö, P. (1999). Liikkeenjohdon konsultointi—nuori ja kasvava toimiala. *Aikuiskasvatus, 19*(1), 48–59.

Lilja, K., Penn, R., & Tainio, R. (1993, July). *Dimensions of consulting knowledge.* Paper presented at the 11th EGOS Colloquium, Paris.

Löwendahl, B.R. (1997). *Strategic management of professional service firms.* Copenhagen: Handelshojskolens Forlag.

Maister, D.H. (1993). *Managing the professional service firm.* New York: Free Press.

Maister, D. (1985). The one-firm firm. *Sloan Management Review, 27*(1), 3–13.

March, J.G. (1991a). Organizational consultants and organizational research. *Applied Communication Research, 19*(1–2), 20–31.

March, J.G. (1991b). Exploration and exploitation in organizational learning. *Organization Science, 2*(1), 71–87.

Miles, R.E., & Snow, C.C. (1992, Summer). Causes of failure in network organizations. *California Management Review, 34*, 53–72.

Miles, R. E., & Snow, C.C. (1986). Network organizations: New concepts for new forms. *California Management Review, 28*, 62–73.

O'Shea, J., & Madigan, C. (1997). *Dangerous company—The consulting powerhouses and the business they save and ruin.* London: NB Publishing.

Payne, A., & Lumsden, C. (1987). Strategy consulting—shooting star? *Long Range Planning, 20*(3). 53–64.

Payne, A., & Poulfelt, F. (1992). *The pathology of M&A in professional service firms.* Paper presented at Strategic Management Society Conference, London, UK.

Poulfelt, F., Payne, A., & Frow, P. (1994). *Developing an international presence: Key issues for management consulting firms.* Paper presented at Academy of Management, Dallas.

Powell, W.W. (1990). Neither market nor hierarchy: Network forms of organization. In B.M. Staw & L.L. Cummings (Eds.), *Research in organizational behavior* (Vol. 12, pp. 295–336). Greenwich, CT: JAI Press.

Ram, M. (1999). Managing consultants in a small firm: A case study. *Journal of Management Studies, 36*(6), 875–897.

Sabath, R.E. (1992). Establishing alliances. *Journal of Management Consulting, 7*(2), 10–14.

Scott, J. (1991). *Network analysis.* London: Sage.

Starbuck, W.H. (1993). Keeping a butterfly and an elephant in a house of cards: The elements of exceptional success. *Journal of Management Studies, 30*(6), 885–923.

Sturdy, A. (1997). The consultancy process—An insecure business. *Journal of Management Studies, 34*(3), 389–414.

Talouselämä 4/1999.

Tienari, J. (1999). Sotakorvaustyön tehostamisesta sähköisen liiketoiminnan kehittämiseen. Liikkeenjohdon konsultoinnin lyhyt historia Suomessa. Lappeenranta: LaTKK, Kauppatieteenosaston tutkimuksia 1.

Tsoukas. H. (1991). The missing link: A transformational view of metaphors in administrative science. *Academy of Management Review, 16*, 566–585.

Viitanen, P. (1993). *Strategian muotoutumisprosessi ja strategiset muutokset tietointensiivisessä yrityksessä.* Turun kauppakorkeakoulu. Turku: Lisensiaattitutkimus.

Whitley, R. (1988). The management sciences and managerial skills. *Organization Studies, 9*(1), 47–68.

Winch, G., & Schneider, E. (1993). Managing the knowledge-based organization: The case of architectural practice. *Journal of Management Studies, 30*(6), 923–937.

Yin, R.K. (1984). *Case study design and methods.* Beverly Hills, CA: Sage.

CHAPTER 2

THE ROLE OF RELATIONAL EXPERTISE IN PROFESSIONAL SERVICE DELIVERY[1]

Kate Walsh

INTRODUCTION

The service organization has become the literal mainstay of the U.S. economy. As the predominant form of U.S.-based business, by 1990 service organizations contributed more than 72% of our GNP (Bowen & Cummings, 1990). Yet, while service organizations have been growing in both size and significance in the United States, it was not until the 1980s that organizational researchers began to specifically examine the nature of services. Most of this research studied transactional service encounters between customers and employees, which are temporary, often impersonal, and sometimes nonrecurring interactions between consumers and many types of service providers, such as supermarket (Rafaeli, 1989) and convenience store cashiers (Sutton & Rafaeli, 1988), as well as flight attendants (Hochschild, 1983), waiters (Mars & Nicod, 1984), fast food clerks (Leidner, 1993) and bank tellers (Schneider, Parkington, & Buxton, 1980).

While important to our understanding of service, transactional encounters between employees and customers represent only one dimension of service (Bowen & Jones, 1986; Gutek, 1995). To date, we understand very little about the service experience created between more professional service providers and their clients. Professional service providers, such as doctors, lawyers, accountants and consultants are acknowledged as and hired by clients as experts in their field. The relationship between the professional and client acts as the medium for delivering this expertise. Yet ways of delivering professional services have rarely been explored. The implicit assumption is that professionals' expertise in their field alone makes them successful or unsuccessful service providers. The actual role that service delivery plays in a professional's ability to apply an expertise and build a successful practice, however, has largely been ignored.

This chapter seeks to add to our understanding of service—and specifically professional consulting service—through considering a particular approach that service professionals use to consult with and create client-based relationships. Applying concepts from gender research, this research delineates a *relational approach* to service delivery. A relational approach, as outlined by Miller and associates at the Wellesley College Stone Center for Research (cf. Jordan, Kaplan, Miller, Stiver, & Surrey, 1991; Miller, 1976, 1991; Surrey, 1987) and refined and applied to organizational research by Fletcher (1994, 1998, 1999), considers ways individuals can think and act in order to invite mutual growth and development in their interactions with others. These concepts are often examined under a gender-based, post-structuralist lens as a way of uncovering how relational ways of working are marginalized and diminished in the public sphere of organizational work (Fletcher, 1998, 1999).

Through a study of fifty service professionals working in the consulting and audit/tax practice of big five accounting firms, this research examines how both men and women use a relational approach within the infrastructure of an individually-based, patriarchal organization. The specific questions that guided this work are:

1. What does a relational approach to expert-based service delivery look like?; and
2. To what extent are such approaches related to organizational success?

The basic goal of this study is to uncover ways relational practices are used and rewarded in work. Through uncovering the ways service providers use a relational approach to provide their service, this research may help us understand one of the reasons why some professionals may be successful in their practice and why others may falter.

SERVICE RELATIONSHIPS

In the 1980s organizational researchers began to examine service in general and the role of service delivery in particular. Their findings suggested that services are vastly different from manufacturing in that: (1) the product for sale is an intangible experience that cannot be possessed (Bowen & Schneider, 1988), (2) the product is simultaneously produced and consumed (Bowen & Cummings, 1990), and (3) the customer plays a key role in both creating and consuming the product for sale (Argote, 1982). Thus the customer acts as a resource, as well as co-producer, buyer, beneficiary and often product of the service (Lengnick-Hall, 1996).

Current Perspective on Long-Term Service Relationships

Professional services generally involve the creation of long-term, ongoing relationships with clients, where the intangible service is simultaneously and continuously produced and consumed. These longer-term relationships are defined by their repeated interactions that, over time, enable professionals to garner knowledge about and understanding of their clients. Ultimately, each professional service relationship is characterized by its high degrees of asset specificity or unique knowledge exchange, where both the professional and client hold specific, highly customized information about the other, and the professional has developed a keen understanding of the client's specific needs. The longer the relationship, the more knowledge they accumulate about each other. This knowledge accumulation usually enables the professional to create a more efficient process of interacting, and eventually deliver a more effective and customized service.

Professional service experiences "create bonds of attachment and trust" where the service provider and client "become dependent on one another… This interdependence causes both provider and customer to look out for the other, because in fact the other is an important factor in one's own success" (Gutek, 1995, pp. 17–18). The client is dependent on the provider to deliver the intended service in a way that will meet the client's unique needs. The provider is dependent on the client not only to clearly articulate his or her needs, both initially and as they evolve, but to also speak positively of the provider to other potential clients. In fact, Gutek (1995, p. 17) claimed that in a "good" relationship, both parties are interdependent and committed to sustaining the association and are "willing to expend energy and resources to preserve the relationship." Over time, the client and professional increase both their investment in and dependency on one another (Gutek, 1995; Winch & Schneider, 1993).

Increased levels of investment and dependency make it difficult for the client to switch providers, even when the client feels less than satisfied with the professional's expertise.

The Relationship as the Medium of Service Delivery

Providing a professional, or as Gutek (1995) termed it "relational" (i.e., long term, mutually dependent), service means that the provider delivers some form of expertise to the client, for example, legal or strategy development advice. Yet, while the relationship between the professional and client acts as the medium for delivering this expertise, the ways in which professionals use client relationships to deliver their expertise or service are rarely mentioned in the literature. Service delivery is, in essence, implicitly assumed to be irrelevant.

Some researchers (cf. Benner, 1984; Gutek, 1995; Pierce, 1995) acknowledge that relationships with clients matter. Yet each of these perspectives offers conflicting positions about what these relationships *should* look like. Their ideas range from the argument that connecting and building a relationship with clients is an important aspect of providing professional service (Noddings, 1984) to the notion that detaching from the client, especially emotionally, and even conveying arrogance is critical to delivering professional work (Pierce, 1996). At one extreme, Noddings' (1984) ideas about the philosophy of care, as well as Benner (1984) and Benner and Wrubel's (1989) work on caring in the nursing profession, for example, discuss the criticality of connecting on both a cognitive *and* emotional level with the patient.

At the middle of the continuum, Gutek (1995) acknowledged that in delivering expertise the provider needs to create an important connection with the client that becomes the means for service delivery. Yet she views this connection or relationship as both helpful to and a hindrance in delivering this service. Gutek argued that because of their relationship, the service provider and client may fight the emotional feelings associated with their connection (such as dislike with the ways the other is behaving) and the professional works to maintain a detached but pleasant persona. In fact, Gutek suggested that emotional labor (Hochschild, 1983) is at work and argued "both customer and service provider are expected to manage the emotional aspect of their relationship and refrain from displaying their felt emotions ... whether the emotions are positive or negative." Gutek (1995, pp. 80–81) went on to suggest that, "for (service providers), emotional labor means putting aside real feelings and displaying other, sometimes less intense or blander, emotions." Thus, this view suggests that while connecting with clients is important to delivering service, the connection carries negative consequences with it that may impede the provider's ability to do so.

At the other extreme, researchers argue that more negative expressions of behaviors and emotions are useful to creating specific kinds of client relationships that enhance service delivery. The more masculine traits of arrogance and intimidation are perceived by some clients to be signals of expertise, and in some professions, such as the law, forms of gamesmanship and dominance are encouraged behaviors (Pierce, 1996). The power balance between the professional and client shifts in favor of the professional, and in return for receiving superior expertise, the client is expected to accept and accommodate their egos (Gutek, 1995). In this instance, the client looks to the professional's arrogance as a signal of expertise. Pierce (1995), for example, termed the lawyers she studied as "rambo litigators." She explored the pressures female attorneys felt to act and not act in manners that supported these behaviors. Leidner (1993) also found that insurance salesmen were encouraged to be aggressive, dominant and manipulative when "outmaneuvering" potential prospects or clients.

Key Questions and Issues

Because the research on relationship building and service delivery runs a wide gamut in identifying seemingly conflicting ideas and behaviors, actual approaches to relationship building are worth exploring in greater detail. The confusion identified through this brief review brings to light an important question: What strategies or approaches do service professionals use to create—or not create—relationships with clients in delivering their service? Especially in the context of management consulting, it is clear that approaches to expert-based service delivery—and the role relationships with clients play—are in need of conceptual grounding and clarification. In fact, in the field of professional service firms, research on the actual process of creating and building service relationships has yet to be conducted.

The Patriarchal Expert

One area that theorizes about ways professionals should think about clients is sociological research on the professions. Research in this field suggests that professional work entails a high degree of knowledge-based expertise (Barber, 1965; Winter, 1988). Professional work is controlled through the creation and maintenance of rigorous industry-level standards (Starbuck, 1992) and, as such, professionals enjoy high status outside the profession (Barber, 1965; Winter, 1988). In fact, professionals hold their authority over their clients and act as the unquestionable expert (Barber, 1965; Carr-Saunders & Wilson, 1941). The client needs the knowledge and through training and experience, the professional provides it. Professionals may assume they know—even better than their clients—what their clients need and desire from them. In fact, as Hanlon (1997, p. 125) argued, "the professional controls the interaction with the client and translates the clients' desires into a professional metalanguage and/or explains to clients what is possible in their situation." In this model, the professional holds some degree of power and control over the client.

The Relational Expert

An alternative way to consider how professionals may interact with clients is to apply concepts from gender research and consider a *power-with* model. Gender research shows that women tend to have an explicit focus on maintaining positive relationships. Inherent in this focus is a relational approach, which encourages both parties in a relationship to focus on their mutual growth and development. In fact, creating growth-enhancing relationships is a key goal of relational practice.

GENDER RESEARCH AND GROWTH-ENHANCING RELATIONSHIPS

Research on gender shows that due to their desire to act in an equitable manner and maintain positive relationships, women tend to focus on and pay attention to their relational processes more than men (Tannen, 1990). In their relationships, research suggests that women typically adopt a greater "care perspective" (Gilligan & Attanucci, 1988), act more ethically (Barnett & Karson, 1989) and display greater "social reasoning" (Jones & Hiltebeitel, 1995) and utilize more cooperative skills (Loden, 1985) than their male counterparts. Women also tend to value building connections with others more than gaining power over them (Gilligan, 1982; Neuse, 1978) and they develop their individual selves through their relationships with others (Loden, 1985). Because processes are so important to women, they tend to support flatter organizational structures and more egalitarian work practices (Neuse, 1978; Rosener, 1990) as well.

Creating Growth Enhancing Relationships

Distinguishing such gender differences provides an initial framework for identifying what relational skills may look like. The work of the Wellesley College Stone Center for Research and, primarily, Jean Baker Miller and associates, gives flesh to (1) what these women's approaches and views mean in terms of building and maintaining strong or growth-enhancing relationships, and (2) the value of these relationships to an individual's psychological growth and development (Jordan et al., 1991; Miller, 1976). These researchers argue that authentic, growth-enhancing relationships provide a context for individuals to create critical human connections and, as a result, to personally grow and develop. Many individual psychological problems, in contrast are rooted in disconnected relationships with others (Surrey, 1987).

The Stone Center researchers identified three characteristics that distinguish such growth-enhancing, "relationally-based" relationships from other forms of relationships: (1) mutuality, (2) interdependence, and (3) reciprocity. *Mutuality* is the respectful commitment of both individuals in a relationship to work on their self-development (Jordan et al., 1991; Josselson, 1992). This dynamic means that individuals must be ready to provide authentic support and encouragement to the other. Additionally, it means that individuals must be willing to try to act in a manner congruent with their thoughts and feelings, and remain open to exploring the barriers that prevent them from doing so. *Interdependence* refers to the belief that creating relationships with others, as opposed to remaining autonomous, is a better approach to learning and growing. *Reciprocity* refers to the expectation that individuals in a relationship will contribute to each other's learning, in essence both having the skills to create these relationships and the motivation to use them. An important aspect of reciprocity is relational competence, "the interest and capacity to 'stay emotionally present with,' to enlarge or deepen the relational context to create enough 'space' for both individuals to express themselves and to allow for possible conflict, tension and creative resolution" (Surrey, 1987, p. 5). Thus, individuals wishing to create growth-enhancing relationships must try to remain adaptable to the changing needs of both themselves and the other person.

These researchers also identified three important relational skills that enable individuals to create conditions of mutuality, interdependence and reciprocity. These skills include the ability and willingness to (1) communicate empathy, (2) feel and express vulnerability and emotions, and (3) help others to develop (Jacques & Fletcher, 1997). The first of these skills, communicating empathy, is a process of trying to understand and respond to another's perspective, taking into account one's own thoughts and reactions in the process. For empathy to be effective, an individual must not only consider themselves and the other individual in the interaction, but they also must address both the affective and cognitive aspects of what they, as well as the other individual, are experiencing (Jordan et al., 1991). Thus, an individual communicating empathy will try to surface and express both what he or she is thinking and feeling in the context of acknowledging the thoughts and feelings the other individual is expressing.

Feeling and expressing vulnerability and emotions are also critical to creating growth-enhancing relationships. This means that individuals in relational relationships recognize their interdependencies with one another and are willing to expand their personal boundaries and share deep felt thoughts or concerns. Those wishing to grow and learn from these relationships must be open to considering their own affective reactions (and the reasons underlying them) to the experience.

Helping others to develop is the third skill important to creating growth-enhancing relationships. This capability does not suggest that individuals need to "have the answers" to others' dilemmas. Rather, it means that in an effort to help others, individuals will try to remain conscious of and willing to share their own perspectives, being attentive to the moment. At the same time, they will try to be aware of and responsive to the other's changing needs, as well as the tensions that differing needs can escalate. All of these skills contribute to what Fletcher (1996, p. 115) calls *fluid expertise* or "skills in enabling others (ability to assume the expert role in guiding, teaching, explaining) and skills in being enabled (ability to step away from the expert role in order to be influenced by and learn from others)." The resulting growth-enhancing relationships are characterized as providing individuals with "five good things": zest, empowered action, increased self-esteem, new knowledge and a desire for more connection (Miller & Stiver, 1997).

Relational Practice in Organizational Settings

Although most of the Stone Center Research is conducted from a clinical perspective, a growing number of researchers (including those at the Stone Center) are beginning to apply these concepts to organizational work. In her study of women engineers, Fletcher (1998, 1999), for example, identified important relational skills that women were using in their work place. These skills not only included behaviors that contributed to the ultimate success of a project but behaviors intended to empower others working on that project as well. Additionally these women worked on their own self-development and improvement, seeking to build and reinforce a sense of unity and team with others.

Despite such positive outcomes, Fletcher (1998, 1999) showed how these behaviors were devalued and marginalized in this particular organization. Members attributed these women's behaviors to their desire to assume care taking and nurturing—"mothering" roles. In doing so, they devalued their use, an action that not so subtly reinforced aggressive, individually-focused behaviors, and rewarded those who displayed them. In other words, while the organization relied on the relational behaviors and skills of these women, it did not publicly or structurally acknowledge them as valuable and, in fact, minimized them by assuming they were due solely to gender differences between men and women, one important assumed difference being women's desire to perform care-taking roles. As Jacques and Fletcher (1997, p. 14) noted, "the benefits of doing the concrete task with these relational dimensions intact—and the costs of doing them without these dimensions—are not typically included in measures of effectiveness." From a poststructuralist perspective, this marginalizing of relational work served to support the dichotomized separation of public and private work, and, in doing so, reified the patriarchal status quo (Fletcher, 1998, 1999).

Relational Skills and Service Delivery

This research considers and demonstrates one sphere of organizational work where the use of relational skills is included in measures of organizational effectiveness and formally recognized and rewarded—the delivery of professional services. In fact, relational skills may have important links with ways professionals interact with clients and deliver their expertise. This study is aimed at uncovering what a relational approach to client service might look like and how it potentially can contribute to a professional's success.

THE RESEARCH STUDY

This study, which took place during 1999, was part of a larger examination of professional work identity and service delivery. The research site is three of the big five public accounting firms and the sample focused on fifty partners, directors and managers directly responsible for generating and managing a client base and its associated revenues. Thirty-five of the fifty respondents were generally involved in the consulting end of the practice and the remaining ten were involved in audit and tax work.

Data Collection

To assess how service professionals approach delivering their expertise to clients, in-depth, structured interviews were conducted with all fifty respondents. These interviews were based on the protocol in Table 1. The goal of the interviews was to uncover service professionals' thoughts about (1) their clients, (2) the type of service they believe their clients expect from them, and (3) ways they go about delivering their expertise. The intent was to uncover the different approaches service professionals both implicitly and explicitly use to service clients. Interviews, on average, lasted between 60 and 90 minutes. With respondents' permission, thirty-five of the interviews were tape recorded and immediately transcribed. To the degree possible, copious note taking was used with the remaining five interviews.

Table 1. Interview Protocol

1   Describe your typical clients.

2   Beyond solving their immediate problem, is there anything else your clients expect from you?

3   What do you expect from your clients? What if any, is their job?

4   If you were training someone to take over your job, what would you tell them about your clients?

5   What if anything, do your clients teach you?

6   Please finish the following statement listing as many descriptors as necessary: "As a consultant, I am..."

7   What words would you use to describe what you do?

8   What is the purpose of your work?

9   What are the most important qualities and skills an accountant should possess?

10   Why do you think your clients seek you out—as opposed to another professional?

11   What do you think nonmembers—such as clients—think of your profession?

12   What do you enjoy most about membership in this profession? What do you enjoy least?

13   What do you think nonmembers—such as clients and other colleagues—think of your firm?

14   What do you enjoy most about membership with this firm? What do you enjoy least?

15   What else is important to know about your clients and client service?

Data Analysis

Using the transcripts and notes, the interviews were coded and content analyzed, drawing out key themes that emerged from the data. While evidence of relational practice was not explicitly sought, key trends did emerge from the data. Specific concepts and ideas embedded in the respondents' answers were coded. After all interviews were analyzed, the codes were compared, creating categories of concepts. The data were then reanalyzed, ensuring that all codes were fairly represented by key categories. When all categories were identified, the themes were reassessed and reviewed with ten of the respondents, checking for accuracy of understanding and credibility of the findings.

Results

Of the fifty consultants interviewed for this study, six (four women and two men) had created a specific consulting approach, one very different from the one used by the others in the sample. This specific consulting approach reflected relationality concepts. Before describing this approach and the differences between these two groups of consultants, it is useful to examine two key commonalities across the respondents.

Value of Experience

Ninety percent of the respondents commented that without experience, consultants do not have much to offer clients. Experience relates mostly to exposure to their clients' industries and, preferably, an underlying familiarity with the challenges and pressures of their clients' jobs, which serves as the source of their expertise. As one respondent commented: "I could never conceive of being a consultant right out of college. I feel pretty comfortable having been in the business 25 years before I decided to try to be a consultant." Another said, "if you don't know what you are doing and you don't have industry knowledge, you don't even get to play. I mean to me, that's a prerequisite … That's what allows you to run the race." When asked about important qualities and skills, one consultant focused on "the ability to convey years of experience into a quantifiable consulting product." According to respondents, experience provides the necessary training and expertise that enable consultants to offer help.

Individual Reputation

A second commonality for 64% of the respondents is the belief that their clients hired them for their individual, as opposed to their firm's, reputation and expertise. Many discussed the reputation they created for themselves, a reputation they believed would follow them if they ever joined another firm. As one respondent said, "a lot of these engagements are folks who I knew, and that as soon as I was available to be a consultant they asked me to work for them. They wouldn't have cared if I was independent or part of (another firm)." Another said, "my clients told me, 'we don't care whose name is on the letterhead, as long we get you.' That's what the investment in the relationships has gotten me. The loyalty in me." Still another commented that, "one of the things that has plagued us through the years is (related to) the rainmakers, the practice leaders, the partners and the directors; our level of activity is directly related to the amount of personal marketing and practice development that they do." The conundrum for big five consulting firms is that they count on their partners to bring in business, yet clients are often more loyal to the partners than to the practice.

Despite these commonalities, the consultants in the sample differed in their views on service delivery. These differences fell along a relational approach versus more traditional expert-based approach, and are distinguished by four specific characteristics (summarized in Table 2).

Table 2.   Relational Approach versus a Traditional Approach

Relational Approach	Traditional Approach
Empower the Client	Advise the Client
Learn from the Client	Take away Knowledge from the Project
We: Dependent on Client	Me: Independent from Client
Ask Questions and Listen	Tell Information

Empowering Versus Advising the Client

The first characteristic of a relational approach to professional service delivery is an intent to empower the client with knowledge and skills that contribute to their personal success. Consultants who use this approach apply their experience and expertise to provide personal support to the client. They refer to themselves as the client's coach. As one respondent said, "what I do is let them know that I understand what their position is in the company, what risks they are taking by embarking on some of these projects, and that I'm going to do everything in my power, single mindedly, to make sure that they come out as heroes in their own business group." Additionally, another consultant mentioned, "if I'm working on a chain of coffee houses, I will do research on coffee house trends, new food and beverage product lines, and new store design that is not part of the deliverables of my project written in any contract, but it continuously allows me to communicate and build a relationship and provide information to the client so that he or she knows that even though it's not of a specific scope of the work, I'm thinking of them and I want them to get smart." Along a similar line, a third respondent noted, "My strategy is different from any other partner here. I figure out the one thing my client needs to do his job well and I give him the tools or information to do it. I'm the behind the scenes person. And my client is the one who looks good."

The more traditional approach, in contrast, is to advise the client. Consultants who adopt the role of advisor believe their job is to use their experience and expertise to provide clients with the answers to their problems. This perspective is the generally held view of most of the consultants interviewed. In fact, 58% of those interviewed referred to themselves as the client's advisor. As an example, one respondent mentioned, "clients expect someone who can articulate 30 years of experience in the business and translate it into telling them something they don't know about the business." Another noted, "all of our clients are looking for experts … somebody to stand up and tell the audience what the right answer is… they need someone else with the credibility to come in and sell it to their boss… they're all looking to you for your expertise." Still a third respondent commented, "we're advisors … clients come in and say how do we get from here to there?" Most respondents spoke about solving clients' problems as the nature of their work. They believed that if they solve the problem well, clients will continue to use them for additional projects.

Learning from Clients Versus Taking Knowledge from a Project

A second distinguishing feature of a relational approach is the belief that clients can teach consultants new things. As one respondent commented, "I always learn so much from my clients, usually about their very specific primary drivers." Another discussed different things his clients teach him. He mentioned, "one of the clients I've worked with is the new president of a private company that's preparing for an IPO. We've talked a lot about the issues in his board of directors and how he got his financing. I don't advise him on any of that, he sort of is just telling me all about those things, so I've learned a lot about it." A third respondent described the collaborative nature of consulting, observing "I look upon it as they (the clients) know something we don't and we know something they don't, but we know a bit about what each other does so you combine it together … You both end up learning and you both end up getting things done." Consultants who hold this view are comfortable letting their clients teach them things. Clients are viewed as sources of new knowledge.

Alternatively, 52% of the consultants in the study did not believe their clients taught them new things. Rather, they phrased it as taking away information from a project. The implicit tone was that, as experts, consultants should not look at their clients as potential teachers. In the course of their work, however, they did observe things or learn new things about the client's industry. One respondent mentioned, "sure, I learn from clients all the time. And at the industry level you learn something about their work. But do they teach me things? No. You have to have the right mindset and have an inquisitive mind. If you don't go looking for it, you don't see it." A second respondent commented, "I'm one of those who always takes, takes away from the experience, and what I think I learn most from my clients is how many, how often at a senior level, they know extremely little or nothing at all about their industry." While these consultants clearly learned things on their engagements, specifically about their clients' industries and business challenges, they do not view their clients as sources of learning. They view the "real" learning as a one-way process, from consultant to client.

We versus Me: View of self as dependent on versus independent from the client.
The consultants who used a relational approach viewed themselves as dependent—in a mutual way—on their clients. This concept is akin to a relationship marketing approach (Berry, 1995; Bitner, 1995), where the consultant seeks to create enhanced value for clients over time through learning about the client and customizing the product to meet the clients' changing needs. One respondent who held this view mentioned how, "to me the relationship is more important than the project. Projects will come and go, but the relationships should stay in place. I nurture my relationships ... And in fact my clients, my handful of very very dear and long-term clients, before I moved to [firm], I went to all of them and asked them how they felt about it. If even one of them said 'no way, we won't follow you over there,' I wouldn't have gone ... the relationship is more important to me than anything." A second respondent mentioned that, "if you build the relationships, the services follow. My job is to keep giving my clients new ideas, new information. Twenty-five percent of the time, something hits. I have to be flexible and creative for them. They are my success." These consultants view themselves as dependent on their clients, and they work very hard to ensure their clients are satisfied with the relationship.

Reflecting a more traditional view, 82% of the consultants in this study see themselves as independent, or partially independent, from their clients. They work with their client, and hope that their projects lead into additional work, but for the most part, these consultants see themselves as the independent eye that moves from project to project, and from client to client. As an example, one respondent, claimed, "in a lot of cases, we'll end up with clients who aren't happy because they don't like the answer. We are a big five accounting firm and we can't forget what the 'P' in CPA stands for—the public—and the public expects that if our name is on the report, I think there's an assumption that it's been looked at with the public in mind, so ... our credibility is critical there ... You don't want to have too close a relationship with your clients ... you need to remain as professional as possible." Similarly, another respondent said, "one of the more important qualities and skills a consultant should have is judgment, being able to make an informed, objective opinion ... that's what I give clients. I've built my reputation around that." A third mentioned, "clients hire us for the independent view. It's this concept of having an independent third party who's an expert in a particular industry and we're viewed as part of due diligence activities ... The client wants to have that independent analysis come from a group like us." These consultants view their independent, objective opinion as critical to their work and their credibility. They do not think of themselves as dependent on their clients. Rather they see their clients as dependent on them for the credibility their expertise and firm name provides.

Demonstrating Expertise Through Asking Questions versus Telling Information

The last distinguishing characteristic of a relationship approach is the way expertise is demonstrated. Consultants who use this approach tend to ask focused, careful questions, using listening skills as a strategy to discern clients' needs and, in doing so, to demonstrate their knowledge. For example, one respondent mentioned how, "my way of letting people know I'm an expert is by asking questions that are thought provoking, that make them know that I'm bringing something to the table because they wouldn't have even known to ask those questions." A second respondent said, "the good partner will take the time to figure out the client's needs, will ask lots of questions and spend lots of time listening to what's important to the client." Additionally, one respondent commented, "it's collaborative, it's me asking questions and then shutting up and hearing what the client has to say. That's how I help them."

Alternatively, those who use a more traditional approach demonstrate their expertise through telling and showing clients how much they know. Sixty percent of the respondents use this approach and demonstrate their expertise through not only what they say, but through how they say it. On consultant, for example, discussed how, "it's important to have good presentation skills … how it's presented and how it's delivered is very important to clients … it's confidence and you have to come back at them a little bit with the, not with the ego, but that you're confident … approach is really important." Another said, "all of our clients are looking for experts, but if you can't get your point across both verbally and in writing with confidence then it's going to be useless to the clients. It's so important. You must be able to stand up in front of a crowd and sell the project, sell our clients, sell them that we're qualified to do the project." A third respondent said, "I explain and teach. But I have to stop if they get Bambi eyes. Then it's all over." In this more traditional view, consultants show their expertise through telling and teaching.

RELATIONAL SERVICE DELIVERY

A limitation of this study is that the data were not as clear as the preceding discussion may suggest. Some respondents gave multiple answers to questions; others offered some responses that indicated a relational approach and other responses that indicated a more traditional one. In addition, some offered responses that did not fall into either category. The distinguishing feature of these results, however, is that six of the fifty respondents offered answers that closely mirrored relational practice, while the majority of respondents offered answers that followed a more traditional approach to consulting and service delivery.

Reflecting on Fletcher's (1998, 1999) research, relational practice at work includes behaviors that contribute to the overall success of a project, empower others working on that project, enhance self-development, and build and reinforce a sense of unity and team. Fletcher's conclusions strongly parallel findings in this research. Those respondents who incorporated a relational approach in their service delivery attempted to create working relationships that fostered questioning, listening and idea sharing. These consultants worked hard to empower their clients, not with information and data per se, but with new knowledge and tools. By doing so, they not only helped them on the assigned project, but also provided a foundation that their clients could use to build success in other aspects of their work as well as other relationships. Moreover, these consultants did not perceive themselves solely as the client's coach or support system, instead viewing their clients as a source of new learning for themselves as well. In fact, these consultants viewed themselves as dependent on their clients and their client relationships. This dependency was seen as a source of their personal success and reputation rather than a weakness. This mutual, shared approach to learning and developing mirrors the concepts that describe growth-enhancing relationships.

The more traditional approach used by the majority of consultants in this study, in contrast, reflected more expert-based, one-way service delivery. These consultants viewed themselves as primarily the client's advisor. Their role was to inform and pass knowledge to the client, and they did so through telling the client new information. These consultants viewed their experience working on projects, not working with clients, as sources of new knowledge. Many also adopted an independent, objective manner that they believed helped contribute to the credibility of their firm, credibility being the primary driver for new business. These concepts support those in the professional literature that suggest experts impart knowledge to clients in a one-way, control-oriented manner, from consultant to client. In fact, one only needs to think of interactions with their doctor or lawyer to see that this approach represents a common way of delivering expertise in certain professions.

These findings suggest one way relational practice is used in professional service delivery by both men and women. This approach reflects the importance of creating and maintaining relationships where both parties grow and develop, illustrating how a "relationship marketing" concept can be applied to consulting, where over time the consultant continuously tailors the product to meet the client's needs and, by doing so, sells the relationship as much as the product.

While strong communication skills have long been viewed as critical to building client relationships, this study suggests that the way in which such communication skills are used is also important. As indicated in the interviews, the capability to create a *power-with* versus a *power-over* mindset—via communication and listening skills—was perceived to enhance the ability of some of the consultant respondents to meet their client's unique needs.

This approach is different from process consultation models of consulting (e.g., Schein, 1988) that focus entirely on co-collaborative process skills. A relational approach blends expertise *and* process. Through the ways they interact with their clients, consultants who use a relational approach deliver their expertise in such a way that enables both parties to grow and develop. The respondents in the study felt that both themselves and their clients were better for the experience.

Does using a relational approach lead to greater success for service professionals, especially consultants? Of the six respondents who identified a using relational approach, three commented that they were the top revenue producers for their group. Of the majority of consultants who reported using the more traditional approach, seven commented that they were one of the top producers in their group. Thus, rather than speculate, the next step in this research is to examine specific consulting approaches in the context of (1) client satisfaction and (2) their relationship to long-term financial success.

These findings offer a different avenue for research on consulting practice. Concepts in the gender and especially relational-practice literature provide a useful framework that can be used to examine and explain novel ways in which professionals and clients can work together. At a minimum, they suggest that the traditional approach to delivering expertise may no longer act as the rule and that today's clients could strongly benefit from a mutually developmental approach to expert-based consulting.

Relational practice, as discussed in gender research, offers an interesting and potentially important framework that can help us better understand the different ways service professionals interact with clients to deliver an expertise. Findings in this study show that consultants who use a relational approach apply a collaborative mind-set and skill-set to create empowering, growth-enhancing relationships with clients, where the client and consultant learn from one another. Paradoxically, the dependency the consultant has on the client is a source of strength and success. These findings offer a different way to think about service delivery, an approach that may become increasingly commonplace in the twenty-first century.

NOTE

1.   An earlier version of this paper was presented at the 2000 Academy of Management Meeting in Toronto, Canada.

REFERENCES

Argote, L. (1982). Input uncertainty and organizational coordination in hospital emergency units. *Administrative science quarterly, 27*, 420–434.

Barber, B. (1965). Some problems in the sociology of professions. In K.S. Lynn (Ed.), *The professions in America* (2nd ed., pp. 15–34). Boston: Houghton Mifflin.

Barnett, J.H., & Karson, M.J. (1989). Managers, values and executive decisions: An exploration of the role of gender, career stage, organizational level, function and the importance of ethics, relationships and results in managerial decision making. *Journal of Business Ethics, 8*, 747–771.

Benner, P. (1984). *Novice to expert: Excellence and power in clinical nursing practice.* Menlo Park, CA: Addison-Wesley.

Benner, P., & Wrubel, J. (1989). *The primacy of caring: Stress and coping in health and illness.* Menlo Park, CA: Addison-Wesley.

Berry, L.L. (1995). Relationship marketing of services: Growing interest, emerging perspectives. *Journal of the Academy of Marketing Science, 23*, 236–245.

Bitner, M.J. (1995). Building service relationships: It's all about promises. *Journal of the Academy of Marketing Science, 23*, 246–251.

Bowen, D.E., & Cumming, T.G. (1990). Suppose we took service seriously? In D.E. Bowen, R.B. Chase, & T.G. Cummings (Eds.), *Service management effectiveness* (pp. 1–12). San Francisco: Jossey-Bass.

Bowen, D.E., & Jones, G.R. (1986). Transaction cost analysis of service organization-customer exchange. *Academy of Management Review, 11*, 428–441.

Bowen, D.E., & Schneider, B. (1988). Services marketing and management: Implications for organizational behavior. In B.M. Staw & L.L. Cummings (Eds.), *Research in organizational behavior* (pp. 43–80). Greenwich, CT: JAI Press.

Carr-Saunders, A., & Wilson, P.A. (1941). *The professions.* Oxford: Clarendon Press.

Fletcher, J.K. (1999). *Disappearing acts: Gender, power and relational practice at work.* Cambridge, MA: MIT Press.

Fletcher, J.K. (1998). Relational practice: A feminist reconstruction of work. *Journal of management inquiry, 7*, 163–186.

Fletcher, J.K. (1996). A relational approach to the protean worker. In D.T. Hall (Ed.), *The career is dead—long live the career* (pp. 105–131). San Francisco: Jossey-Bass.

Fletcher, J.K. (1994). Castrating the female advantage: Feminist standpoint research and management science. *Journal of Management Inquiry, 3*, 74–82.

Gilligan, C. (1982). *In a different voice.* Cambridge, MA: Harvard University Press.

Gilligan, C., & Attanucci, J. (1988). Two moral orientations: Gender differences and similarities. *Merrill-Palmer Quarterly, 34*, 223–237.

Gutek, B.A. (1995). *The dynamics of service.* San Francisco: Jossey-Bass.

Hanlon, G. (1997). A shifting profession: Accountancy. In J. Broadbent, M. Dietrich, & J. Roberts (Eds.), *The end of the professions? The restructuring of professional work* (pp. 123–139). London: Routledge.

Hochschild, A.R. (1983). *The managed heart: Commercialization of human feeling.* Berkeley: University of California Press.

Jacques, R., & Fletcher, J.K. (1997). *Relational practice: An emerging stream of theorizing and its' significance for organizational studies.* Paper presented at the 1997 Academy of Management Meeting, Boston.

Jones, S.K., & Hiltebeitel, K.M. (1995). Organizational influence in a model of the moral decision process of accountants. *Journal of Business Ethics, 14,* 417–431.

Jordan, J.V., Kaplan, A., Miller, J.B., Stiver, I., & Surrey, J. (1991). *Women's growth in connection.* New York: The Guilford Press.

Josselson, R. (1992). *The space between us: Exploring the dimensions of human relationships.* San Francisco: Jossey-Bass.

Leidner, R. (1993). *Fast food, fast talk: Service workers and the routinization of everyday life.* Berkeley: University of California Press.

Lengnick-Hall, C.A. (1996). Customer contributions to quality: A different view of the customer-oriented firm. *Academy of Management Review, 21,* 791–824.

Loden, M. (1985). *Feminine leadership or how to succeed in business without being one of the boys.* Toronto: Random House.

Mars, G., & Nicod, M. (1984). *The world of waiters.* Boston: George Allen.

Miller, J.B. (1976). *Toward a new psychology of women.* Boston: Beacon Press.

Miller, J.B. (1991). Aren't you idealizing women? Aren't you idealizing relationships? In J. Jordan, A. Kaplan, J.M. Miller, I. Stiver, & J. Surrey (Eds.), *Some misconceptions of a relational approach.* Work in progress No. 49. Wellesley, MA: Stone Center Working Paper Series.

Miller, J.B., & Stiver, I. (1997). *The healing connection.* Boston: Beacon Press.

Neuse, S. (1978). Professionalism and authority: Women in public service. *Public Administration Review, 38,* 436–441.

Noddings, N. (1984). *Caring: A feminist approach to ethics and moral education.* Berkeley: The University of California Press.

Pierce, J. (1996). Rambo litigators: Emotional labor in a male-dominated occupation. In C. Cheng (Ed.), *Masculinities in organizations* (pp. 1–28), Thousand Oaks, CA: Sage.

Pierce, J. (1995). *Gender trails: Emotional lives in contemporary law firms.* Berkeley: University of California Press.

Rafaeli, A. (1989). When cashiers meet customers: An analysis of the role of supermarket cashiers. *Academy of Management Journal, 32,* 245–273.

Rosener, J. (1990). Ways women lead. *Harvard Business Review, 68,* 119–125.

Schein, E.H. (1988). *Process consultation.* Reading, MA: Addision-Wesley.

Schneider, B., Parkington, J.J., & Buxton, V.M. (1980). Employee and customer perceptions of service in banks. *Administrative Science Quarterly, 24,* 638–649.

Starbuck, W.H. (1992). Learning by knowledge-intensive firms. *Journal of Management Studies, 29,* 713–740.

Surrey, J. (1987). What do we mean by mutuality in therapy? In J. Jordan, A. Kaplan, J.M. Miller, I. Stiver, & J. Surrey (Eds.), *Some misconceptions of a relational approach*. Work in progress No. 49. Wellesley, MA: Stone Center Working Paper Series.

Sutton, R.I. & Rafaeli, A. (1988). Untangling the relationship between displayed emotions and organizational sales: The case of convenience stores, *Academy of Management Journal, 31,* 461–487.

Tannen, D. (1990). *You just don't understand: Women and men in conversation.* New York: Baltimore Books.

Winch, G., & Schneider, E. (1993). Managing the knowledge-based organization: The case of architectural practice. *Journal of Management Studies, 30,* 923–937.

Winter, M.F. (1988). *The culture and control of expertise.* New York: Greenwood Press.

CHAPTER 3

TOWARD A THEORY OF KNOWLEDGE ARBITRAGE

Examining Management Consultants as Knowledge Arbiters and Arbitragers[1]

Matthew Semadeni

INTRODUCTION

Few topics have captivated both the academic and practitioner communities as much as the study of knowledge (Davenport, 1997; Hargadon, 1998; Mahajan & Peterson, 1985; Spender & Grant, 1996; Swan & Newell, 1995). This fascination has led to the recent proliferation of both theory and research, focusing on such areas as intra-firm knowledge transfer (Szulanski, 1997; Zander & Kogut, 1995), inter-firm knowledge diffusion (Mansfield, 1985; Mowery, Oxley, & Silverman, 1996; Teece, Pisano, & Schuen, 1997), and multinational and cultural knowledge issues (Almeida, 1996; Appleyard, 1996; Kogut & Zander, 1993; Lam, 1997). Much of the research in this area has also focused on the role of knowledge in gaining and sustaining competitive advantage (Galunic & Rodan, 1998; Lado & Zhang, 1998; Liebeskind, 1996). This dynamic is often accomplished through the constant monitoring of competitors to stay abreast of the competitive environment (Greve, 1996;

Porter 1980, 1985; Reger & Huff, 1993) with substantial knowledge being involuntarily diffused (Mansfield, 1985; Winter, 1987).

Such knowledge diffusion often occurs via third parties referred to as "knowledge brokers" (Brown & Duguid, 1998; Hargadon, 1998; Hargadon & Sutton, 1997). According to Hargadon (1998, p. 10), the task of a knowledge broker is to move knowledge "from where it is known to where it is not." Studies of such knowledge brokers include investment bankers (Haunschild & Miner, 1997), board members (Haunschild, 1993), public officials (Skok, 1995), agents (Valley, White, Neale, & Bazerman, 1992), and product designers (Hargadon & Sutton, 1997). Hargadon's (1998) definition suggests that knowledge brokers are engaged in what might be thought of as knowledge *arbitrage*. The idea of knowledge arbitrage has recently been addressed by both academics (e.g., Kao, 1996) and the popular press (e.g., *McKinsey Quarterly*, 1998; Yeo, 1997), and has generally been defined as a multinational issue, with individuals who span national and cultural boundaries capitalizing on the arbitrage of knowledge from one country or culture to another (Kao, 1996; Kraar, 1994).

This chapter argues for another perspective of knowledge arbitrage, that the knowledge broker engaging in knowledge arbitrage plays two distinct roles: the role of knowledge arbitrageur and knowledge arbiter. The first role is one of *action*, where the knowledge broker becomes the conduit, diffusing knowledge from a source to a recipient (Burt, 1992; Powell, Koput, & Smith-Doerr, 1996). The second role is more problematic, involving the *judgment* of the knowledge broker (Abrahamson, 1996). In this role, the arbiter has much discretion as to what knowledge is and is not subjected to arbitrage.

The discussion focuses on these two roles of the knowledge broker by examining client knowledge arbitrage performed by management consulting firms. It is intriguing to note that while many researchers tacitly acknowledge the knowledge broker position that management consultants occupy in the arbitrage of client knowledge (e.g., Abrahamson 1991, 1996; Abrahamson & Rosenkopf, 1993; Hargadon, 1998; O'Neill, Pouder, & Buchholtz, 1998; Reger & Huff, 1993), the details surrounding how knowledge arbitrage occurs and what knowledge receives arbitrage by management consultants, as well as the consequences of the arbitrage itself, are still largely unexplored.

This void in the knowledge literature is interesting and relevant to all parties to the knowledge arbitrage for several reasons. First, firms that use management consulting services are potentially exposing the knowledge from which they derive competitive advantage to arbitrage by management consultants. Second, firms engaging management consultants could be susceptible to knowledge arbitrage motivated by management fad or fashion or consultant methodologies. Third, given their size and the diversity of their client base, arbitrage of competitive client knowledge by management consultants is not constrained to a particular industry, potentially leading to knowledge cross-pollination. Finally, long-term clients of management consulting firms may undergo knowledge isomorphism as they are exposed to knowledge arbitrage over a long period of time. Thus, the study of knowledge arbitrage by management consulting firms has important implications for a wide array of organizations.

Building upon work done in the areas of knowledge management and management consulting, this chapter initially examines the theory surrounding knowledge arbitrage. Second, the role and nature of the consultant and the consulting engagement will be briefly explored, with particular emphasis placed on the consulting relationship. Next, client knowledge arbitrage by the consulting firm will be discussed, yielding several propositions regarding client knowledge arbitrage and its consequences. Finally, the chapter closes with a discussion of potential areas for future research.

THE THEORY OF KNOWLEDGE ARBITRAGE

Theory surrounding the concept of knowledge brokering is fairly well developed (Burt, 1992, 1997; Hargadon, 1998; Hargadon & Sutton, 1997; Marsden, 1982). Burt (1992, 1997) describes how knowledge brokers establish networks and social capital that enable them to effectively execute their responsibilities. Through these networks, knowledge brokers transmit and receive knowledge that is not readily available to all organizational members. By transacting in this manner, individuals acquire and spend social capital (Burt, 1997; Nahapiet & Ghoshal, 1998) that they use to facilitate knowledge arbitrage. Since knowledge brokers also play a gatekeeper role (Allen, 1977; Granovetter, 1973; Pagett & Ansell, 1993), they are able to exploit their situations, extracting rents from their advantageous position (Marsden, 1982). Hargadon and Sutton (1997), for example, found that design engineers at IDEO engaged in knowledge arbitrage by leveraging their past experiences and contacts on new projects in dissimilar areas (e.g., using design principles from ceiling fans to develop cooling mechanisms for personal computers).

As knowledge brokers, individuals or organizations perform two fundamental roles. First, the knowledge broker is an arbitrageur, engaged in the arbitrage of knowledge from one area to another. While this arbitrageur role may not be interesting *per se*, it raises intriguing issues when the knowledge broker is *the link* between two otherwise unconnected parties and the knowledge transferred is of value to the parties involved (Hargadon, 1998; Marsden, 1982). Furthermore, while some knowledge sources may be ambivalent to the knowledge arbitrage performed by knowledge brokers (e.g., Leonard-Barton, 1995), other knowledge sources may be put at substantial risk by knowledge arbitrage, especially if the knowledge conveyed relates to the competitive advantage of the organization (Porter, 1980, 1985). Additionally, knowledge arbitrage may have a substantial impact upon the knowledge recipient, potentially influencing strategies and processes through the introduction of new or disparate knowledge (Hargadon, 1998; Walsh & Ungson, 1991).

In addition to the role of knowledge arbitrageur, knowledge brokers also act as knowledge arbiters, selecting what knowledge will *and* will not undergo arbitrage (Abrahamson, 1991, 1997; Abrahamson & Fombrun, 1994). Given this advantageous position, knowledge brokers may exploit the ignorance of other network members to their own advantage (Burt, 1992; Marsden, 1982). An illustration of this dynamic is found in Abrahamson's work (1991, 1996) on the influence of fads and fashions on management. Abrahamson (1991, p. 591) describes how "unclear goals and high uncertainty" among managers drive a frenetic search for "the next big thing" in management. Such an environment is fertile ground for the planting of management fad and fashion seeds by knowledge arbiters. Much of Abrahamson's (1996) critique centered on the time-to-market approach to new management concepts and ideas, with trend-setting management "fashion setters" racing to get their fashions out to market before their competitors. Fashion setters who delay in advocating new concepts risk being labeled as "laggards" and having their contribution marginalized. This dynamic reflects the "norm of progress" (Abrahamson, 1996, p. 262) assumption held by management, which states that managers must continually innovate and evolve or risk being left behind. The management fashion setters described by Abrahamson (1996, p. 264) feed upon this assumption, continually supplying new management fashions through a four phase process of creation, selection, processing, and dissemination (based on DiMaggio & Hirsch, 1976). Only knowledge deemed "valuable" to the fashion-setting firms survives the selection process. Commenting on this, Abrahamson (1991, p. 596) stated:

> fashion-setting organizations may select only administrative technologies they believe they can market profitably, regardless of how technically efficient the technologies would be for organizations. Fashion-setting organizations may, therefore, impel the diffusion of inefficient technologies or the rejection of efficient ones.

Thus, if knowledge brokers act as purveyors of management fads and fashions, knowledge arbitrage could be significantly impacted through the self-interested arbiter role of the knowledge broker.

Thus far, discussion has focused on the dual roles of the knowledge broker as knowledge arbitrageur and knowledge arbiter. The emphasis now turns to the knowledge arbitrage process performed by knowledge brokers, a process that consists of three fundamental components: knowledge acquisition, knowledge arbitrage, and the consequences of the knowledge arbitrage.

Knowledge Acquisition

Shackle (1955, p. 18) stated that knowledge "is a very peculiar commodity... for knowledge would not be [acquired] if it were already possessed; and when we [acquire] knowledge we do not know what we are going to get." In this regard, knowledge brokers act much like alert entrepreneurs (Kirzner, 1979), seeking knowledge sources that will provide them with the collateral necessary to engage in knowledge arbitrage. The acquisition and arbitrage of knowledge is particularly attractive given knowledge's "positive-sum, increasing-return qualities" which cause knowledge to expand and increase in value when it is shared (Lado & Zhang, 1998, p. 490).

Knowledge acquisition is facilitated and constrained by such items as organizational routines, dominant logic, knowledge stickiness, redundant knowledge and absorptive capacity. These facilitators and constraints are critically important in the knowledge arbitrage process since they, in large measure, determine the knowledge that is acquired and made available for arbitrage.

First, organizational routines are established over time as organizations increase their ability to replicate performance (Hannan & Freeman, 1984). As such, much tacit organizational knowledge is trapped in routines (Nelson & Winter, 1982) that act as both assets (Dierickx & Cool, 1989) and liabilities (Henderson & Clark, 1990; Leonard-Barton, 1992). As assets, the knowledge broker is able to use organizational routines to exploit existing "stocks" of knowledge as well as to potentially create new stocks (Nonaka, 1994). On the other hand, routines may lock firms into certain trajectories (Henderson & Clark, 1990) or paths (Arthur, 1989) that will constrain their ability to capitalize on existing knowledge stocks or to acquire new knowledge (Leonard-Barton, 1992).

Second, and very closely related to organizational routines, is the concept of "dominant logic" (Bettis & Prahalad, 1995; Prahalad & Bettis, 1986). Prahalad and Bettis (1986) describe dominant logic as being shaped by experiences and expertise. Like organizational routines, dominant logic may be an asset or liability to the organization. While dominant logic can be a strong force for the institutionalization of organizational culture (Ochi, 1980), enabling firms to replicate past performance, it may also lead knowledge brokers to approach dissimilar situations in a uniform fashion. This tendency, which is captured by the adage "when you have a hammer, every thing looks like a nail," suggests that although the logic applied to the situation is not relevant, the individual does not perceive the irrelevance due to the influence of the dominant logic base. A potential hazard to knowledge acquisition occurs when *new* or *divergent* knowledge, with which the knowledge broker has not previously dealt, confronts dominant logic (Prahalad & Bettis, 1986). When this occurs, dominant logic may act as a filter (Bettis & Prahalad, 1995), giving rise to two issues. First, important knowledge may be unconsciously filtered out by the dominant logic, thereby precluding that knowledge from acquisition. Second, dominant logic could lead individuals to overemphasize certain knowledge, focusing too much attention of some factors to the possible exclusion of others (Ocasio, 1997). Both issues will have substantial influence on the knowledge acquired by the knowledge broker.

Knowledge acquisition may also be plagued by knowledge "stickiness" (von Hippel, 1994), the inherent difficulty associated with the acquisition of certain kinds of knowledge. While knowledge stickiness, which has been examined at both the intra-firm (Szulanski, 1997; Zander & Kogut, 1995) and inter-firm levels (Mansfield, 1985; Mowery et al., 1996; Teece et al., 1997), is influenced by many factors (Szulanski, 1995), the *type* of knowledge being acquired is especially important. Knowledge is generally regarded as either tacit or explicit (Polanyi, 1967), with tacit knowledge being far more difficult to articulate and transfer than explicit knowledge (Nonaka, 1994). The difference between tacit and explicit knowledge clearly raises a number of issues for knowledge brokers. Kogut and Zander (1992), for example, identified the paradox of replication and imitation: if a firm can replicate knowledge, that knowledge can also be imitated by a competitor. This reality was found to influence what operations multinational firms retain as wholly owned versus shared through joint venture (Kogut & Zander, 1993). Similarly, knowledge acquisition is shaped by the type of knowledge being acquired, with explicit knowledge acquisition generally transpiring with less stickiness than tacit knowledge. In fact, Nonaka (1994) asserts that for tacit knowledge to be acquired, it must be "externalized" through metaphor and analogy into explicit knowledge. Invariably some knowledge is lost in the process, supporting Polanyi's (1967, p. 4) assertion that "we can know more than we can tell." Thus, since knowledge stickiness influences knowledge acquisition by a knowledge broker, certain types of knowledge may be favored due to their lack of stickiness.

Fourth, knowledge brokers must possess prior redundant knowledge for knowledge acquisition to take place. Redundant knowledge, sometimes referred to as social knowledge (Kogut & Zander, 1996; Miller & Shamsie, 1996; Spender, 1996), is defined as common knowledge held within an organization that facilitates dialogue (Nonaka, 1994). Through redundant knowledge, a common frame of reference is established enabling the diffusion of knowledge among organizational members (Galunic & Rodan, 1998). Redundant knowledge is thus acquired by knowledge brokers as they interact with various parties over time and establish a shared means of exchange based on a common understanding of relationships and symbols (Kogut & Zander 1992; Tushman & Scanlan, 1981; Walsh & Ungson, 1991). To discharge their position, knowledge brokers are required to possess redundant or overlapping knowledge with multiple groups (Brown & Duguid, 1998; Hargadon, 1998; Hargadon & Sutton, 1997), allowing them to communicate effectively with various knowledge sources and recipients. Through redundant knowledge, knowledge brokers are able to acquire knowledge from a source *and* communicate it to a recipient. Consequently, the amount of redundant knowledge shared by the knowledge broker with the knowledge source will affect the degree to which knowledge acquisition will take place, with knowledge arbitrage being hampered by a lack of redundant knowledge.

Finally, the absorptive capacity of the knowledge broker will influence the amount of knowledge arbitrage that will occur. Cohen and Levinthal (1990, p. 128) define absorptive capacity as "the ability of a firm to recognize the value of new, external information, assimilate it, and apply it to commercial ends." In looking at absorptive capacity in terms of the redundant knowledge of an organization, they (1990, p. 129) argue that "the premise of the notion of absorptive capacity is that the organization needs prior knowledge to assimilate and use new knowledge." Thus, existing knowledge facilitates the acquisition and integration of new knowledge. Szulanski (1997) found that a lack of recipient absorptive capacity was the most significant obstacle to intra-firm transfer of best practices. Although the study design precluded any derivation of causality, Szulanski theorized that this knowledge "stickiness" was due to the lack of absorptive capacity by the knowledge recipient. As such, absorptive capacity is perhaps the defining characteristic of the knowledge broker (Hargadon, 1998) and will determine how effectively they will engage in knowledge arbitrage.

In summary, organizational routines, dominant logic, knowledge stickiness, redundant knowledge and absorptive capacity act as facilitators of or constraints to knowledge acquisition by knowledge brokers. Although knowledge brokers may be unaware of the effects these variables have on the knowledge arbitrage in which they are engaged, each item could have considerable impact not only upon the knowledge acquired, but also upon the knowledge brokers themselves.

Knowledge Arbitrage

Much of the prior discussion regarding the dual role of the knowledge broker as knowledge arbiter and knowledge arbitrageur subsumes the fundamental concepts of the knowledge arbitrage process, with a few notable exceptions. First, knowledge arbitrage may occur at multiple levels, from the individual level (Blackler, 1995) to the firm level (Szulanski, 1997) to the inter-firm level (Hargadon, 1998; Hargadon & Sutton, 1997). Though much of the work surrounding knowledge brokers and the knowledge arbitrage they effectuate has focused on individual knowledge brokers (e.g., individual design engineers at IDEO (Hargadon & Sutton, 1997) or individual board members of the board (Davis, 1991; Haunschild, 1993; Westphal, 1999), knowledge arbitrage may also take place at more macro levels, with firms acting as knowledge brokers (Davenport, 1997). In this capacity, knowledge broker firms leverage the individual knowledge possessed in one area of the firm into other areas, accomplishing both *internal* and *external* knowledge arbitrage. Internal knowledge arbitrage occurs when knowledge conveys within the firm (Szulanski, 1997) while external knowledge arbitrage occurs when the knowledge broker organization conveys knowledge between previously disconnected organizations (Hargadon, 1998).

Next, since knowledge arbitrage occurs at various levels, it follows that knowledge arbitrage at different levels will have different implications. For example, knowledge arbitrage occurring at the individual level will generally involve interchange mechanisms distinct from those utilized at the firm or inter-firm levels, with different interchange mechanisms causing different knowledge arbitrage. At an individual, interactive level, more analogy and metaphor may be involved (Nonaka, 1994), whereas firm and inter-firm level exchanges may be more formal and standardized (e.g., reports, presentations). At the individual level, Brown and Duguid (1998, p. 103) state that knowledge brokering "involves participation rather than mediation" where knowledge brokers "are a feature of overlapping communities." At more macro levels, knowledge arbitrage is constrained by the ability of the knowledge broker to convey knowledge to a wide audience. This conveyance involves opportunity costs and is often less effective than arbitrage effectuated at more micro levels given the knowledge lost through standardization. Knowledge standardization requires the knowledge broker to adopt a "least common denominator" approach to the knowledge, potentially causing the loss of much knowledge richness or divergence through simplification. Thus, while the knowledge may enjoy a wider audience, the relative value of knowledge imparted will be lower.

Finally, knowledge arbitrage may be affected by knowledge broker biases based in competition or rivalry. Given that knowledge broker power is derived primarily by the broker's ability to move knowledge among otherwise unconnected parties, the advent of other knowledge brokers may initiate rivalry, potentially leading to competition. Although this rivalry and subsequent competition could lead to increased knowledge arbitrage, it could also lead knowledge brokers to discount the contributions of competing knowledge brokers while promoting their own (Katz & Allen, 1982), as occurs with management fads and fashion (Abrahamson, 1991, 1996) in an effort to maintain their reputation and social capital (Burt, 1992, 1997; Nahapiet & Ghoshal, 1998). Analogously, knowledge brokers may fall prey to "bandwagon effects" (Abrahamson & Rosenkopf, 1993) that cause them to engage in knowledge arbitrage that is perhaps less efficacious for the knowledge recipient in order to maintain the power derived from their knowledge broker position.

Knowledge Arbitrage Consequences

The final component in the knowledge arbitrage process is an examination of the consequences of knowledge arbitrage. In a competitive market (Porter, 1980, 1985), the potential loss of competitive advantage through knowledge arbitrage is a genuine concern. Competitive environments lead many firms to engage in constant competitor monitoring (Greve, 1996; Reger & Huff, 1993) through mechanisms such as benchmarking or competitor analysis (Ghoshal & Westney, 1991). Many times the source of this competitive information is a knowledge broker who has access to knowledge not publicly available. If knowledge brokers occupy positions that allow them to acquire knowledge not otherwise available, and then subject that knowledge to arbitrage, the competitive knowledge of the knowledge source may be imperiled. Although the arbitrage of this knowledge may be beneficial for the economy,[2] it can be devastating to the source firm, literally bleeding away its competitive advantage.

As knowledge brokers perform knowledge arbitrage, substantial power accrues to the brokers through their gatekeeper position (Allen, 1977; Granovetter, 1973). Conceptually, power denotes capacity or ability (Barnes, 1988; Haugaard, 1997); in the case of knowledge brokers, this capacity is derived from joining two otherwise unconnected parties (Burt, 1992). From this position the broker is able to exact rents for the knowledge arbitrage performed (Marsden, 1982), with these rents based more on the recipient's perceptions of the knowledge rather than the knowledge itself (Kirzner, 1979). In this sense, any resulting power is derived from managing the impressions of the knowledge recipients (Brown, 1997). This power may be thought of as social capital (Burt, 1992, 1997; Nahapiet & Ghoshal, 1998) that may be used to further the objectives of the knowledge broker and solidify their power in the network (Pagett & Ansell, 1993).

Next, firms subjected to knowledge arbitrage over extended periods may undergo knowledge isomorphism, "a constraining process that forces one unit in a population to resemble other units" (DiMaggio & Powell, 1983, p. 149). DiMaggio and Powell (1983) hypothesized that uncertainty and ambiguity would lead to isomorphism and reliance upon boundary-spanning organizations. Such conditions exist during knowledge arbitrage when the knowledge recipients rely upon the knowledge provided by the broker to dispel uncertainty and ambiguity. Furthermore, knowledge brokers operate in boundary-spanning positions (Tushman & Scanlan, 1981), relying on their reputation (Clark, 1995) in performing knowledge arbitrage to perpetuate their position. Consequently, firms engaging in knowledge arbitrage may, over time, experience knowledge isomorphism, which could lead to increased knowledge homogeneity between knowledge sources and recipients.

Finally, although the discussion thus far has focused on unidirectional knowledge arbitrage, bidirectional arbitrage is not only possible but it is more probable than unidirectional knowledge arbitrage. As such, bidirectional knowledge arbitrage could lead to knowledge cross-pollination (Hargadon & Sutton, 1997), the combination of existing firm knowledge with new knowledge received from outside the firm's boundaries—potentially yielding positive or negative effects. Positive effects include the adaptation of the new knowledge to the firm's own purposes (Teece et al., 1997) potentially sparking innovation (Galunic & Rodan, 1998). Negative effects include the possible perpetuation of ineffectual or questionable knowledge to areas that would be otherwise shielded, yielding substandard performance (Hayes & Abernathy, 1980). In this sense, knowledge brokers play a key role, going as it were like bees from flower to flower, in the process distributing knowledge both within and beyond industry groups (Appleyard, 1996).

In summary, the consequences of knowledge arbitrage will affect all parties involved. The potential arbitrage of competitive knowledge, the accrual of power to knowledge brokers, knowledge isomorphism, and knowledge cross-pollination each have significant impacts upon the knowledge source, the knowledge broker, and the knowledge recipient. Furthermore, an understanding of the knowledge arbitrage process illuminates many important points and issues that are important for the type of specific knowledge arbitrage performed in management consulting.

THE MANAGEMENT CONSULTING PROFESSION

Few trends have impacted firms in the past decade as much as the increase in the use of management consultants. Global consultant revenues are exploding, rising from $51 billion in 1995 to a projected $113 billion in 2000 (Kennedy Research Group, 1998), with some firms such as AT&T spending more on management consulting services than R&D (McKenna, 1995). This rise in the use of external management expertise has led to concern about the overall efficacy of consultants (Chen, Farah, & Mac-Millan, 1993), a proliferation of management fads (Abrahamson, 1991, 1996), discussion of consultant-client friction (Kesner & Fowler, 1997), and even calls for management consultant licensure and regulation (State of Nevada, 1999). Although investigation into the use of management consultants is not new (Higdon, 1969; Tilles, 1961), one area that has yet to be explored is the knowledge arbitrage function performed by management consultants. As a result of their intimate contact with the competitive aspects of client organizations, management consulting firms often have access to client knowledge not otherwise available, a reality that places management consultants in a knowledge broker position, functioning as both knowledge arbitrageurs and knowledge arbiters.

The Role and Nature of Management Consulting

A brief examination of the management consulting profession illuminates several key aspects of the knowledge arbitrage function it performs. Greiner and Metzger (1983, p. 7) define management consultant services as:

advisory service[s] contracted for and provided to organizations by specially trained and qualified persons who assist, in an objective and independent manner, the client organization to identify management problems, analyze such problems, recommend solutions to those problems, and help, when requested, in the implementation of solutions.

This definition connotes the intimate relationship established between a firm and its management consultants, with the consultants in close contact not only with the issues or opportunities facing the firm, but also the proposed remedies.

Next, the question arises as to why organizations employ consultants. Procurement of management consulting services hinges on three factors: uncertainty, time compression, and legitimacy and reputation. Stinch-combe (1990, p. 17) refers to the first factor of uncertainty mitigation as the utilization of the "expertise of analyzers" who sort through the "noise" in organizational information to provide coherence to otherwise chaotic events. Dierickx and Cool (1989) described the second concept, time compression, in their discussion of asset stocks. In essence, the organization does not have the necessary asset stocks (e.g., managerial or technical talent) to resolve the problem nor the time required to build up such stocks. The third factor influencing the retaining of management consultants is that of legitimacy and reputation (Clark, 1995) where the client organization derives social capital (Nahapiet & Ghoshal, 1998) or status in addition to the consulting services rendered when a prestigious management consulting firm is retained. Through their use of prestigious management consultants, organizations can garner stakeholder support, both internal and external, for initiatives such as reorganization, diversification, or new product development.

Knowledge Arbitrage and The Consulting Engagement

To clearly understand the knowledge arbitrage of management consulting firms one must examine the consulting engagement process. The process utilized here is described in the generic sense and does not address the particularities of the various forms of management consulting (e.g., strategic consulting, process consulting, technology consulting, etc.) due to the high degree of homogeneity among the approaches of the various management consulting firms (O'Shea & Madigan, 1997). In addition, the firms described by this model are generally larger, composed of multiple groups that each work in different areas, generally according to industry (O'Shea & Madigan, 1997). Smaller consulting firms, consisting of fewer consultants, would exhibit knowledge arbitrage dynamics different from those presented in this chapter. Finally, the difference between the firm and the assigned team creates two units of analysis. The consulting team is a subunit of the consulting firm, generally working within an industry group (e.g., oil and gas, manufacturing, utilities) or in a functional specialty (e.g., change management, strategic planning). Although consulting teams may become quite large, they are usually rather cohesive in regards to knowledge diffusion (Hansen, Nohria, & Tierney, 1999). Many of the dynamics that will be discussed in subsequent sections will deal with issues at the *consulting firm* level, where individuals who did not participate on a particular consulting engagement are recipients of the client knowledge from that engagement through intra-firm knowledge arbitrage.

There are essentially two parties to the consulting engagement: the consultant firm (represented by a team of consultants) and the client organization (Greiner & Metzger, 1983; Robertson & Swan, 1998). The client organization provides explicit organizational knowledge (in the form of organizational data, policy manuals, organizational charts, etc.). The consulting team provides standardized methodologies, the training and experience (i.e., personal prior engagement knowledge) of the individual team members, and the client knowledge that the firm has garnered from *other* previous consulting engagements in which the consulting team members have not participated (Abramson, 1999; Stewart, 1995).

During the consulting engagement, the consulting team and client organization work together to achieve the purpose of the engagement (e.g., strategy development, change management, reengineering). During this process, explicit knowledge is cataloged along with tacit knowledge that is generally extracted or harvested by consultants as part of the consulting engagement. Much tacit organizational knowledge is embedded in organizational routines (Nelson & Winter, 1982), architectures (Henderson & Clark, 1990), or individuals (Nonaka, 1994), and may not be readily perceptible to the client organization. As objective outsiders, management consultants work to capture this tacit knowledge through interviews, observation, or other forms of collection. This knowledge is then codified according to the methodologies the management consultants apply to the engagement (Byrne, 1994; Higdon, 1969).

The knowledge product of the consulting engagement is twofold. First, the individuals participating in the engagement gain tacit knowledge through the consulting experience that can be carried forward to the next engagement[3] (if consultants) or can be applied to future client organization problems or issues (if client organization members). Second, explicit knowledge and tacit knowledge that has been made explicit during the engagement is captured into "deliverables" (formal reports or summaries of findings) that are presented to the client organization. Additionally, management consulting firms retain the deliverables from their consulting engagements that they amass into large, cross-sectional, multi-industry databases (Abramson, 1999; Davenport, 1997; Hansen et al., 1999; Stewart, 1995). Thus, while the individual or consulting team tacit knowledge arbitrage from client to client may be bounded, both by memory and stamina, the arbitrage of much of the explicit knowledge gained through the engagement is not. This client knowledge becomes a resource to the consulting firm for subsequent consulting engagements.

Client Knowledge Acquisition

Although knowledge acquisition by management consulting firms is a multifaceted topic, three main themes emerge as germane to knowledge arbitrage: the use of knowledge management routines, the types of knowledge available in the consulting relationship, and the prior experiences of the consulting team and consulting firm. These themes largely determine the degree to which client knowledge is successfully acquired, stored and subsequently used in knowledge arbitrage.

First, the popular press contains numerous references to the use of knowledge management processes to facilitate knowledge arbitrage within management consulting organizations (Abramson, 1999; Davenport, 1997; Ross, 1996; Stewart, 1995). These processes, which may be manual or automated, are fundamentally organizational routines (Hannan & Freeman, 1984; Nelson & Winter, 1982) framed by the dominant logic (Bettis & Prahalad, 1995; Prahalad & Bettis, 1986) of a management consulting firm. Management consulting firms have put enormous resources into information technology approaches to acquire and diffuse knowledge within their organizations (Abramson, 1999; Davenport, 1997; Ross, 1996), investments that have had mixed success (Hansen et al., 1999). These knowledge management technologies are efficient at acquiring knowledge the consulting firm *recognizes* as valuable. In other words, client knowledge that either supports existing firm knowledge or converges with it is likely to be acquired (Cohen & Levinthal, 1990). However, knowledge management systems are also susceptible to structural rigidity (Leonard-Barton, 1992) and path dependency (Arthur, 1989) that may preclude knowledge acquisition if the knowledge is atypical or structured in a format divergent from that used by the system. For example, atypical or divergent knowledge could include knowledge acquired from clients in industry groups not previously penetrated or from clients in countries or cultures not previously serviced. In this case, knowledge management technologies may act as filters (Bettis & Prahalad, 1995), hampering the perception of client knowledge. These tendencies lead to the following propositions:

Proposition 1. Established knowledge management processes will positively affect the acquisition of knowledge that supports existing client knowledge or converges with it.

Proposition 2. Established knowledge management processes will negatively affect the acquisition of knowledge that does not support existing client knowledge or diverges from it.

Notwithstanding the efforts of management consulting firms to holistically acquire knowledge from their client engagements, some client knowledge may resist acquisition. For example, although tacit client knowledge is generally of greater value than explicit knowledge (Kogut & Zander, 1993), it is much "stickier" and will resist acquisition (Szulanski, 1997), potentially leading firms to favor explicit knowledge that is more readily acquired. Indeed, Hansen and colleagues (1999, p. 113) cite a partner at Bain & Company as stating that the firm's knowledge acquisition and diffusion efforts "offered a picture of the cake without giving the recipe." The "recipe" in this case would require tacit knowledge that was not acquired when the explicit knowledge "picture" was taken. A lack of tacit knowledge will substantially impact the value of the acquired knowledge given that *both* tacit and explicit knowledge are necessary for the knowledge dialogue process described by Nonaka (1994), leading to the following proposition:

> **Proposition 3.** The ease of explicit client knowledge acquisition will increase its acquisition by management consulting firms vis-à-vis tacit client knowledge.

Finally, the redundant knowledge and absorptive capacity of the management consulting firm will substantially impact knowledge acquisition, with absorptive capacity determined to a large degree by the amount of redundant knowledge (Cohen & Levinthal, 1990) that exists within the firm and that exists between the consulting firm and its clients. Prior consulting engagements with particular clients will increase the amount of redundant knowledge between the consulting firm and the client organization and will also increase the absorptive capacity of the consulting firm. Conversely, a lack of redundant knowledge will make client knowledge "sticky" and will hamper its acquisition (Szulanski, 1997). Subsequently, I offer the following proposition:

> **Proposition 4.** Prior consulting engagements with a client will increase the redundant knowledge between the consultant and client organizations, increasing the absorptive capacity of the management consulting firm and the knowledge acquisition from that client.

Thus, client knowledge acquisition by the management consulting firm will be effected by the firms knowledge acquisition routines, by the stickiness of the client knowledge, and by the absorptive capacity and redundant knowledge of the firm.

Client Knowledge Arbitrage

In performing client knowledge arbitrage, management consulting firms act as both arbitrageurs and arbiters. They are arbitrageurs in the sense that as knowledge brokers they move knowledge from where it is to where it is not (Hargadon, 1998). They are arbiters in the sense that they adjudicate the knowledge acquired, deciding which knowledge will and will not undergo arbitrage.

Although several external factors influence client knowledge arbitrage, perhaps no factor is as salient to the management consulting field as Abrahamson's discussion of management fad and fashion (1991, 1996). Management fashion setters such as management consultant firms feed upon the perpetual change in management approaches, continually supplying new management fashions. As discussed earlier, a four-phase process of creation, selection, processing, and dissemination (Abrahamson, 1996, p. 264; DiMaggio & Hirsch, 1976) is readily apparent in the arbitrage of client knowledge by management consulting firms. First, knowledge is generated during the consulting engagement, with tacit knowledge retained by the engagement participants and explicit knowledge captured in deliverables. The tacit knowledge created may be shared with others in the firm through consultant rotation, but tacit knowledge will not receive as wide a diffusion as the explicit knowledge captured in the deliverables. Second, client knowledge is scrutinized for its profit-generating value, with the knowledge deemed marketable or reusable retained while the balance of the knowledge is discarded or ignored. Third, the explicit knowledge selected is packaged or processed in preparation for its reuse (Bahrami & Evans, 1995). Finally, the selected client knowledge is disseminated to other consultants as the next management fad or fashion.

The capability to choose what knowledge is and is not significant places management consulting firms in the position of knowledge arbiter, providing the basis for the following proposition:

> **Proposition 5.** Client knowledge arbitrage will be positively affected by perceived market value or reusability of the knowledge with other clients, and negatively affected by uncertain market value or singular applicability.

Next, from the client knowledge acquired, consulting firms build a repertoire of general explicit knowledge that they can then leverage on other consulting engagements. Much of this knowledge is codified, distributed, and inculcated into individual management consultants in the form of methodologies (Higdon, 1969; O'Shea & Madigan, 1997). Consulting firms continually author and update these methodologies that they promote not only as their solution to management problems, but also as a means by which a firm may obtain sustained competitive advantage vis-à-vis its competitors (Byrne, 1994). These methodologies become selling tools (Clark, 1995; Greiner & Metzger, 1983) that are used within and across industries to exhibit the consulting firm's explicit knowledge. Additionally, such methodologies act to legitimate (Pfeffer, 1981) the processes employed by the consultants. Consequentially, methodologies are influential in directing the knowledge arbitrage of the consulting firm, with knowledge that agrees or converges with the methodological approach receiving greater weight compared to knowledge that disagrees or diverges from the methodological approach, leading to the following proposition:

> **Proposition 6.** Existing consulting firm methodologies will affect knowledge arbitrage by filtering client knowledge according to methodological

applicability, with convergent or affirming knowledge favored over divergent or disaffirming knowledge.

Finally, competition or rivalry among the various management consulting firms acting as knowledge brokers may color the knowledge arbitrage performed by the consulting firm. In the highly competitive environment of management consulting (O'Shea & Madigan, 1997), firms may focus their arbitrage activity toward knowledge in areas of firm-specific competitive advantage (Abrahamson, 1996). This may also lead firms to discount or ignore knowledge different from their area of specialty. Furthermore, although rivalry at times leads to imitation (e.g., Katz & Shapiro, 1987), in the high-reputation environment of management consulting (Clark, 1995), partners and managers may be loath to copy a rival for fear of lending credence to the rival's knowledge broker position. Thus, the arbitrage affected by the management consulting firm is vulnerable to influences completely external to the efficacy of the knowledge, leading to the following proposition.

Proposition 7. Competition and rivalry among management consulting firms will bias client knowledge arbitrage.

In summary, the client knowledge arbitrage process is significantly influenced by the knowledge broker roles of arbiter and arbitrageur, with management fad and fashion, consulting methodologies, and inter-firm rivalry influencing the arbitrage performed.

Client Knowledge Arbitrage Consequences

Several consequences emerge from the arbitrage of knowledge, consequences that influence all parties involved in the arbitrage process. These consequences include the loss of competitive knowledge by the knowledge source, accrual of power by the knowledge broker, and knowledge isomorphism and knowledge cross-pollination among the knowledge recipients.

First, a consulting engagement exposes or generates significant client knowledge, knowledge that often pertains to the competitive advantage of the client organization. During the engagement, the consulting team must "translate" such firm-specific information and jargon into a form that they and other consultants within the firm can understand (Greiner & Metzger, 1983). The product of this translation process is in part the deliverables that are ultimately given to the client organization and retained by the consulting firm. By making explicit knowledge that would otherwise be trapped within the organizational routines and processes of the organization (Henderson & Clark, 1990; Nelson & Winter, 1982), consultants liberate this knowledge so that it may be applied to other clients through arbitrage. Thus, the competitive advantage of the client knowledge source is endangered by the arbitrage of their competitive knowledge through the use of management consulting services, which leads to the following proposition:

Proposition 8. Loss of competitive client knowledge will increase through client knowledge arbitrage by management consulting firms.

Another consequence of client knowledge arbitrage by management consulting firms is the accrual of power to the management consulting firms due to their knowledge broker position. Power is represented by the consulting firm's ability or capacity to move knowledge among their client group. Management consulting firms are able to extract rents (Marsden, 1982) from their position as well as use their knowledge broker position to build their reputation (Brown, 1997). This reputation can then be used to further consolidate their position as a knowledge broker. Consequentially, I offer the following proposition:

Proposition 9. Through repeated client knowledge arbitrage, the management consulting firm's knowledge arbitrage power will increase.

Finally, over time knowledge arbitrage will affect the knowledge recipients by causing knowledge isomorphism, leading to knowledge homogeneity as well as cross-pollination of knowledge among the firms experiencing knowledge arbitrage. First, isomorphism generally occurs due to uncertainty and ambiguity (DiMaggio & Powell, 1983). These factors are all generally present in the consulting relationship (Byrne, 1994; Clark, 1995), with consultants engaged when uncertainty and ambiguity are high (Stinchcombe, 1991). Furthermore, as consultants transfer their approach via their methodologies to their client base, firms adopt similar approaches to common management problems (*The Economist*, 1996). An example of this is found in a statement from a CEO, describing the knowledge isomorphism that occurs through the use of management consultants:

> Recently ... I have found that [my management consultants] are trying to push cookie-cutter solutions. It's almost as if they are simply changing the names on the same set of presentations. While some of their advice is useful, I am not sure if that's enough. Frankly, I expect more. (Hansen et al., 1999, p. 113)

Consequentially, some argue that extended exposure to this knowledge isomorphism may be detrimental to client organizations in the long run (e.g., Hayes & Abernathy, 1980). Thus, it is proposed that:

Proposition 10. Through client knowledge arbitrage, management consultant client organizations will, over time, experience knowledge isomorphism resulting in increased knowledge homogeneity.

Management consulting firms also fill a boundary-spanning role among their client group (Tushman & Scanlan, 1981). This role is accomplished by individual consultants who often consult to multiple industries and by the consulting organization's access to large, cross-sectional, multi-industry databases (Abramson, 1999; Davenport, 1997; Stewart, 1995) which contain client knowledge that has survived the selection process described earlier. Thus, management consultants facilitate the cross-pollination (Hargadon & Sutton, 1997) of ideas and industry specific knowledge to which their client group would not otherwise have access. The effects of this cross-pollination could be either positive (Hargadon, 1998) or negative (Hayes & Abernathy, 1980) for the organizations involved. Positive effects include the introduction of new approaches or novel thinking to otherwise closed industries, while negative effects could include the spread of ineffective or deleterious knowledge or practices among otherwise isolated or insulated industries. Hence, I offer the following proposition:

Proposition 11. Through client knowledge arbitrage, management consulting firms will cross-pollinate industry-specific client knowledge to client organizations outside the knowledge source's industry.

The consequences of client knowledge arbitrage extend to all parties involved, affecting them through the potential loss of competitive knowledge, through an increase in the power of the knowledge broker, and through knowledge isomorphism and cross-pollination.

SUMMARY

The contribution of this chapter is threefold. First, the chapter introduces a new perspective on the concept of knowledge arbitrage, one based on the dual roles of knowledge arbiter and knowledge arbitrageur. Next, the discussion advances the knowledge literature by developing theory surrounding the knowledge arbitrage process, examining knowledge acquisition, knowledge arbitrage, and the consequences of knowledge arbitrage. Finally, the theory is applied to the well known, but as of yet unexamined, area of client knowledge arbitrage by management consulting firms.

Several prospective research areas exist in the study of client knowledge arbitrage by management consulting firms. First, the empirical test of the propositions presented in this chapter will add significantly to the extant literature on knowledge arbitrage by professional organizations. While such testing will not be easy, especially given the secretive nature of client-consultant relationships (Higdon, 1969; O'Shea & Madigan, 1997), proxies are available (e.g., the Big 5 accounting firms generally expand their audit relationships [which are declared in 10-K filings] into consulting relationships). Also, the adaptation of the heterogeneous diffusion model (Greve, 1995, 1996; Greve, Strang, & Tuma, 1995) discussed by Drazin and Schoonhoven (1996) could be used to model the network and contagion effects of knowledge arbitrage by management consulting firms. Through the heterogeneous diffusion model, both effects could be modeled simultaneously, providing more robust empirical results.

Another area of research, not directly addressed in this chapter, focuses on how the client knowledge selected for arbitrage is packaged and diffused to the consultants and thereafter to clients. Examination of this area may be most appropriately approached from an information technology perspective given the high investment by consulting firms in information technology to support their knowledge management initiatives (Abramson, 1999; Ross, 1996). This examination could be explored from the dichotomous perspectives of simply *knowing* client knowledge versus having possessing the actual *technical competence* needed to implement that knowledge, what Attewell (1992, p. 4) refers to as the difference between the knowledge "signal" and the actual "know-how."

In conclusion, knowledge arbitrage, especially within the management consulting profession, represents a fascinating dimension of the knowledge literature and provides an excellent milieu for the examination of this phenomenon, especially given the explosive growth in the use of management consulting services. This chapter has endeavored to initiate an examination of knowledge arbitrage in management consulting, hopefully serving as a point-of-departure for further work in this area.

NOTES

1.   The author wishes to thank Bert Cannella, Javier Gimeno, Ann McFadyen, Aswin van Oijen and the participants of a seminar in Strategy at Texas A&M University for their contribution to this chapter. An earlier version was presented at the 2000 Academy of Management meeting in Toronto, Canada.

2.   In 1924 the Supreme Court ruled that such exchanges were in the public's interest "because the making available of such information tends to stabilize trade and industry, to produce fairer prices, and to avoid the waste which inevitably attends the unintelligent conduct of economic enterprise" (*Maple Floor Mfrs. Assn. v. United States*, 268 U.S. 563, 582–583).

3.   Consultant knowledge benefit is illustrated by a statement from an Anderson Consulting manager who said "every time you go to a customer, you learn something and it increases your value, your knowledge grows" (Hargadon, 1998, p. 15).

REFERENCES

Abrahamson, E. (1996). Management fashion. *Academy of Management Review, 21*(1), 254–285.

Abrahamson, E. (1991). Management fads and fashions: The diffusion and rejection of innovations. *Academy of Management Review, 16*(3), 586–612.

Abrahamson, E., & Fombrun, C.J. (1994). Macrocultures: Determinants and consequences. *Academy of Management Review, 19*(4), 728–755.

Abrahamson, E., & Rosenkopf, L. (1993). Institutional and competitive bandwagons: Using mathematical modeling as a tool to explore innovation diffusion. *Academy of Management Review, 18*(3), 487–517.

Abramson, G. (1999). On the KM midway. *CIO, 12*(15), 62–70.

Allen, T.J. (1977). *Managing the flow of technology.* Cambridge, MA: The MIT Press.

Almeida, P. (1996). Knowledge sourcing by foreign multinationals: Patent citation analysis in the U.S. semiconductor industry. *Strategic Management Journal, 17,* 155–165.

Appleyard, M.M. (1996). How does knowledge flow? Interfirm patterns in the semiconductor industry. *Strategic Management Journal, 17,* 137–154.

Arthur, W.B. (1989). Competing technologies, increasing returns, and lock-in by historical events. *The Economic Journal, 99,* 116–131.

Attewell, P. (1992). Technology diffusion and organizational learning: The case of business computing. *Organization Science, 3*(1), 1–19.

Bahrami, H., &. Evans, E. (1995). Flexible recycling and high tech entrepreneurship. *California Management Review, 37*(3), 62–89.

Barnes, B. (1988). *The Nature of power.* Urbana: University of Illinois Press.

Bettis, R.A., &. Prahalad, C.K. (1995). The dominant logic: Retrospective and extension. *Strategic Management Journal, 16*(1), 5–15.

Blackler, F. (1995). Knowledge, knowledge work, and organizations: An overview and interpretation. *Organization Studies, 16*(6), 1021–1046.

Brown, A.D. (1997). Narcissism, identity, and legitimacy. *Academy of Management Review, 22*(3), 643–686.

Brown, J.S., & Duguid, P. (1998). Organizing knowledge. *California Management Review, 40*(3), 90–111.

Burt, R. (1997). The contingent value of social capital. *Administrative Science Quarterly, 42,* 339–365.

Burt, R. (1992). The social structure of competition. In N. Nohria & R.G. Eccles (Eds.), *Networks and organizations* (pp. 57–91). Boston: Harvard Business School Press.

Byrne, J.A. (1994, July 25). The craze for consultants. *Business Week,* pp. 60–66.

Chen, M-J., Farah, J-L., & MacMillan, I.C. (1993). An exploration of the expertness of outside informants. *Academy of Management Journal, 36*(6), 1614–1632.

Clark, T. (1995) *Management consultants: Consultancy as the management of impressions.* Philadelphia: Open University Press.

Cohen, W.M., & Levinthal, D.A. (1990). Absorptive capacity: A new perspective on learning and innovation. *Administrative Sciences Quarterly, 35,* 128–152.

Davenport, T.H. (1997). *Information ecology: Mastering the information and knowledge environment.* New York: Oxford University Press.

Davis, G.F. (1991). Agents without principles? The spread of the poison pill through the intercorporate network. *Administrative Science Quarterly, 36*(4), 583–613.

Dierickx, I., & Cool, K. (1989). Asset stock accumulation and sustainability of competitive advantage. *Management Science, 35,* 1504–1511.

DiMaggio, P.J., & Hirsch, P. (1976). Production organizations in the arts. In R.A. Peterson (Ed.), *The production of culture* (pp. 73–90). Beverly Hills, CA: Sage.

DiMaggio, P.J., & Powell, W.W. (1983). The iron cage revisited: Institutional isomorphism and collective rationality in organizational fields. *American Sociological Review, 48*(2), 147–160.

Drazin, R., &. Schoonhoven, C.B. (1996). Community, population, and organization effects on innovation: A multilevel perspective. *Academy of Management Journal, 39*(5), 1065–1083.

Economist. (1996, May 4). Andersen's androids. *The Economist,* p. 72.

Galunic, D.C., & Rodan, S. (1998). Resource recombinations in the firm: Knowledge structures and the potential for Schumpeterian innovation. *Strategic Management Journal, 19,* 1193–1201.

Ghoshal, S., & Westney, D.E. (1991). Organizing competitor analysis systems. *Strategic Management Journal, 12*(1), 17–31.

Granovetter, M.S. (1973). The strength of weak ties. *American journal of sociology, 78,* 1360–1380.

Greiner, L.E., & Metzger, R.O. (1983). *Consulting to management.* Englewood Cliffs, NJ: Prentice-Hall.

Greve, H.R. (1996). Patterns of competition: The diffusion of a market position in radio broadcasting. *Administrative Science Quarterly, 41*(1), 29–60.

Greve, H.R. (1995). Jumping ship: The diffusion of strategy abandonment. *Administrative Science Quarterly, 40,* 444–474.

Greve, H.R., Strang, D., & Tuma, N.B. (1995). Specification and estimation of heterogeneous diffusion models. In P.V. Marsden (Ed.), *Sociological methodology* (pp. 377–420). Cambridge, MA: Blackwell.

Hannan, M.T., &. Freeman, J. (1984). Structural inertia and organizational change. *American Sociological Review, 49*(2), 149–164.

Hansen, M.T., Nohria, N., & Tierney, T. (1999). What's your strategy for managing knowledge? *Harvard Business Review, 77*(2), 106–116.

Hargadon, A.B. (1998). Firms as knowledge brokers: Lessons in pursing continuous innovation. *California Management Review, 40*(3), 209–227.

Hargadon, A., & Sutton, R.I. (1997). Technology brokering and innovation in a product development firm. *Administrative Science Quarterly, 42*(4), 716–750.

Haugaard, M. (1997). *The constitution of power: A theoretical analysis of power, knowledge and structure.* New York: Manchester University Press.

Haunschild, P.R. (1993). Interorganizational imitation: The impact of interlocks on corporate acquisition activity. *Administrative Sciences Quarterly, 38*(4), 564–592.

Haunschild, P.R., & Miner, A.S. (1997). Modes of interorganizational imitation: The effects of outcome salience and uncertainty. *Administrative Science Quarterly, 42*(3), 472–500.

Hayes, R.H., & Abernathy, W.J. (1980). Managing our way to economic decline. *Harvard Business Review, 58*(4), 67–77.

Henderson, R., & Clark, K. (1990). Architectural innovation: The reconfiguration of existing product technologies and the failure of established firms. *Administrative Science Quarterly, 35*, 9–30.

Higdon, H. (1969). *Business healers.* New York: Random House.

Kao, J.J. (1996). *Jamming: The art and discipline of business creativity.* New York: Harper Business.

Katz, M.L., & Shapiro, C. (1987). R&D rivalry with licensing or imitation. *American Economic Review, 77*(3), 402–420.

Katz, R., & Allen, T.J. (1982). Investigating the "Not-Invented-Here" syndrome: A look at the performance, tenure, and communication patterns of 50 R&D project groups. *R&D Management, 12*(1), 7–19.

Kennedy Research Group. (1998, January 7). Kennedy Research predicts $114 billion consulting market by 2000. *Kennedy Research Group,* Fitzwilliam, NH.

Kesner, I.F., & Fowler, S. (1997). When consultants and clients clash. *Harvard Business Review, 75*(6), 22–38.

Kirzner, I.M. (1979). *Perception, opportunity, and profit: Studies in the theory of entrepreneurship.* Chicago: University of Chicago Press.

Kogut, B., & Zander, U. (1996). What firms do? Coordination, identity, and learning. *Organization Science, 7*(5), 502–518.

Kogut, B., & Zander, U. (1993). Knowledge of the firm and the evolutionary theory of the multinational corporation. *Journal of International Business Studies, 24*(4), 625–645.

Kogut, B., & Zander, U. (1992). Knowledge of the firm, combinative capabilities, and the replication of technology. *Organization Science, 3*, 383–397.

Kraar, L. (1994). The overseas China. *Fortune, 130*(9), 91–114.

Lado, A.A., & Zhang, M.J. (1998). Expert systems, knowledge development and utilization, and sustained competitive advantage: A resource-based model. *Journal of Management, 24*(4): 489–509.

Lam, A. (1997). Embedded firms, embedded knowledge: Problems of collaboration and knowledge transfer in global cooperative ventures. *Organization Studies, 18*(6), 973–997.

Leonard-Barton, D. (1995). *Wellsprings of knowledge: Building and sustaining the sources of innovation.* Boston: Harvard Business School Press.

Leonard-Barton, D. (1992). Core capabilities and core rigidities: A paradox in managing new product development. *Strategic Management Journal, 13*: 363–380.

Liebeskind, J.P. (1996). Knowledge, strategy, and the theory of the firm. *Strategic Management Journal, 17*, 93–107.

Mahajan, V., & Peterson, R.A. (1985). *Models for innovation diffusion.* Beverly Hills, CA: Sage.

Mansfield, E. (1985). How rapidly does new industrial technology leak out? *Journal of Industrial Economics, 34*(2), 217–223.

Marsden, P.V. (1982). Brokerage behavior in restricted exchange networks. In P.V. Marsden & N. Lin (Eds.), *Social structure and network analysis* (pp. 201–218). Beverly Hills, CA: Sage.

McKenna, C.D. (1995). The origins of modern management consulting. *Business and Economic History, 24*(1), 51–58.

McKinsey Quarterly. (1998). Industrial venture capitalism: Sharing ownership to create value. *McKinsey Quarterly,* (1), 26–34.

Miller, D., & Shamsie, J. (1996). The resource-based view of the firm in two environments: The Hollywood film studios from 1936 to 1965. *Academy of Management Journal, 39*(3), 519–543.

Mowery, D.C., Oxley, J.E., & Silverman, B.S. (1996). Strategic alliances and interfirm knowledge transfer. *Strategic Management Journal, 17,* 77–91.

Nahapiet, J., & Ghoshal, S. (1998). Social capital, intellectual capital, and the organizational advantage. *Academy of Management Review, 23*(2), 242–267.

Nelson, R.R., & Winter, S.G. (1982). *An evolutionary theory of economic change.* Cambridge, MA: Belnap Press of Harvard University Press.

Nonaka, I. (1994). A dynamic theory of organization knowledge creation. *Organization Science, 5,* 14-37.

O'Neill, H.M., Pouder, R.W., & Buchholtz, A.K. (1998). Patterns in the diffusion of strategies across organizations: Insights from the innovation diffusion literature. *Academy of Management Review, 23*(1), 98–114.

O'Shea, J., & Madigan, C. (1997). *Dangerous company: The consulting powerhouses and the businesses they save and ruin.* New York: Random House.

Ocasio, W. (1997). Toward an attention-based view of the firm. *Strategic Management Journal, 18,* 187–206.

Ochi, W.G. (1980). Markets, bureaucracies, and clans. *Administrative Sciences Quarterly, 25,* 129–141.

Pagett, J.F., & Ansell, C.K. (1993). Robust action and the rise of the Medici, 1400–1434. *American Journal of Sociology, 98*(6), 1259–1319.

Pfeffer, J. (1981). *Power in organizations.* Boston: Pittman.

Polanyi, M. (1967). *The tacit dimension.* London: Routledge & Kegan Paul.

Porter, M.E. (1985). *Competitive advantage: Creating and sustaining superior performance.* New York: Free Press.

Porter, M.E. (1980). *Competitive strategy: Techniques for analyzing industries and competitors.* New York: Free Press.

Powell, W.W., Koput, K.W., & Smith-Doerr, L. (1996). Interorganizational collaboration and the locus of innovation: Networks of learning in biotechnology. *Administrative Science Quarterly, 41*(1), 116–145.

Prahalad, C.K., & Bettis, R. (1986). The dominant logic: A new linkage between diversity and performance. *Strategic Management Journal, 7,* 485–501.

Reger, R.K., & Huff, A.S. (1993). Strategic groups: A cognitive perspective. *Strategic Management Journal, 14,* 103–124.

Robertson, M., & Swan, J. (1998). Modes of organizing in an expert consultancy: A case study of knowledge, power, and egos. *Organization, 5*(4), 543–564.

Ross, C.F. (1996, July 15). Knowledge management. *Gartner Group Report.*

Shackle, G.L.S. (1955). *Uncertainty in economics, and other reflections.* Cambridge: Cambridge University Press.

Skok, J.E. (1995). Policy issue networks and the public policy cycle: A structural-functional framework for public administration. *Public Administration Review, 55*(4), 325–332.

Spender, J-C. (1996). Making knowledge the basis of a dynamic theory of the firm. *Strategic Management Journal, 17,* 45–62.

Spender, J-C., & Grant, .M. (1996). Knowledge and the firm: Overview. *Strategic Management Journal, 17*, 5–9.

State of Nevada. (1999). *Provide for regulation of professional management consultants.* Nevada State Legislation Proceedings, Senate Bill 220.

Stewart, T.A. (1995). Mapping corporate brainpower. *Fortune, 132*(9), 209–111.

Stinchcombe, A.L. (1990). *Information and organizations.* Berkley, CA: University of California Press.

Swan, J.A., & Newell, S. (1995). The role of professional associations in technology diffusion. *Organization studies, 16*(5), 847–874.

Szulanski, G. (1997). Exploring internal stickiness: Impediments to the transfer of best practice within the firm. *Strategic Management Journal, 17*, 27–43.

Szulanski, G. (1995). *Appropriating rents from existing knowledge: Intra-firm transfer of best practice.* Unpublished Ph.D. dissertation. France INSEAD.

Teece, D.J., Pisano, G., & Schuen, A. (1997). Dynamic capabilities and strategic management. *Strategic Management Journal, 18*(7), 509–533.

Tilles, S. (1961, November-December). Understanding the consultant's role. *Harvard Business Review*, pp. 87–99.

Tushman, M.L., & Scanlan, T.J. (1981). Boundary spanning individuals: Their role in information transfer and their antecedents. *Academy of management journal, 24*(2), 289–305.

Valley, K.L., White, S.B., Neale, M.A., & Bazerman, M.H. (1992). Agents as information brokers: The effects of information disclosure on negotiated outcomes. *Organizational Behavior & Human Decision Processes, 51*(2), 220–236.

von Hippel, E. (1994). "Sticky information" and the locus of problem solving: Implications for innovation. *Management Science, 40*(4), 429–439.

Walsh, J.P., & Ungson, G.R. (1991). Organizational memory. *Academy of Management Review, 16*(1), 57–91.

Westphal, J.D. (1999). Collaboration in the boardroom: Behavioral and performance consequences of CEO-board social ties. *Academy of Management Journal, 42*(1), 7–24.

Winter, S.G. (1987). Knowledge and competence as strategic assets. In D. Teece (Ed.) *The competitive challenge* (pp. 159–184). Cambridge, MA: Ballinger.

Yeo, G. (1997). Keep bridging cultural boundaries. *Asian Business, 33*(9), 14.

Zander, U., & Kogut, B. (1995). Knowledge and the speed of transfer and imitation of organizational capabilities: An empirical test. *Organizational Science, 6*(1), 76–92.

PART II

TRENDS AND TECHNIQUES IN MANAGEMENT CONSULTING

CHAPTER 4

CONSULTING AND EQ

Enhancing Emotional Intelligence in the Workplace

Aaron J. Nurick

INTRODUCTION

Much has been said and written about the term "emotional intelligence" since the publication of Daniel Goleman's (1995) popular volume on the concept. The business world, ever quick to catch onto a growing trend, responded with special enthusiasm leading Goleman (1998) to follow up with a second book titled *Working With Emotional Intelligence* that focuses on applying emotional intelligence to organizational life. As Goleman (1998, p. 3) suggests in his introduction, "The new measure takes for granted having enough intellectual ability and technical know-how to do our jobs; it focuses instead on personal qualities, such as initiative and empathy, adaptability and persuasiveness." Not surprisingly, many organizations have launched programs designed to improve the emotional intelligence or "EQ" of their members, ranging from such well-known corporations as American Express to the U.S. Air Force (Schwartz, 2000).

   The whole area of emotional intelligence has become a fertile ground for consultants working to improve organizational effectiveness and helping organizations anticipate and cope with major changes. This chapter presents a model that consultants may find useful as they engage client organizations around these issues. The central focus is an application of a well-recognized measurement instrument, the Bar-On Emotional Quotient Inventory (EQ-i), developed by Israeli psychologist, Reuven Bar-On (1997). Before developing that framework, it is necessary to gain a theoretical appreciation of the term *emotional intelligence*, and its relevance to modern organizational life and as a foundation for consultation.

DEFINING EMOTIONAL INTELLIGENCE

Although emotional intelligence has become a very popular term since the publication of Goleman's (1995) book on the topic and it does have the "feel" of a new concept, there are multiple definitions and understandings about its meaning. Given the amount of attention in the media and the multiplicity of websites and EQ measures and seminars that currently exist, one might conclude that a whole new field of inquiry has been established. Yet, as Goleman (2000) observes, this apparently new field actually has roots that are well embedded in psychological thought during the last century.

The current concept of emotional intelligence has followed a progression beginning with the work of Reuven Bar-On (1997) in the 1980s on measuring "EQ" with the Emotional Quotient Inventory (EQ-i) and Howard Gardner (1983), who introduced the idea of multiple intelligences including "personal" (or emotional) intelligence. The term "emotional intelligence" was first used by Salovey and Mayer (1990) and then transported into the popular culture by Goleman (1995, 1998). Since that time, the term has become the latest in a series of "buzzwords" that are part of the national conversation. According to Mayer, Salovey, and Caruso (2000a,b), emotional intelligence may be viewed from three perspectives: (1) as a cultural trend or part of the cultural and political zeitgeist; (2) as a group of personality traits that are important to success in life such as persistence and achievement motivation; and (3) as a set of abilities identified by scientific literature concerning the processing of emotional information.

The zeitgeist approach to emotional intelligence captures the current cultural tension between emotion and reason that echoes such debates throughout history. The fusing of the term "emotion" with understood notions of "intelligence" seemed to provide a necessary integration of seemingly competing pathways to success in work and life. It also suggested a certain egalitarian spirit that enabled a wider definition of success, counteracting the narrow focus of *The Bell Curve* (Herrnstein & Murray, 1994) by implying that EQ might not only be more important than IQ, but that it could be learned and enhanced as well. As Mayer et al. (2000, p. 97) conclude, "emotional intelligence has been suggestive of a kinder, gentler, intelligence—an intelligence anyone can have."

The most widely used definitions of emotional intelligence focus more on a mixture of personality and socioemotional factors (Mayer et al., 2000). Goleman's (1995) conceptualization included five factors: knowing emotions, managing emotions, motivating oneself, recognizing emotions in others, and handling relationships. In his later work, Goleman (1998, pp. 26–28) expanded the model to twenty-five competencies that incorporate more work-related aspects such as political awareness, service orientation, and achievement drive (the latter reflecting Goleman's early association with David McClelland). By contrast, Bar-On (1997, p. 14) provides a rather simple definition of emotional intelligence as "an array of non-cognitive capabilities, competencies and skills that influence one's ability to succeed in coping with environmental demands and pressures." The emphasis here is on psychological health and emotional well-being reflected in ten key components: self-regard, interpersonal relationship, impulse control, problem solving, emotional self-awareness, flexibility, reality testing, stress tolerance, assertiveness, and empathy. In addition to these core components, Bar-On (2000) describes and measures five "facilitators" of emotionally and socially intelligent behavior: optimism, self-actualization, happiness, independence, and social responsibility. Cooper and Sawaf (1996) present yet another component model with four "cornerstones" of emotional literacy, emotional fitness, emotional depth and emotional alchemy, each with subcomponent measures ranging from emotional honesty to resilience and renewal to creating the future.

The most comprehensive approach to EQ is provided by Mayer et al. (2000a,b) who present an ability theory of emotional intelligence concerned with processing emotions. Their process model operates across the cognitive and emotional domains and forms a system consisting of four branches, beginning with emotional perception and identification and sequentially moving through the processes of emotional facilitation of thought and emotional understanding, culminating in emotional management. This systems approach to emotional intelligence recognizes the "messy, fuzzy" aspects of emotions and the need to be flexible as one considers the unpredictable nature of relationships and the varying emotional paths one may pursue. Mayer et al. (2000a,b) provide evidence—and a strong argument—that this increasingly popular term is indeed an intelligence that can be measured and applied to how people function in various settings, including organizations.

EQ AND THE CURRENT WORK ENVIRONMENT

As we enter the twenty-first century, there are a number of reasons why emotional intelligence has special resonance in today's business world. With the exponential growth of information technology and its dramatic effects on how business operates, individuals are increasingly feeling the stress of constant change in their organizations. Turbulent environments, once an obscure theoretical concept in the 1960s, have become the new corporate reality. Organizations are moving to flatter and more fluid structures that require greater levels of interdependence and, as a result, more interpersonal competence to get work done. The current generation of workers, mostly coming of age in the last 20 years and comprising more women, is generally more comfortable with emotional expression and less likely to draw a sharp and immutable line between work and personal life as their forebears were. Whatever the causes, it is clear that there continues to be a need to more fully develop the human aspects of corporate life.

Two Metaphors for Change

Change is recognized as the constant in modern organizations. Managers are faced with increasing uncertainty and turbulence, reflecting the increased pace of world events, the competitive pressures posed by a dynamic, global economy, and instant and ubiquitous communication enabled by technology. These forces led Peter Vaill (1989) to use the metaphor "permanent whitewater" to depict this experience. Drawing upon the earlier work of Emery and Trist (1965), who coined the term "turbulent environments," Vaill (1989, p. 2) describes the visual appeal of this metaphor that he suggests:

> vividly conveys a sense of energy and movement. Things are only very partially under control, yet the effective navigator of the rapids is not behaving randomly or aimlessly. Intelligence, experience, and skill are being exercised, albeit in ways that we hardly know how to perceive, let alone describe.

We can begin to see this experience as a precursor to understanding both the appreciation and application of emotional intelligence in the workplace.

In similar fashion, Shapiro and Carr (1991) captured the experience of being "lost in familiar places" as a way of being that recognizes how individuals feel unstable even in familiar institutions such as social organizations and the family. They speak of rapidly changing systems that have moved beyond their inhabitants' ability to comprehend them. Shapiro and Carr

(1991, p. 4) conclude that individuals "awash, therefore, in a sea of complex and overlapping contexts" are constantly faced with the task of redefinition, adjusting identities that are rooted in very deeply held and often unconscious values and beliefs.

These combined metaphors point to the need for human skills that can both adapt to and even thrive in increasingly turbulent, changing and unpredictable environments. Individuals must be flexible and open to new ideas and more willing to work in collaborative, team environments. The challenge for managers in these complex and fluid structures is not to fall prey to natural human resistance to change. Managers in such environments become increasingly vulnerable to stress, leading to more defensive behavior in the form of over-controlling rigidity (i.e., "micro-managing") or projecting their own weaknesses onto employees. Such behavior can result in dysfunctional behavior patterns and toxic organizational cultures. Emotional intelligence is thus becoming an increasingly critical factor in creating successful and productive organizations in rapidly changing environments.

EQ AND CONSULTING

Given the changing nature of organizations and the growing interest in emotional intelligence as both a scientific and cultural phenomenon, there are numerous opportunities for consultants to assist organizations and their members in dealing with emotional difficulties in the workplace. It could be argued, of course, that there is nothing really new here. After all, consultants have worked with these issues for years under the general banner of "human relations," and, in the relatively near future, EQ could join other acronyms such as MBO (Management by Objectives) and TQM (Total Quality Management) as short-lived fads. While this danger is ever present, EQ seems to hold a deeper meaning for business, especially as it affects individual and organizational performance. There is growing recognition that "soft skills"—such as the capacity to listen to new ideas and problems and to act assertively—are important to bottom-line results and not simply feel-good techniques reminiscent of sensitivity training. Moreover, since EQ is measurable and changeable—two aspects of the construct that bode well for consultants—organizations and their members have a basis to assess changes and related progress.

An EQ Consultation Model

Accepting the fact that EQ is part of the cultural lexicon and that emotional intelligence is a growing part of a national conversation, it is important to carefully delineate how consultants can effectively work with these issues. Each of the theoretical approaches noted earlier lends itself to certain paths to intervention. As it was with Quality of Work Life in the 1970s and Total Quality Management and Reengineering in the 1980s and 1990s, a consultant can pass off any training program as an "EQ program," hoping to ride and profit from the wave of popular sentiment. To avoid such shallow and potentially harmful approaches, it is necessary to establish some general criteria for effective work in this area.

1. *The program must be based on a sound theoretical foundation.* As discussed above, there are several theoretical approaches to understanding and working with emotional intelligence. Whether one wishes to work with a cultural, personality, or ability approach, or a combination of these approaches, it is useful to have a framework to provide a lens of understanding for both the consultant and client. While it is not necessary to adhere to a rigid, dogmatic program or set of ideas, having a set of well-grounded precepts lends credibility to the experience and avoids the "latest bag of tricks" perception.

2. *The program should begin with diagnosis.* Assessment can be the basis for both understanding and change. Levinson (1991) states that even though many consultants claim that they do not diagnose, every intervention is based on an implicit diagnosis based on some set of assumptions. The purpose of formal diagnosis is to collect enough data to understand the presented problem and to begin to clarify these assumptions by basing inferences on the data. Whether accomplished by observation, interviews, measurement instruments or a combination of these techniques, the consultant develops a knowledge base from which to draw preliminary conclusions, ask new questions, and prepare action steps.

3. *The program should focus on targeted interventions.* Following diagnosis, the consultant should develop a sense of where the most important needs are and focus on interventions that specifically address those needs. Such interventions can be quite varied, taking the form of presentations, training around specific issues or skills, group and individual feedback, and coaching. The most important aspect is that the client understands and feels the need for intervention, buys into the program, and can see the relevance for organizational functioning. This avoids the feeling of a "canned" program where one size fits all—no matter what the issues are.

4. *The program should provide the basis for continued learning.* With a sound conceptual and diagnostic base, the consultant can develop a continuing relationship with the organization whereby the issues and skills can be revisited. Some interventions may take a while to

sink in and work through the organization. Also, new issues arise as the organization faces new and perhaps unforeseen challenges. Once the client has a framework and a language to think clearly about the issues, the consultant can provide meaningful follow-up and assist the organization in adapting to changes.

A Diagnostic Model for EQ Consulting

Based on the above criteria, the model proposed here builds on Bar-On's (1997) definition of emotional intelligence and uses the Emotional Quotient Inventory (EQ-i) as an assessment and diagnostic instrument. The underlying rationale is that EQ has been empirically demonstrated to be an important factor in effective organizational performance and leadership (Stein & Book, 2000) and that Bar-On's (1997) definition emphasizes adapting to change. Stein and Book (2000) report findings based on the administration of the EQ-i to 42,000 people from 36 different countries. Although there are other measures of EQ, including the Emotional Competence Inventory (ECI) based on Goleman's framework (Boyatsis, Goleman, & Rhee, 2000), the EQ-i is a well-established instrument with a 20-year history and a large database. As with similar measures, the EQ-i requires a consultant to go through a training program and certification process to learn to administer and interpret the instrument. According to those familiar with the questionnaire, it provides a very precise and subtle measure that captures the factors related to success across group categories, including occupations, gender, race, and socioeconomic levels (Stein & Book, 2000).

The Emotional Quotient Inventory (EQ-i)

Bar-On (1997) developed the EQ-i to measure five major components or "realms" of EQ including: Intrapersonal, Interpersonal, Adaptability, Stress Management, and General Mood. Each component will be defined along with its subscales according to descriptions found in Bar-On (1997) and Stein and Book (2000).

Intrapersonal

The intrapersonal realm focuses on the "inner self," how well one expresses feelings, lives and works independently, and has confidence expressing ideas and beliefs. The intrapersonal scales are:

- *Emotional Self-Awareness:*   The ability to recognize and differentiate between feelings and emotions.
- *Assertiveness:*   The ability to express feelings, beliefs, and thoughts, and defend one's rights in a nondestructive manner.
- *Independence:*   The ability to be self-directed and self-controlled in thought and action, and to be free of emotional dependency.
- *Self-Regard:*   The ability to respect and accept oneself as basically good, with a knowledge one's of strengths and weaknesses.
- *Self-Actualization:*   The ability to realize one's potential capacities, manifested by becoming involved in pursuits that lead to a meaningful, rich and full life.

Interpersonal
Included in the interpersonal realm are the "people skills" that enable one to relate well to others in a variety of situations as measured by:

- *Empathy:*   The ability to be aware of, to understand and to appreciate the feelings and thoughts of others.
- *Social Responsibility:*   The ability to be a cooperative, contributing, and constructive member of a social group, doing things for and with others, accepting others, and acting in accordance with one's conscience and upholding social rules.
- *Interpersonal Relationships:*   The ability to establish and maintain mutually satisfying relationships characterized by intimacy and by giving and receiving affection.

Adaptability
This realm comprises the ability to size up and respond to a wide range of difficult situations, the ability to grasp problems, devise effective solutions, and deal effectively with conflicts. The component scales are:

- *Problem-Solving:*   The ability to identify and define problems, and to generate and implement potentially effective solutions.
- *Reality Testing:*   The ability to assess the correspondence between what is experienced and what objectively exists, in essence "tuning in" to the immediate situation and seeing it the way it is rather than the way one wishes or fears it is.
- *Flexibility:*   The ability to adjust one's emotions, thoughts, and behavior to changing situations and conditions.

Stress Management
The realm of stress management concerns the ability to withstand stress without caving in, falling apart, losing control or going under. It involves

the ability to remain calm instead of reacting impulsively under pressure. The scales consist of:

- *Stress Tolerance.*   The ability to withstand adverse events and stressful situations without falling apart by actively and positively coping with stress.
- *Impulse Control.*   The ability to resist or delay an impulse, drive or temptation to act.

General Mood

This realm concerns one's outlook on life, the ability to enjoy oneself and others, and overall feelings of contentment or dissatisfaction as measured by:

- *Happiness.*   The ability to enjoy life, oneself and others, and to have fun.
- *Optimism.*   The ability to look at the brighter side of life and to maintain a positive attitude even in the face of adversity.

Each of the subscales listed above is measured by a self-report inventory of 133 items or statements on a 5-point scale, ranging from "Very seldom or not true of me" to "Very often true of me or true of me." Administration of the inventory follows usual conventions of informed consent and debriefing. Bar-On (1997) reports very favorable reliability (overall internal consistency average of .76) and validity as measured by nine different validity measures (see Bar-On, 1997 for the detailed studies). Because of the depth of the database, the EQ-i results can also be compared to norms according to many subgroups, including gender, age, race, and many occupations. Stein and Book (2000) provide examples of the most important components for several job categories, including consultants and top managers. Management consultants, for example, are highest on the following scales in descending order: assertiveness, emotional self-awareness, reality testing, self-actualization, and happiness.

Engaging the Client

Once a contact is made, the consultant can listen for EQ themes as part of initial discussions with the client. Consultants, for example, are often asked to work with a group around issues of strategic planning or coping with change. The organization might be experiencing unproductive levels of conflict or stress manifested in high turnover, hostile interactions, or passive-aggressive inertia such as not showing up for meetings or other organizational events. If such concerns begin to emerge, which are often discussed in more implicit and subtle ways, the consultant can suggest a diagnostic process that involves initial measurement. Since the EQ-i has many uses, ranging from selection, clinical diagnosis, and career development (Bar-On, 1997), the instrument can be used to collect data along with other means such as interviews to provide a leverage point for interventions.

Administering the Instrument

Two very important factors in successfully administering any measurement instrument, especially one that deals with such potent issues as emotional functioning, are *informed consent* and *confidentiality*. The EQ-i can be administered either individually or in a group. At the first meeting, it is important for the consultant to provide a frame or context for the measurement process by explaining that it is part of an overall organizational diagnosis and development program. It is most important for participants to know how the results will be used, that individual data will not be disseminated without their knowledge, and that they will be debriefed on their results on each of the scales. While remote administration is possible, it is best to administer the instrument on-site, with the consultant available for questions or concerns. It is also important to avoid providing too much initial information that could have the potential effect of biasing the results. The 133-item self-report questionnaire takes about 45 minutes to complete. Complete guidelines for administration are presented in Bar-On (1997).

Feedback and Interpretation

Feedback from the EQ-i is available in several forms and the consultant may choose the most appropriate format for the client's needs. At the basic level, standardized scores (with 100 as the mean score with a standard deviation of 15) are provided on overall EQ and each component scale and subscales in bar chart format. The consultant may request the normative group for the scores so that participants know whether they are being compared to the general population or to a particular subgroup. More elaborate and customized reports are also available depending on the consultant's and client's needs. These reports can range from simple bar charts to a more in-depth "development report" that has computer-generated interpretations of each subscale tailored to the individual.

During this process, the consultant should review the psychometric properties that are provided with the scores to ensure that the validity and consistency measures are acceptable. The instrument, for example, statistically detects and adjusts scores for positive and negative impression, that is, individual tendency to answer in a positive or negative way. The results indicate whether or not the scores fall within an acceptable range of positive and negative impression and are internally consistent.

After becoming familiar with the data, the consultant may then arrange a half-day to day with the organization that includes the following:

1. A brief overview of the concept of emotional intelligence, how it is defined, and a description of the EQ-i scales and their meaning.
2. A description of the feedback report that each participant will receive. At this point the consultant may provide the overall group with its EQ score and scale results.
3. Follow-up meetings with each participant to go over individual scores and their interpretation.

Receiving the individual feedback report can be a daunting experience and a powerful intervention in itself and must be done carefully and sensitively. It is very typical for participants to view the results as a scorecard or a pass-fail exam. This tendency may even be more pronounced in highly competitive business cultures. It is important, therefore, to place the results in the context of strengths and areas in need of development in comparison to the normative group. Most individuals will show a range of scores that can vary quite widely, although about two-thirds of the respondents are expected to fall within two standard deviations from the mean or a range of 85 to 115 on the scales (Bar-On, 1997).

The consultant can look for patterns that emphasize a particular theme. For example, a respondent may score lower on assertiveness and independence and higher on flexibility, indicating that he or she may have some difficulty expressing ideas and beliefs and may yield too easily to others in meetings and discussions. A person scoring lower on empathy and social responsibility, in contrast, may need to examine how they relate to others. Bar-On (1997) recommends examining individual items on scales with low scores to determine particular aspects of a problem. It is critical at this juncture to use the data as a stimulus for discussion rather than final analysis. In many instances, clients quickly recognize the implicit patterns and can talk about how the data relate to their work life. If a person is shown as experiencing stress (as shown by lower stress tolerance, intrapersonal and general mood scores), the consultant may engage him or her in a conversation about sources of stress and its impact. Together they might learn about aspects of the culture that are creating the stress and develop strategies for coping with it.

Targeted Interventions

The consultant can use the data from the EQ-i either at the group or individual level to plan targeted interventions that focus on developing appropriate interpersonal skills. Such training or mini courses may focus on enhancing particular skills and behaviors that are related to the scales, such as problem solving, identifying and dealing with feelings, and building and maintaining effective relationships. It may also be useful to provide more generalized training in key interpersonal areas such as listening, assertiveness, and conflict management that relate to several of the scales. If the organization is going through a particularly stressful period that involves high levels of change (and implied loss), the consultant can also engage the group in productive discussions that can help the emotional issues to surface in a safe atmosphere. The consultant can offer strategies that legitimize uncertainty and "not knowing" as a normal part of adapting to complex changes. The consultant can also develop a portfolio of exercises and presentations that addresses the most salient and meaningful themes based on the profiles. Stein and Book (2000), for example, provide a number of exercises and techniques that address each subscale of the EQ-i, ranging from emotional self-awareness, stress tolerance, and empathy to reality testing.

A more tailored portfolio approach develops more of an ongoing "coaching" relationship that is growing in popularity in our business culture (Hall, Otazo, & Hollenbeck, 1999). While training in specific skills such as listening and problem solving can be useful, companies need to put the training in the context of developing competencies over time in relation to behavioral and organizational change (Caudron, 1999). Ongoing practice and support *after* training becomes more crucial to gain proficiency in skills that develop over time (Laabs, 1999). This dynamic is why coaching can be such an effective mechanism to ensure ongoing development in areas designed to improve emotional intelligence. Kilburg (2000, p. 65), for example, provides a working definition of executive coaching as:

> a helping relationship formed between a client who has managerial authority and responsibility in an organization and a consultant who uses a wide variety of behavioral techniques and methods to assist the client to achieve a mutually identified set of goals to improve his or her professional performance and personal satisfaction and consequently to improve the effectiveness of the client's organization within a formally defined coaching agreement.

The typical goals of executive coaching include such things as increasing the range, flexibility, and effectiveness of the client's behavioral repertoire, increasing specific managerial tasks such as planning, decision making and staffing, and improving psychological and social competencies.

Through the coaching relationship, the client and consultant essentially build a working alliance within which the client can achieve behavioral mastery by practicing new skills over time, exploring the impact on organizational relationships and performance (Kilburg, 2000). Based on their study of executive coaching in *Fortune* 100 companies, Hall et al. (1999) found that executives benefitted most from honest, realistic and challenging feedback and the listening and action ideas from the coach. These executives acquired new skills through coaching that included new attitudes, more patience and feeling comfortable being more personal with employees, and greater adaptability. As a consequence, they were better able to deploy staff to fit different situations and do more mentoring and teaching rather than doing the job themselves. The key long-term benefit was that the executives became more reflective and able to observe and think before acting, a major component of emotional intelligence.

Concerns and Limitations

Although the concept of emotional intelligence has captured the imagination of a considerable part of our culture and has special appeal to business, it also has its detractors and critics for reasons alluded to above. The main focus of the criticism has to do with the wide popularity of the term as it has spread throughout the cultural milieu and the extravagant claims of its proponents, particularly Daniel Goleman. In a recent critique, Fineman (2000) warns of turning emotional intelligence into a commodity or another product to be sold by the academic and consulting industries. Goleman and other "purveyors of emotional intelligence stress its performance benefits and mutability, a bait for performance-hungry, competitively anxious, managers and executives..." (Fineman, 2000, p. 105). Fineman also questions the underlying moral and value base of EQ, which posits that high emotional intelligence is valued because it feeds into a competitive market that values winning and stars. Indeed, the focus of Stein and Book's (2000) work is on measuring and developing "star performers." By extension, the less emotionally intelligent are considered "rescuable" through competency training. As Fineman (2000, p. 109) observes, "Constructing emotional intelligence in the benign language of 'competencies' and 'training' may lessen the personal anxiety of being categorized as low on emotional intelligence, but it does not release the manager from contrived dependence on the consultant to improve matters."

Even Goleman (1998) himself has criticized the management training industry as "the billion-dollar mistake" that wastes both time and money without much result. As he laments, many training programs use a "spray and pray" approach that does not focus on specific behavior or evaluating outcomes. Such an orientation provides ample opportunity for slick presentations that focus more on selling a product than on developing effective skills that will benefit the individual and the organization. The dilemma and potential trap for consultants who focus on emotional intelligence is one that is not new: how to sell a product while maintaining its (*and* the consultant's) integrity. Goleman (1998) provides a set of guidelines for emotional competence training that includes assessing both the job and the individual, gauging readiness, developing clear goals, creating performance feedback, and providing organizational support for the effort.

As should be apparent from the theoretical formulations discussed earlier, emotional intelligence is far from a simple concept, despite its general appeal as a path to success. Even though instruments with such sound psychometric properties as the EQ-i provide valuable data, the bar charts and standardized scores can give the illusion of scientific, complete and accurate knowledge. It is also important to remember, as Schwartz (2000) realized, that the EQ-i is a self-assessment instrument and subject to all of the limitations of self-perception. A "360" version of the EQ-i is under development that will attempt to balance self-ratings with those of other co-workers to provide a more accurate picture.

Ironically, much of the writing about emotional intelligence has a more rational-cognitive orientation (e.g., Stein & Book's emphasis on the work of Albert Ellis and Rational Emotive Behavioral Theory), when in fact emotions most often defy our conscious knowledge (Fineman, 2000). It becomes very easy to provide the quick surface fix to a phenomenon that is very rich and complex in texture. For this reason, the real value of the model presented above emanates from the interaction between the consultant and the client around the meaning of the data and the potential for an ongoing relationship. The consultant, by asking the question "What does this score mean for *you*?" can begin an important conversation and help the client grapple with what Lawrence (1999), building on the work of Bollas (1987), has identified as the "unthought known" in much the same way that a therapist helps a client analyze a dream. The consultant helps the client give voice to information that is known at some level (and thus revealed in the EQ-i), but not fully captured in actual thoughts and words.

CONCLUSION

A new conversation has begun as corporations are realizing that emotional awareness and competence are significant sources of energy that needs to be more fully tapped. The concept of emotional intelligence in its varying forms and definitions has crystallized much of this thinking and has provided a base for an array of new organizational interventions. The consultation model and process presented in this chapter are built upon a sound theoretical and empirical foundation that uses the EQ-i as a starting point for targeted interventions designed to enhance emotional and interpersonal competence. Although there are inherent pitfalls and limitations to this approach, consultants can work with clients around data that highlight their particular strengths and weaknesses, and tailor a plan to improve emotional functioning. By focusing more on the process than the product, the consultant can temper some of the exorbitant claims that have endangered emotional intelligence as another passing fad or panacea. Perhaps the most useful outcome is an ongoing coaching relationship designed to derive mutual understanding of the meaning of the scores and then working to improve specific skills within the context of rapid organizational change. Interpersonal competence is never fully learned or perfected; rather, as French and Simpson (1999) suggest, it is a continuous learning process that takes place at the "edge of knowing and not knowing."

REFERENCES

Bar-On, R. (2000). Emotional and social intelligence: Insights from the Emotional Quotient Inventory. In R. Bar-On & D. Parker (Eds.), *The handbook of emotional intelligence* (pp. 363–388). San Francisco: Jossey-Bass.

Bar-On, R. (1997). *Bar-On Emotional Quotient Inventory technical manual.* Toronto: Multi-Health Systems.

Bollas, C. (1987). *The shadow of the object.* London: Free Association Press.

Boyatsis, R., Goleman, D., & Rhee, K. (2000). Clustering competence in emotional intelligence: Insights from the emotional competence inventory. In R. Bar-On & D. Parker (Eds.), *The handbook of emotional intelligence* (pp. 343–362). San Francisco: Jossey-Bass.

Caudron, S. (1999, July). The hard case for soft skills. *Workforce,* pp. 60–66.

Cooper, R., & Sawaf, A. (1996). *Executive EQ: Emotional intelligence in leadership and organizations.* New York: Grosset/Putnam.

Emery, F., & Trist, E. (1965). The causal texture of organizational environments. *Human Relations, 18,* 21–32.

Fineman, S. (2000). Commodifying the emotionally intelligent. In S. Fineman, (Ed.) *Emotion in organizations* (pp. 101–114). London: Sage.

French, R., & Simpson, P. (1999). *Our best work happens when we don't know what we're doing.* Paper presented at the International Society for the Psychoanalytic Study of Organizations Symposium, Toronto.

Gardner, H. (1983). *Frames of mind: The theory of multiple intelligences.* New York: Basic Books.

Goleman, D. (1995). *Emotional intelligence.* New York: Bantam.

Goleman, D. (1998). *Working With emotional intelligence.* New York: Bantam.

Goleman, D. (2000). Foreword. In R. Bar-On & D. Parker (Eds.), *The handbook of emotional intelligence* (pp. vii-viii). San Francisco: Jossey-Bass.

Hall, D., Otazo, K., & Hollenbeck, G. (1999, Winter). Behind closed doors: What really happens in executive coaching. *Organizational Dynamics*, pp. 39–53.

Herrnstein, R., & Murray, C. (1994). *The bell curve: Intelligence and class in American life.* New York: Free Press.

Kilburg, R. (2000). *Executive coaching: Developing managerial wisdom in a world of chaos.* Washington, DC: American Psychological Association.

Labbs, J. (1999, July). Emotional intelligence at work. *Workforce*, pp. 68–71.

Lawrence, W.G. (1999). *Thinking refracted in organizations: the finite and the infinite/the conscious and the unconscious.* Paper presented at the International Society for the Psychoanalytic Study of Organizations Symposium, Toronto.

Levinson, H. (1991). Diagnosing organizations systematically. In M. Kets de Vries (Ed.) *Organizations on the couch: Clinical perspectives on organizational behavior and change* (pp. 45–68). San Francisco: Jossey-Bass.

Mayer, J., Salovey, P., & Caruso, D. (2000a). Emotional intelligence as zeitgeist, as personality, and as a mental ability. In R. Bar-On & D. Parker (Eds.), *The handbook of emotional intelligence* (pp. 92–117). San Francisco: Jossey-Bass.

Mayer, J., Caruso, D., & Salovey, P. (2000b). Selecting a measure of emotional intelligence: the case for ability scales. In R. Bar-On & D. Parker (Eds.), *The handbook of emotional intelligence* (pp. 320–342). San Francisco: Jossey-Bass.

Salovey, P., & Mayer, J. (1990). Emotional intelligence. *Imagination, Cognition, and Personality, 9*, 185–211.

Schwartz, T. (2000, June). How do you feel? *Fast Company*, pp. 297–312.

Shapiro, E., & Carr, W. (1991). *Lost in familiar places.* New Haven, CT: Yale University Press.

Stein, S., & Book, H. (2000). *The EQ edge: Emotional intelligence and your success.* Toronto: Stoddart.

Vaill, P. (1989). *Managing as a performing art.* San Francisco: Jossey-Bass.

CHAPTER 5

THE CHANGING ROLE OF CONSULTING IN PROJECT MANAGEMENT

Hans J. Thamhain

INTRODUCTION

The emergence of modern project management has outpaced the understanding of how and why project-oriented interventions work, creating value in some situations while leading to disappointment or even outright disaster in others. There is little argument among business leaders that project management provides an important tool set for implementing multidisciplinary ventures, ranging from new product-, service- and process-development initiatives, to acquisitions and foreign assistance programs. Yet, there is also a growing sense of disappointment and frustration that not all techniques work equally well, nor are all equally applicable to all projects (cf. Iansiti & MacCormack, 1997; Rasiel, 1999; Thamhain, 1994). Realizing both the complexities and the significance for business performance, many companies have established an *internal* project management consulting group or sought consulting help from the *outside*. Merely engaging consultants—whether internal or external—however, does not automatically guarantee project success. To be effective as change agents, these consultants must be capable of more than understanding the tools and techniques of modern project management. They must also understand

87

the infrastructure of their client's organization and deal with the complex social, technical and economic issues that determine the culture and value system of the enterprise as summarized in Table 1 (cf. Gupta & Govindarjan, 2000; Thamhain & Wilemon, 1999). A traditional focus on project management tools alone will seldom be sufficient to compete effectively in today's dynamic world of business.

Table 1.   Project Consulting: Complexities and Challenges

- Dealing with project complexities and challenges
- Understanding client needs and communicating a vision
- Aligning tools and techniques with existing business process, organizational culture and values
- Dealing effectively with organizational conflict, power and politics
- Dealing effectively with the human side of project management
- Obtaining senior management buy-in and commitment
- Aiming at long-term improvements while maintaining existing operating efficiency
- Dealing with process improvement challenges that often requires total organizational involvement and broad commitment to change
- Developing effective team leaders and project managers
- Creating sustainable improvements
- Improving project operations with minimum business interference

PROJECT MANAGEMENT IN A CHANGING WORLD

The business environment is quite different from what it used to be. For one thing, new technologies, especially computers and communications, have radically changed the workplace and transformed our global economy, reorienting them toward service and knowledge work, with higher mobility of resources, skills, processes, and technology itself. In a concomitant change, new project management techniques have evolved which are often better integrated with business processes, offering more sophisticated capabilities for project tracking and controlling in culturally-diverse environments that contain a broad spectrum of contemporary challenges. Such challenges include time-to-market pressures, accelerating technologies, pressures for innovation, resource limitations, technical complexities, social and ethical issues, operational dynamics, risk and uncertainty (cf. Bishop, 1999; Deschamp & Nayak, 1995). As summarized in Table 2, facing such a dynamic environment often makes it difficult to manage projects through traditional, linear work processes or top-down controls.

Table 2. Today's Projects: Characteristics and Challenges

- Changing business models and structures
- Complex joint ventures, alliances and partnerships
- Complex project performance measurements and data processing requirements
- Complexity of defining project success and deliverables
- Obtaining multi-functional buy-in and commitment
- Global markets
- Integrating broad spectrum of functions and support services
- Integrating project and business processes
- Large groups of stakeholders
- Managing beyond immediate results
- Need for continuous improvement of project operations
- Need for integration across functions, dealing with different organizational cultures and values
- Need for sophisticated human relations skills
- Ability to deal with organizational conflict, power and politics
- Critical role of organizational members in successful project implementation
- Project complexities, implementation risks and uncertainties
- Resource constraint, tough performance requirements
- Self-directed teams
- Tight, end-date driven schedules
- Total project life-cycle considerations
- Virtual organizations, markets and support systems

In response to these challenges, many companies and their management have formed new alliances through mergers, acquisitions and joint ventures, and have explored alternative organizational designs, business processes and leadership styles, such as concurrent engineering, design-build, and stage-gate protocols. While these concepts have the potential for organizations to become more agile and responsive, they also require more intense cross-functional teamwork and cooperation, with high levels of resource and power sharing, and complex lines of authority, accountability and control (Gupta & Govindarajan, 2000; Thamhain & Wilemon, 1999). As a result, the focus of project management has shifted over the past decades from simply tracking schedule and budget data, to the integration of human factors and organizational interfaces into the project management process. The new generation of project leaders must deal effectively with the new challenges and realities of today's business environment, which include highly complex sets of deliverables, as well as demanding timing, environmental, social, political, regulatory and technological factors. Working effectively in such an intricate environment requires new skills in both project administration and leadership, especially for complex, technology-based and R&D-oriented projects, that rely to an increasing extent on innovation, cross-functional teamwork and decision making, intricate multi-company alliances and highly complex forms of work integration. Project success often depends to a considerable extent on member-generated performance norms and work processes, rather than supervision, policies and procedures (Bahrami, 1992; Thamhain & Wilemon, 1999). As a result, self-directed and commitment-based concepts are gradually replacing the traditional, more hierarchically structured project organization.

Forces for Effective Project Management

In the past, project performance was measured by-and-large in terms of achieving agreed-on results within given time and resource constraints. Today, these measures have become little more than threshold competencies for companies that espouse project management as a core capability—very important, but unlikely to provide a true competitive advantage. Yet, many firms, and many consultants, still measure overall project performance by these threshold factors. Focusing on these factors alone, however, is unlikely to overcome a firm's project management deficiencies. To the contrary, such focus may mask crucial competitive factors such as innovative results, technological breakthroughs, time-to-market capabilities, flexibility and responsiveness to changing requirements, future business positioning, and client satisfaction.

As summarized in Table 3, there are eight major forces that are driving the nature of today's project consulting environment, forces that must be understood in order to build an effective project management system.

Table 3.   Changes in the Current Project Environment

Shift from...	*to...*
• mostly linear work processes	• highly dynamic, organic and integrated project systems
• efficiency	• effectiveness
• extensive use of IT	• more process-integrated use of IT
• information	• decision support
• project management tools	• integrated systems
• managerial control	• self-direction and accountability
• executing projects	• enterprise-wide project management
• project management as a support system	• established standards and professional status

Shift from Linear Processes to Dynamic Project Systems

In the past, project management concepts were based on predominately linear models, typically exemplified by production lines, sequential product developments, scheduled services and discovery-oriented R&D. Managing projects in the present environment, in contrast, requires more dynamic and interactive relationships, involving complex sets of interrelated, nonlinear and often difficult to define processes. These changes have not only increased the complexity of the project environment, but they also demand a far more sophisticated management and consulting style which rely strongly on group interaction, resource and power sharing, individual accountability, commitment, self-direction and control. Consequently, many of today's projects and their integration rely to a considerable extent on member-generated performance norms and evaluations, rather than on hierarchical guidelines, policies and procedures. While this paradigm shift is driven by changing organizational complexities, capabilities, demands and cultures, it also leads to a radical departure from traditional management philosophy on organizational structure, motivation, leadership and project control. As a result, traditional "hard-wired" project organizations and processes are being replaced by more flexible and nimble networks. These networks are usually derivatives of the conventional matrix organization, but with more permeable boundaries, more power and resource sharing, and more concurrent project integration.

Shift from Efficiency Toward Effectiveness

Many companies have broadened their focus from *efficient* execution of projects—emphasizing job skills, teamwork, communications, and resource optimization at the project level—to include *effectiveness* of their project organizations. This shift responds to the need for better integration of project activities into the overall enterprise, making sure the organization is "doing the right thing." Companies are trying to leverage project management as a core competency, integrating closely with other functions such as marketing, R&D, field services and strategic business planning. While this shift is enhancing the status and value of project management within the enterprise, it also raises the overall level of responsibility and accountability, placing more demands on project management to perform as a full partner within the integrated enterprise system.

Shift Toward More Integrated Information Technology

The availability and promise of technology have led to an enormous acquisition of IT-based tools and techniques by managers at all levels. These managers are eager to leverage these tools for true value added, increasing the effectiveness of their operations rather than simply generating more data. The challenge for consultants is to look beyond project management software per se to fully understand and *apply* the technology to the firm's business process, helping project managers solve their problems and increase operating efficiency, rather than just replacing traditional forms of communication, interactions and problem solving that, in many cases, still play a crucial role in project success.

Shift from Information to Decision Support

Today's technology provides managers in any part of the enterprise with push-button access to critical information on project status and performance. In addition, IT-based project management tools, in conjunction with well-maintained data bases, offer powerful support for resource estimating, scheduling and risk analysis. These tools provide better data integrity and decision-support, from project initiation to execution, affecting the quality of project control and predictability across the entire enterprise.

Shift from Project Management Tools to Integrated Systems

Effective project management today requires far broader skill sets than just dealing with budgeting and scheduling issues. While critically important, these abilities are strongly supported by modern information technology and have become core competencies for project leaders, literal requirements to enter the professional field. Managerial focus has shifted from the mechanics of controlling projects according to established schedules and budgets, to optimizing desired results across a wide spectrum of performance measures that integrate with total enterprise performance. An underlying ideal is movement toward developing a true learning organization. The need for understanding project management as an integrated part of the overall business process—its human side and company-external components—all have a profound impact on the type and scope of project management training, consulting needs and organizational development required for leveraging project management as an enterprise-wide resource.

Shift from Managerial Control to Self-direction and Accountability

With increasing project complexities, advances in information technology, changing business cultures, and new market structures, companies must look *beyond* traditional managerial control for effective project execution. Especially top-down project controls, based on centralized command and communications, while critically important, are no longer sufficient for generating satisfactory results. Projects rely, to an increasing extend, on technology, innovation, cross-functional teamwork and decision making, intricate multi-company alliances and highly complex forms of work integration. The dynamics of these project environments foster to a considerable extent member-generated performance norms and work processes, and a shift toward more team ownership, empowerment and self-control (Barner, 1997; Kruglianskas & Thamhain, 2000; Thamhain & Wilemon, 1999). All of this has a profound impact on the way project leaders must manage and lead, and how consultants must analyze the work environment for effective intervention. Methods of communication, decision making, soliciting commitment, and risk sharing are shifting constantly away from a centralized, autocratic management style to a team-centered, more self-directed form of project control.

Shift from Executing Projects to Enterprise-wide Project Management

Many companies use project management far more extensively than just for implementing projects. A growing number of organizations are relying on project management as a core competency for leveraging their resources, achieving accelerated product developments, capturing higher levels of innovation, ensuring better quality, and, in general, securing better resource utilization. To accomplish this level of competency, companies must integrate their project operations with the strategic goals and business processes across the total enterprise.

Shift from Project Management as a Support Function Toward Full Operational Responsibility and Professional Status

With its own body of knowledge, norms and worldwide standards, professional certification, and formal education programs at the master's and Ph.D. level, project management has established its professional position over the last two decades. Today, the principles of project management apply across industries and around the globe, virtually in all types of situations. Companies can choose from a growing pool of formally educated project management professionals and consultants, with access to professional training that follows well-established operational, managerial, quality, and ethical standards.

New Tools, Techniques and Management Philosophy

With the increasing complexities of today's projects and their business environments, companies have moved toward more sophisticated tools and techniques for effectively managing their multidisciplinary activities. These tools and techniques available to consultants range from computer software for sophisticated schedule and budget tracking to intricate organizational process designs, such as concurrent engineering and stage-gate protocols. Even conventional project management tools, such as schedules, budgets and status reviews, are being continuously upgraded and effectively integrated with modern information technology systems and overall business processes. As part of this evolution, organizations must also shift their focus from simply tracking schedule and budget data, to integrating human factors and organizational interfaces into project-control formulae. The new generation of project management consultants have a broad range of tools that are designed to deal more effectively with the new challenges and realities of today's business environment, which include highly complex sets of deliverables, as well as timing, environmental, social, political, regulatory and technological factors.

While the shift to more sophisticated project management processes is the result of changing business cultures, project complexities, technological capabilities and market structures, it also requires radical departures from traditional management philosophy and operating practices on organization, motivation, leadership and project control. As a result, the traditional management style, designed largely for top-down control, centralized command and one-way communication, is no longer sufficient for managing effectively in today's team-based environment. The new breed of managers that evolved with these contemporary organizations is often more connected with the organization and its business process, and can deal with a broad spectrum of contemporary challenges, such as time-to-market, accelerating technologies, innovation, resource limitations, technical complexities, project metrics, operational dynamics, risk, and uncertainty, more effectively than their colleagues in the past. All of this has a profound impact on the way project leaders must manage and lead. It also explains in part the reasons why the methods of communication, decision making, soliciting commitment, and risk sharing are continuously shifting away from a centralized, autocratic management style, to a team-centered, more self-directed form of project leadership.

Few companies rush into consulting services, which are often viewed as costly and disruptive, at times even in conflict with deeply-held organizational beliefs about the way things should be done. Given the increasing complexities associated with the myriad projects organizations are dealing with today, however, a growing number of companies literally have no choice. They have exhausted their expertise in dealing with the given challenges and see consulting services as a possible lifeline for finding solutions. Others take a more strategic view toward continuing improvement, trying to push the frontier of their project environment. These managers realize the complexities of their organizations and the limitations of general management. These companies, in turn, often hire specialists who are experts in particular business areas *and* have effective diagnostic skills (Block, 1999; Reimus, 2000). Achieving benefits in this arena, however, involves complex organizational issues, administrative tools and human factors. Companies that make the process work are able to attract and engage consulting services that can help the enterprise to augment expertise and skills in specialty areas, benchmark internal and external capabilities, and challenge conventional wisdom and stimulate innovative thinking.

A MODEL FOR PROJECT PERFORMANCE

Based on the preceding discussion, the issues affecting project performance can be analyzed in terms of eight principal categories as shown in Figure 1: (1) the *people* on the project team and its support organizations, (2) *leadership*, (3) *project tools and techniques*, and (4) *business processes* that power and support the project activities; these four categories are overlapping and intricately affected by (5) *the organizational infrastructure and support systems*, (6) *managerial support*, (7) *project complexity*, and (8) the *overall business environment*. These categories not only determine project performance, but also hold the DNA for the type of consulting services that are best suited for improving specific project management situations.

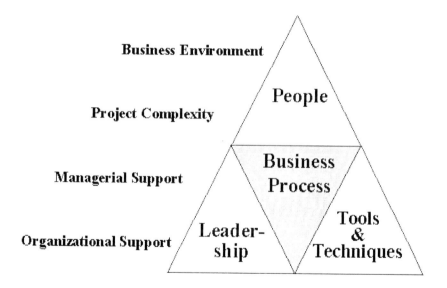

Figure 1.   Influences on project performance

Criteria for Effective Project Management Consulting

Companies do not go lightly into reorganizing their established business processes. At best, it is inconvenient, painful, disruptive and costly. At worst, it can destroy any existing operational effectiveness and the ability to compete successfully in the marketplace. Achieving benefits from project management consulting involves complex organizational issues, administrative tools and human factors. Companies and consultants that make the process work, see consulting as an intervention tool for building and fine-tuning the project system as part of the overall business process (Thomas, Delisle, Jugdev, & Buckle, 2001). Yet, engaging the organization in an evaluation of the current system, and aiming for improvements, can be a threatening process. Such threats increase with the perception of the people that the new environment will deviate significantly from the current situation.

What senior consultants and managers find consistently is that for the consulting processes to work effectively it must blend with the culture and value system of the organization. Project management consultants cannot ignore the human side of the enterprise. That is, consultants must work to establish an environment conducive to mutual trust, respect, candor, and risk sharing. Equally important, consultants must foster effective two-way communication and cross-functional linkages capable of connecting people, processes and support functions, and resolving inevitable conflict.

A number of suggestions have been derived from various field studies in project management consulting (Block, 1997; Bower, 1997; Deschamps & Nayak, 1995; Rasiel, 1999; Sarvary, 1999; Thamhain, 1994). These suggestions are aimed at helping both managers and consultants to understand the complex interaction of organizational and behavioral variables involved in creating change and improvements in today's intricate project management systems. The findings also help to increase our awareness of what is and is not effective in terms of building high-performance project management systems. Finally, this discussion is intended to help scholars who study these concepts to better understand the complexities involved in project management consulting, and to use some of the conclusions reached here as building blocks for further research.

Align Project System Improvements with Company Goals

It is critical to identify value from the start. Organizational members are more likely to engage in a development initiative if they perceive it to be clearly related to the goals and objectives of the company. Clear linkages between the intervention and company mission, goals, and objectives create enthusiasm and desire to participate, as well as lowering anxieties and helping to unify the people behind the intervention. Thus, it is important for the consultant to both understand and communicate the significance of the project to the company mission. Explicitly securing senior management support and endorsement further enhances these benefits.

Take a Systems Approach

Many project management improvement efforts fail due to a poor understanding of the need to integrate project management with the total business process and its management systems. Subsystems, such as specific project management initiatives, are easier and quicker to develop than the overall organizational system to which they belong. Yet, they function sub-optimally, at best, unless they are designed as an integrated part of the total enterprise. System thinking, as described by Senge (1990), provides a useful tool for front-end analysis and organization design.

Define Clear Objectives and Direction

Consulting leaders must ensure that the people in the organization perceive the objectives of the intervention to be attainable, with a clear sense of direction toward reaching those ends. This perception can be influenced by both the consultant and the organization's managers, and should be continuously reinforced during the implementation cycle. More than any other tool, well-articulated business performance metrics—ranging from product plans to mission statements, technology objectives and financial goals—can cut through the complexities and fog of "management performance," further connecting the project to the mission and strategic direction of the enterprise.

Define Implementation Plan

Implementation of a new process or management system requires a clear plan with specific milestones and metrics that indicates where the team should be going and how it can get there. Consultants can facilitate this process by establishing plans characterized by incremental measurability, early problem detection ability, visibility of accomplishments, recognition, and rewards.

Custom-design

Even for apparently simple situations, the new or improved tool should be customized to fit the host organization and its culture, needs, norms and processes. Consultants should ensure that the new tool is consistent with the established norms of the existing management system. Consultants have a better chance for smooth implementation and for gaining organizational acceptance of the new system if they can show that the newly developed process is consistent with already established values, principles and practices, rather than a new order to be imposed without reference to the existing organizational history, values or culture. Particular attention should be paid to the workability of the tools and techniques in cross-functional applications. Further, working with the organization's management team, consultants should ensure consistency of documentation and reporting formats with established organizational standards.

Involve People Affected by the Intervention

While expert-based consulting has dominated the project management field, it is critical to also engage in more process-oriented consulting (O'Connell, 1990), ensuring that relevant organizational members are part of the intervention. Consultants should act as facilitators of the organization's development, encouraging the client to help itself. Operational procedures, quality standards and management practices must be generated from within the organization as a prerequisite for becoming institutionalized. Key project personnel and managers from all functions and levels of the organization should be involved in assessing the situation, searching for solutions, and evaluating new tools and techniques. Consultants need to ensure organizational acceptance of any changes, including the introduction of new tools and methods, especially in self-directed team environments. While direct participation in decision-making is the most effective way to obtain buy-in toward a new system, it is not always possible, especially in large organizations. Critical factor analysis, focus groups and process action teams are also good vehicles for team involvement and collective decision-making, leading to ownership, greater acceptance, and willingness to work toward continuous improvement.

Assess Benefits and Challenges

Before introducing a new project management tool or technique to an organization, it is important to conduct a thorough assessment of the potential benefits, problems and challenges that can be anticipated. A focus group—selected from the project population at-large or specific project team—can provide valuable insight into the challenges of getting the new tool accepted and working at the team level. This assessment can also provide many of the necessary inputs for customizing the new tool to the organization, identifying the support systems and interfaces needed for effective implementation.

Build on Existing Management Systems

Radically new methods are usually greeted with great anxiety and suspicion. If at all possible, the introduction of new management tools and techniques should be consistent with established project management practices within the organization. The more that the new order of operation is congruent with already existing practices, procedures, and distributed knowledge of the organization, the higher the probability that the change intervention will be successful and self-sustaining. The highest level of acceptance and success is found in areas where new tools are *added incrementally* to already existing management systems. These situations should be identified and addressed first. An example for building on existing organizational processes and management systems could be the implementation of a stage-gate process. Consultants should make an effort to integrate already established and proven procedures for project definition, documentation, status reports, reviews, and sign-offs into the new process. Such integrative efforts tend to make new management processes appear more evolutionary rather than a radical change. Building upon an existing project management system also facilitates incremental enhancement, testing and fine-tuning of the new managerial tools or process.

Encourage Project Teams to Fine-tune and Integrate Tools and Techniques

Successful implementation of new project management tools and processes often requires modifications of organizational structures, policies and practices. In many of the most effective organizations, project teams have the power and are encouraged to make changes to existing organizational procedures, reporting relations, decision and work processes. It is crucial, however, that these team initiatives are integrated with the overall business process and supported by management. True integration, acceptance by the people, and sustaining of a new organizational process will only occur through the collective understanding of all the issues and a positive feeling that the process is helpful to the work to be performed. To optimize the benefits of a new project management tool or technique, it must be perceived by all the parties as a "win-win" proposition, an outcome that can be facilitated by providing people with an active role in the implementation and utilization process. Consultants should carefully plan and drive the involvement of key stakeholders during all phases of the project, starting with needs assessment, through new system development and its implementation. Focus teams, review panels, open discussion meetings, suggestion systems, pilot test groups and management reviews are examples for providing such stakeholder involvement. An underlying objective of stakeholder involvement is the development of proper user skill sets and the collective fine-tuning of the new management system toward most effective applications.

Pretest New Tools and Techniques

Preferably, new concepts should be pilot tested on small projects with experienced project teams. Asking a team to test, evaluate and fine-tune a new tool or technique is not only often seen as an honor and professional challenge but it usually starts the implementation with a positive attitude, creating an environment of open communications and candor. Equally important, consultants should "prototype" new project management systems early and obtain feedback from experienced project personnel whom they trust. Incorporating this feedback into the next system prototype cycle can accelerate the organizational adoption of the new management technique.

Anticipate Anxieties and Conflicts

Although project management-oriented changes have not generally been associated with the same intensity of anxieties, conflicts and politics, that are common with broader organizational transformations, they are often disruptive to the organization and generate negative reactions due to uncertainties associated with new working conditions and requirements. These responses can range from personal discomfort with skill requirements to dysfunctional anxieties over the impact of the tool on work processes and performance evaluation. Effective consulting leaders know this intuitively, anticipating these problems and attacking them aggressively as early as possible. Consultants should seek-out the type of norms and practices imbedded in the new management system that have caused conflict and problems in other areas of the local business process. Assessment efforts should then focus on determining how these practices impacted operational effectiveness and business performance, and what, if anything, had been done about it in the past. By building on these existing "case studies," valuable lessons can be learned for future interventions. As a way of facilitating this process, consultants can help in developing guidelines for conflict resolution and establishing conflict resolution processes, such as information meetings, management briefings and workshops featuring the experiences of early adopters. Consultants can also work with the organization's management to foster an environment of mutual trust and cooperation. Cooperation with new tools and techniques can be expected only if its use is relatively risk-free. Unnecessary references to performance appraisals, tight supervision, reduced personal freedom and autonomy, and overhead requirements should be avoided, and any concerns dealt with promptly on a personal level.

Invest Time and Resources

The host company must invest time and resources for developing a new tool or technique, or improving an existing one. Most project management techniques cannot be effectively implemented via directive, but instead require the broad involvement of the people who are part of the project, helping to define metrics and project controls. Consultants must work together with upper management to implement any action plan. This demonstrates management confidence, ownership and commitment to the project. This focus also helps to integrate the new system with the overall business process. As part of the implementation plan, consultants must build-in processes for dealing with the inevitable challenges of organizational change. They must also allow time for organizational members to buy-in to the new vision and process. Training programs, pilot runs, internal consulting support, fully-leveraged communication tools such as groupware, and best-practice reviews are examples of action tools that can help in both institutionalizing and fine-tuning the new management system. Most important, these tools can help in building the necessary user competencies, management skills, organization culture, and personal attitudes required for the organization development to succeed.

Define Checks and Balances

Consultants should set up system supports that enable organizational members to monitor, validate and audit the implementation of the new system, and to assess its impact on organizational performance. Such checks-and-balances also provide in-process feedback, early warnings of potential problems, and the opportunity of in-process correction and fine-tuning of the new management system.

Foster a Culture of Continuous Support and Improvement

The key to a successful project intervention centers on people's behavior and their role within the project itself. Companies that are effective in creating and integrating new management processes into their organizations have cultures and support systems that demand broad participation in their organization developments. While ensuring that organizational members are more proactive and aggressive toward change is not an easy task, this process must be facilitated systematically—by both consultants and key managers. Any project management tool or technique must be integrated into the continuously changing business process. Provisions should be made for updating and fine-tuning these tools on an ongoing basis to ensure relevancy to today's project management challenges. Therefore, it is important to establish support systems—such as discussion groups, action teams and suggestion systems—to capture and leverage the lessons learned, and to identify problems as part of a continuous improvement process. Consultants should work with senior management to establish incentives, norms and practices for going beyond just encouraging meetings and dialogue, but for organizational members to take proactive approaches toward continuous organizational improvement.

Ensure Management Direction and Leadership

Organizational improvements require top-down support to succeed. Team members will be more likely to help implement new management processes, tools and techniques, and cooperate with necessary organizational requirements, if management clearly articulates the criticality to business performance and the benefits to the organization and its members. Senior management approval and encouragement are often seen as recognition of team competence and a validation of effective team leadership. Throughout the implementation phase, both senior management and consultants can influence the attitude and commitment of their people toward a new concept by their own actions. Concern for project team members, assistance with the use of the tool, enthusiasm for the project and its administrative support systems, proper funding, the ability to attract and retain the right personnel in support of the new system, all fosters a climate of high motivation, involvement, open communications, and willingness to cooperate with the new requirements and to help with its continuous improvements.

CONCLUSION

In today's dynamic and hyper-competitive environment, project management consultants must understand the cutting edge tools and techniques of project management, being able to fully leverage these tools to provide tangible value added to their client organizations. Creating such benefits requires more than just writing a new procedure, delivering a best-practice workshop, or installing new information technology. It requires the ability to engage the organization in a systematic evaluation of its specific competencies, assessing opportunities for improvement and linking existing competencies with the overall enterprise system and its strategy. Effective consultants understand the complex interaction of organizational and behavioral variables. They can work with the client organization, creating mutually beneficial and rewarding situations between the people affected by the intervention and senior management. By involving the firm's most experienced and respected project personnel and business managers and by analyzing the critical functions that drive project performance, these people can shake-up conventional thinking and create a vision for their clients. Through interaction with key stakeholders, consultants can help management to gain insight into the critical functions and cultures that drive project performance, and identify those critical components that could be further optimized. It is important to keep in mind that proactive participation and commitment of relevant stakeholders are critical to success. It also requires congruency of the intervention with the overall business process and its management system.

Too many clients end-up disappointed that the latest management technique did not produce the desired result. Regardless of their conceptual sophistication, any management tool, such as tracking software, concurrent engineering, design-build, stage-gate, voice-of-the-customer and theory of constraints, is *just a framework* for processing project data, aligning organizational strategy, structure and people. To produce benefits to the firm, these tools must be fully customized to the business process and congruent with the organizational system and its culture. As a result, few firms hire consultants just based on their knowledge of the management tools or techniques. Such knowledge is considered a threshold competency that is expected. True value is added to the client firm by helping managers to identify the areas that hold potential for improvement and by designing the new tool or system as an integrated part of the business process, fully leveraged with all other organizational functions.

Most important, project management consultants must pay attention to the human side of organizations. While such an emphasis has not traditionally been a strong point of experts in this area, if project management consultants are to enhance cooperation among project stakeholders they must foster a work environment where people see the significance of the intervention for the enterprise and its mission. One of the strongest catalysts to change and cooperation is the professional pride and excitement of organizational members, fueled by visibility and recognition. Such a professionally stimulating environment seems to lower anxieties over organizational change, reduce communication barriers and conflict, and enhance the desire of those involved to cooperate and to succeed. Effective consultants are social architects who can foster a climate of active participation by involving people at all organizational levels in the assessment of the current project management system, and in the planning and implementation of change processes. They also can build alliances with support organizations and upper management to assure organizational visibility, priority, resource availability, and overall support for sustaining the organizational improvement beyond its implementation phase. If the project management consulting process is to work effectively, these individuals must merge management tools, techniques and technology, creating value in today's demanding business environment.

REFERENCES

Bahrami, H. (1992). The emerging flexible organization: Perspectives from Silicon Valley. *California Management Review, 34*(4), 33–52.

Barner, R. (1997). The new millennium workplace. *Engineering Management Review (IEEE), 25*(3), 114–119.

Bishop, S.K. (1999). Cross-functional project teams in functionally aligned organizations. *Project Management Journal, 30*(3), 6–12.

Block, P. (1999). *Flawless consulting.* San Francisco: Jossey-Bass.

Bower, M. (1997). *Will to lead: Running a business with a network of leaders.* Cambridge, MA: HBS Press.

Deschamps, J., & Nayak, P.R. (1995). *Product Juggernauts.* Cambridge, MA: HBS Press.

Gupta, A., & Govindarajan, V. (2000). Knowledge management's social dimension. *Sloan Management Review, 42*(1), 71–80.

Iansiti, M., & MacCormack, A. (1997). Developing product on Internet time. *Harvard Business Review, 75*(5), 108–117.

Kruglianskas, I., & Thamhain, H. (2000). Managing technology-based projects in multinational environments. *IEEE Transactions on Engineering Management, 47*(1), 55–64.

O'Connell, J.J. (1990). Process consulting in a context field: Socrates in strategy. *Consultation, 9*(3), 199–208.

Rasiel, E. (1999). *The McKinsey way.* New York: McGraw-Hill.

Reimus, B. (2000). Knowledge sharing within management consulting firms. *Report*, Fitzwilliam, NH: Kennedy Information, Inc.(http://www.kennedy-info.com/mc/gware.html).

Sarvary, M. (1999). Knowledge management and competition in the consulting industry. *California Management Review, 41*(2), 95–107.

Scott, B. (200). *Consulting from the inside.* New York: American Society for Training and Development.

Senge, P.M. (1990). *The fifth discipline: The art and practice of the learning organization.* New York: Doubleday/Currency.

Thamhain, H.J. (1994). Designing project management systems for a radically changing world. *Project Management Journal, 25*(4), 6–7.

Thamhain, H.J., & Wilemon, D.L. (1999). Building effective teams for complex project environments. *Technology Management, 5*(2), 203–212.

Thomas, J., Delisle, C., Jugdev, K., & Buckle, P. (2001). Selling project management to senior executives. *pmNetwork, 15*(1), 59–62.

CHAPTER 6

A SYSTEM-WIDE, INTEGRATED METHODOLOGY FOR INTERVENING IN ORGANIZATIONS

The ISEOR Approach

Henri Savall, Veronique Zardet, Marc Bonnet, and Rickie Moore

INTRODUCTION

In general, the domain of management advice has been judged primarily on the methods used by management consulting firms. Academicians, more often than not, have largely concentrated on explicative research models rather than prescriptive models in the area of organizational performance. The objective of this chapter is to present an example of research that attempts to highlight the links between academically-oriented study and consulting. It focuses on research programs undertaken by the Socio-Economic Institute of Organizations (ISEOR) since 1976 that took place in many different environments and contexts. These experiments have resulted in a number of hypotheses that integrate organizational interventions, the possibility of significant economic results, involvement of key organizational participants and stakeholders in the firms, and enhanced conditions in which these individuals carry out their work.

THE NEED FOR A GLOBAL APPROACH TO MANAGEMENT CONSULTING

There are two basic types of interventions in the area of management consulting. First, there are focused interventions by experts, by definition, specialists in their given field. They specialize, for example, in recommending software packages, strategic advice and benchmarking, advice on productivity and cost reductions, remuneration packages and specialist audits. The second type is when consultants take a more global view of the firm, focusing on implementing improved functioning in the organization (Ackoff, 1997; Savall, 1989). These interventions are typically concerned with broader foci, such as Total Quality Management (TQM) and Organizational Development (OD).

In the first type of management consulting, consultants tend to use highly formalized methodologies, which correspond with the specialist modules of an organization's functional areas, from accountancy and finance to marketing, corporate strategy, and human resources. These interventions have the advantage of assisting firms to compensate for their lack of competence in particular specialist areas. A firm, for example, could implement an enterprise resource planning (ERP) software system through the long-term use of consultants without the need to recruit additional personnel or ERP experts. One of the main problems posed by this type of expert-based solution, however, is that it may not necessarily result in coherence between the different dimensions of the organization and its management. Prime examples are often found in the information systems arena, when a consultant might tell a dissatisfied client, "if you are experiencing difficulties in putting the software into operation, it's not our fault; it's due to the fact that you are not well organized enough to understand the procedures or to sufficiently train your staff." A similar refrain is often something along the lines of, "My recommendations were perfectly acceptable in Firm X, but if they don't work in your company it's because you did not specify or request enough of my expertise in our agreed proposal." Yet, even though the managers may be disappointed because the outcome of the consultant's intervention falls short of what they had hoped for, they typically do not confront the management consulting firm in question due to the fact that they themselves made the decision to seek out a "quick fix." Instead, they typically turn their attention to another consulting firm specializing in another area of expertise they require. The aftermath—witnessed by ISEOR from this type of practice in many countries—is that the firm is left with the expense of numerous management consulting interventions, without obtaining any satisfactory results or evaluating performance against costs.

In the second type of intervention, consultants have the advantage of focusing their role on the broader aspects of facilitating change (e.g., Ackoff, 1974; Bay & MacPherson, 1998; Osborne & Gaebler, 1993). This approach forces them to take account of the more global aspects of the firm and related systematic changes, which are often avoided by managers despite being disappointed by past OD efforts. The resulting lack of tangible results often leaves firms and their management still searching for rapid results. In the same way, the cornerstones of TQM and OD may have allowed firms to develop, but managers typically have a hard time reconciling these methods with budgetary constraints.

From the point of view of the management researcher, academic models often link efforts to improve organizational performance with multiple actions or "bundles of actions" that are simultaneously implemented at various levels in the organization (see, e.g., Ackoff & Emery, 1982; Buckley, 1968; Gharajedaghi, 1985, 1999). Such research, however, is rarely able to highlight specific operational or change processes that create a global or comprehensive view of the organization, especially from the perspective of different levels of organization and management. Yet, while the knowledge base of management consultants allows them to assist managers in carrying out specified changes, their expertise, to a large extent, exists in a "black box" that is removed from the basic objective of "knowledge management." Managers, in essence, need to understand the interactions between different management domains, but by relying on consultant intervention such knowledge transfer and development are often lacking.

As an illustration of this dynamic, consider how TQM is typically introduced into an organization. Consultants are brought in to assist the firm to use management tools that integrate marketing and human resources, attempting to provide an enhanced view of customer needs by all the employees of the firm. Such advisory methods for global, system-wide management, however, are usually limited because they stop short of sufficiently integrating all dimensions of change management—from company strategy and human resource management to management information systems. The consultants also tend to use supposedly global management tools that could be classified under the heading of "fads." These methods end up disappointing the managers who implement them because they are not sufficiently system-wide in practice. While many management consultants, especially from large consulting firms, try to exchange informal or formal experiences they have encountered, this practice does not create a global model that transcends cultural contexts or different types of organizations. Instead, it tends to reinforce the view that contingency approaches, rather than a truly global approach, are the most realistic way to proceed.

Faced with these challenges, difficulties and orientations, ISEOR has developed a global, system-wide intervention method that can be used in organizations to enhance their overall performance and functioning.

ISEOR AND A SOCIOECONOMIC APPROACH TO CHANGE MANAGEMENT

ISEOR is a research center that provides a theoretical body of information concerning a socioeconomic approach to change management.[1] Since its creation in 1976, the Institute has carried out more than 1,000 experiments in a broad array of industries and organizations: (1) industrial companies from steel and engineering to agriculture and food; (2) service companies from transportation to banks and insurance; and (3) public sector organizations, including hospitals, schools and universities, and other public administration entities. These interventions have occurred in both small and large enterprises, ranging from a one-man business to a 300,000-employee corporation, in a number of different continents and countries, including Africa (Algeria, Angola, Benin, Burkina Faso, Ivory Cost, Madagascar, Morocco, and Tunisia), the Americas (Brazil, Canada, Colombia, Mexico, Venezuela, and the United States), Asia (China and Vietnam), and Europe (Belgium, Germany, France, Portugal, Romania, Slovenia, Spain, and Switzerland).

The continuous accumulation of research data (more than 400,000 pages of case studies and archives) has allowed ISEOR researchers to progressively identify the dominant socioeconomic factors that cut across organization and industry types (see, Savall, Zardet, & Bonnet, 2000). The resulting analysis makes it possible to formulate scientific rules that are transferred through university teaching from the undergraduate level to doctoral programs.[2]

To better understand the framework and methodology of ISEOR's socioeconomic management framework (see, also, Etzioni, 1988), it is worth briefly looking at the development of this approach since the mid-1970s. Wide-ranging experiments were carried out to test and improve these new management tools. The research agenda focused on testing hypotheses and improving our understanding about the relevance of different variables on organizational performance.

A Brief History of ISEOR and its Intervention Approach

The ISEOR Center endeavored to ground theory in the data available and search for methods to identify and evaluate the hidden costs of organizational dysfunctions. The underlying objective was to develop management tools that would facilitate a dialogue between senior-level managers, human resource managers, and other line managers. A typology was created that analyzed these hidden costs under five main headings: absenteeism, industrial injuries, staff turnover, poor quality, and low productivity. The costs of dysfunctions were seen to result from the informal power of the actors who react to the enterprise structures, as shown in Figure 1, which represents the fundamental hypothesis of the socioeconomic approach to management (SEAM).

Such hidden costs have been identified and evaluated in many industries and enterprises, and the results typically show that the average costs are *higher* than the payroll costs. For purposes of financial evaluation, hidden costs are divided into six categories: over-wages, over-consumption, time wasted, non-production, non-creation of potential gains, and risks. In-depth diagnoses have shown that the dysfunction costs are due to the social

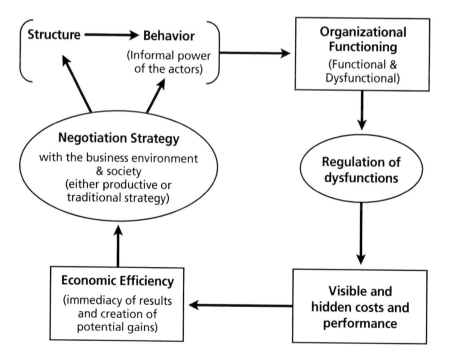

Figure 1.   The SEAM model (*Source:* H. Savall, *Reconstruire l'entreprise.* Paris: Dunod, 1979.

performance of the enterprise defined by six domains: working conditions, work organization (communication-coordination-conciliation), time management, integrated training and strategy implementation.

Since 1978, ISEOR has experimented with various change management interventions, including a diagnosis and project method aimed at reducing hidden costs and creating potential gains (Savall, 1978, 1981; Savall & Zardet, 1989). For management consulting interventions, the model presents two principal advantages. First, the approach shows managers the importance of their own actions and interventions. The diagnostic process enables managers to evaluate hidden costs, which often indicates that organizational dysfunctions cost companies considerably more than speculated. As an illustration, Figure 2 portrays an evaluation of such costs in an aeronautical firm—the cost of a seemingly unimportant dysfunction is $12,000 per year. Based on an organization-wide analysis, the total of other hidden costs in the firm amounted to the equivalent of 86% of the company's total salary costs.

A second advantage of this approach is to demonstrate to managers that there are multiple performance factors involved and that they cannot concentrate solely on one particular aspect of the problem. The root causes of

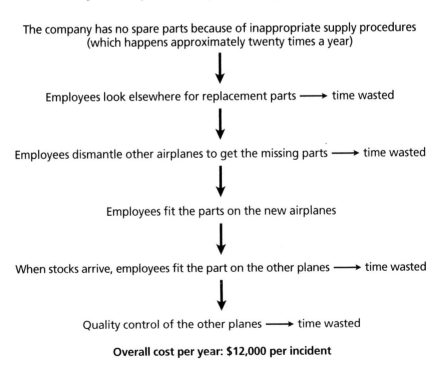

Figure 2.   Example of the calculation of rework in an aircraft company

organizational dysfunctions are multifaceted, and often include financial politics, stock control, commercial management issues, and human resource management. In the case of the aeronautical firm (Figure 2), for example, the senior managers attempted to better control the budgeting process by requesting a reduction in stock—which increased the risk of late delivery of orders due to an inadequate supply of components, while the salespeople were promising on-time delivery. The solution to this problem required a number of different action points: improvement in communication between the different departments of the firm, improvements in the computer system to take into account the needs of the production line workers, an improvement in purchasing training for the buyers, and so forth.

During the 1980s, ISEOR continued to work on such integrated approaches to organizational problems, developing intervention methods that were consistent with a system-wide appreciation of organizations rather than concentrating on one particular service or one particular aspect of the management team. This approach was developed as the HORIVERT method and will be expanded on later in the chapter.

Other management tools were also experimented with during this period that allowed organizational members to better manage the interfaces between different dimensions of their companies. These tools, which will also be outlined in the next section of the chapter, included internal and external strategic planning, priority action plans, a skills inventory, time management, strategic piloting indicators, and periodically negotiable activity contracts.

Since 1990, ISEOR experiments have focused on the concept of strategic management intervention engineering. Two major foci have been developed as part of this emphasis:

1. *Stimulating the will to change in order to avoid resistance to change.* This method combines internal and external management interventions in order to create the dynamics for change. The method contains rules pertaining to the pace of change through:

    • the "mirror effect" and "expert advice" which are used in diagnosis at the beginning of the intervention; the goal is to enable participants to more fully comprehend the need for change; and
    • an assessment method that energizes the change process.

2. *Synchronizing three axes of the intervention to accelerate the pace of change within the enterprise.* The three key axes or dimensions are:

    • The *improvement process* that focuses on the dysfunctions experienced by participants. The objective is to illustrate how organizational improvement projects can be financed mainly by cuts in hidden cost and the creation of added value.

- *Management tools*, which deal with reorienting the role of managers toward improvement, development actions, and leadership.
- *Policy and strategic decisions*, which include structures for improvement efforts and behavioral ethics.

SEAM AS A SYSTEMWIDE APPROACH TO MANAGEMENT CONSULTING INTERVENTIONS

In this section, the discussion focuses on three different aspects of the integrated, global nature of the SEAM framework (see Figure 3) as a management consulting intervention method:

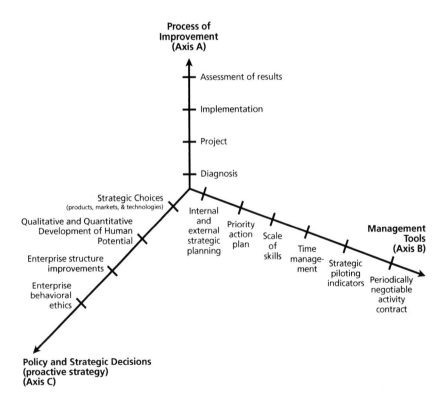

Figure 3.   The three axes of socio-economic intervention (*Source:* Reproduced with permission; © ISEOR 1981. Also published in H. Savall and V. Zardet, "Maîtriser les couts et performances caches," *Economica*, 1989.)

1.   An integrated approach that evaluates the costs of visible *and* hidden performances throughout the intervention process;

2. A technique that covers the whole organization (the HORIVERT method); and
3. The socioeconomic tools used by ISEOR consultants to assist managers to control the different dimensions and levels of their company.

Taking Account of Visible and Hidden Costs

Throughout the intervention process, ISEOR's socioeconomic method relies heavily on the calculation of performance costs, especially those that allow managers to eliminate contradictory indicators. The logic of change, in essence, is based on active improvements and appropriate budgeting. This approach, which shares common ground with both OD and the sociotechnical method, includes the integration of an explicit economic dimension (see Demming, 1975; Gummesson, 2000).

As an illustration, we can use the example of a food company going through four stages of improvement: diagnosis, project development, implementation, and evaluation.

Diagnosis

The diagnosis phase consists of examining the full range of possible dysfunctions and the subsequent costs. Hundreds of dysfunctions might be gathered together with their possible causes. Table 1 illustrates an example of calculated costs and the possible causes of dysfunctions that created hidden costs of $47,000 per year. In this instance, the total of these costs corresponded to the firm's monthly payroll costs, which demonstrates to senior management and frontline managers the necessity of organizational change. This type of economic analysis facilitates the role of consultant intervention because of the value-added nature of the outcome; without such economic evaluation participants often view change in terms of added costs rather than cost reduction and a true change in performance.

Table 1.   An Example of the Costs of Dysfunctions in an Agri-Food Company

Dysfunction Cost Observed	Frequency of Problem	Reasons for the Dysfunction	Components of the Financial Consequences
Poor Quality of the Dough	Twice a week	• The dough may be too wet • The baker did not respect some of the production process parameters • Differences in temperature and humidity	• Non production • Time wasted • Over-consumption (misuse of raw materials) ***Cost per year $47,000***

The sum of $47,000 was based on a four-week study of the round-the-clock production line that found:

1. The poor quality dough (raw materials) being used resulted in an average loss of seven hours on average per person per week on the line (which was manned by six people).
2. Multiplied by 52 weeks, the time wasted per year amounted to 2,184 hours.

Each hour wasted meant lost production and lost sales. The average cost of each hour wasted resulted in loss of margin on variable costs (consisting mainly of the cost of idle equipment and the cost to the payroll of an idle workforce) that was calculated as follows:

1. Sales for the line: $7,000,000 a year
2. Variable costs: $3,000,000 a year
3. Margin on variable costs: $4,000,000 a year
4. Average margin on variable costs per hour: $20 per hour.

The cost of time wasted was therefore $20 x 2,184 hours = $43,680. In addition, the over-consumption of ingredients (flour, yeast, sugar, eggs etc.), which could not be recycled, was taken into account at a cost of $0.8 per pound:

5. 4,150 pounds were thrown away on this production line each year.
6. Resulting in a loss of $3,320 per year.

Total loss per year thus equaled $43,680 (time wasted) and $3,320 (over-consumption of ingredients) for a total of $47,000.

Project Development and Implementation

The role of the consultant is not limited to providing methodological assistance to organizational members looking for solutions within the project groups. The consultant's role is also targeted at evaluating the costs of these solutions and their implementation—in the context of capturing hidden costs and improving performance. Using the example of the food company, an illustration of such a role is outlined in Table 2. In this example, the company has integrated specified levels of production with improved equipment technology and production processes, training of production line personnel, and an enlargement in their roles through the introduction of certain quality control measures. A method that is not as systemic in nature, in contrast, might focus on technological improvements alone, to the detriment of training and the changing roles of line personnel. This latter approach, with its emphasis on a purely technological investment, may appear less expensive ($14,000), but it might not result in the same level of performance and savings.

Table 2.   Evaluating the Costs and Performance Benefits of Project Solutions: Economic Balance

Costs		Performance (Outcomes)	
Investment in New Equipment (tangible investment)	$14,000	Reduction in costs for poor quality	$39,000
Cost of integrated training (intangible investment)	$27,000	Reduction in production line stoppages and improved product quality (835 hours instead of 2,184 hours lost. 1,350 hours × $20)	$27,000
Cost of time spent in implementing the improvement process (intangible investment)	$4,200		
Cost of the assistance by provided by the management consultant	$7,800		
Totals	$53,000		$66,000

Improvement in cash flow achieved in the first year: $13,000

Based on our analysis, the cost of integrated training was:

1. Preparation of materials—120 hours spent by management × $20 $2,400
2. Training sessions: 1,230 hours 12,000 (30 employees, 20 hours each at $20 per hour)
3. Cost of assistance provided by the management consultant 12,600

Cost of time spent in implementing the improvement process:

1. Interviews (2 hours × 30 persons × $20 per hour) $1,200
2. Project groups : 50 hours x $20 3,000
3. Cost of the assistance provided by the management consultant 7,800

As shown in Table 2, the cost of the tangible investment in new equipment ($14,000) is relatively easy to calculate since it is recorded in the company accounts. The cost of intangibles is mainly calculated according to the cost of time spent in the training sessions and in the improvement process, and also in the cost of assistance provided by the management consultant.

The reduction in cost due to poor quality was $39,000 a year. This was due to a 25% decrease in returned sales, which had previously amounted to $156,000 a year. Reduction in production line stoppages and improved product quality amounted to $39,000 (25% × $156,000 = $39,000). The number of working hours lost, previously 2,184, was effectively reduced to 834 hours as a result of the improvement process. Therefore 1,350 hours were saved, worth $20 per hour arriving at the figure of $27,000.

Evaluation

Interventions by management consultants should be considered as part of a global investment by a company to improve its performance in the same way as tangible investments in new technology. In the case of the agri-food company discussed above, the range of performance factors was evaluated at more than $2,000,000 per year as summarized in Table 3. The total cost of the investment in the change process was $462,000, which not only gave the organization an immediate return on investment in the first year but also contributed to increased surpluses in the following years.

Table 3. Evaluation of the Results of a Management Consulting Intervention in an Agri-Food Company

Production Department

• Increase in Productivity (Production)	$ 80,000
• Cutting Production Waste by 25%	165,000
• Cutting Absenteeism by 45% in the Packaging Department	43,000
• Streamlining the Production Line based on information taken from improvement indicators	740,000
	125,000
	184,000
• Better Time Management due to more organized production	Not quantified
• Cut in Maintenance Costs	120,000

Logistics Department

• Improved Inventory Management, allowing a cut in the need for bank loans and, as a result, lower interest payments	$ 83,000
	112,000
• Reduction in delivery delays resulting in increased sales	140,000

Sales Department

• Increased margins due to better selling techniques and sales training	$170,000
	26,000
• Improved time management of the sales representatives enabling them to focus their efforts on sales rather than administrative procedures	40,000
Total	**$2,028,000**

A GLOBAL VIEW OF THE ORGANIZATION: THE HORIZONTAL AND VERTICAL METHOD (HORIVERT)

Assessments of change management interventions typically reveal that actions aimed at improving only one part of a company or using separate solutions for a number of different dysfunctions tend to be disappointing. As an illustration, a chemical company was involved with a number of different management consultants who had implemented a range of programs in different parts of the organization, including:

1. Teambuilding centering on the top management team, including the recruitment of new executives;
2. Reengineering of the data processing department;
3. Creation of a corporate structure in order to have a better control of subsidiaries;
4. Safety training schemes in the production department;
5. Implementation of quality procedures and total quality management; and, in general,
6. Actions aimed at enhancing productivity in all departments.

Despite these myriad activities, the company continued to encounter problems and difficulties due to a lack of coherence and synergy between their actions. For instance, the lack of appropriate planning of the different actions resulted in overworked executives and a decrease in the quality of the individual interventions. Similarly, the software chosen by the new data processing manager did not meet the needs of the different departments, and quality procedures did not filter down through the company.

As a way of coping with these difficulties, ISEOR's intervention consisted of two simultaneous actions:

- A *horizontal action* consisting of methodological assistance focused on the top management team. This intervention was mainly based on training the team to (1) select those actions that would yield the highest value added and (2) ensure the coherence and feasibility of these actions. The managers, for example, learned how to create a Priority Action Plan focused on improved cross-departmental coordination in developing new products, a process that prevented delays in scheduled launch times. This first tier of actions was mainly aimed at improving communication and cooperation between the different departments of the chemical company and improving coordination between the different projects implemented in the company.
- *Vertical actions* in multiple units (project teams of departments) were also undertaken. Three main steps were the (1) development of an in-house training scheme in the sales department, (2) diagnosis and

accompanying project planning efforts focused on preventing problems (dysfunctions) in one of the company's plants, and (3) a project focused on preventing production stoppages.

Both sets of actions—horizontal and vertical—were synchronized at the top-management team level, assisted by the management consultant who implemented a pilot test of the intervention. The horizontal actions increased the awareness of the board of directors concerning the technical and commercial environment. One of the ways this was accomplished was through the use of "indicators of strategic vigilance," that is, data on the environment that provide relevant information for enhancing strategic decisions. Each of the departments was also involved in this process through "vertical" actions: many employees, sales representatives and front line managers, for example, were given tasks to capture and marshal data in their areas of responsibility. One team was assigned to study a given competitor and try to predict its next move. At the same time, this team had to relay this information to colleagues who were dealing with other competitors. In order to succeed in this cross-departmental (horizontal) initiative, departments and services had to be reorganized at the vertical level. If this kind of horizontal intervention had not been supported by vertical actions, the policy could have resulted in little more than an organizational "checkmate." In this case, the horizontal action consisted of implementing strategic vigilance indicators, with top management team assuming responsibility for this objective. Vertical actions focused on sharing the information with the other teams. Such vertical actions that cut across teams and work units can readily reduce delivery delays by accelerating communication and reducing bottlenecks. In the case of the chemical company, this action was accompanied by horizontal activities aimed at improving the supply chain and coordination between the supply department and other company departments.

This type of system-wide consulting intervention enabled the company to formulate and implement its strategy more efficiently and more effectively. Specific results included increased production, reduction in the time needed to start new production processes, reduction in maintenance costs, reduction in the need for spare parts, savings in the purchasing process, gain in new clients, improvement of strategic awareness throughout the company, and an increase in the sales representatives' efficiency. Figure 4 illustrates the limits of either vertical or horizontal approaches and the need for a globally-oriented, system-wide approach that integrates the two perspectives (HORIVERT). In the case of vertical actions alone, which might be focused on a single department or project of the company, the change project is not extended to other units and does not profit from the participation of top management and other relevant groups. With only a horizontal action—focused, for example, on the top management team—

lower levels of the company are not involved in the intervention and resistance to the concomitant changes is often observed. By combining horizontal *and* vertical interventions, in contrast, a foundation can be created that can readily enhance higher levels of organizational performance.

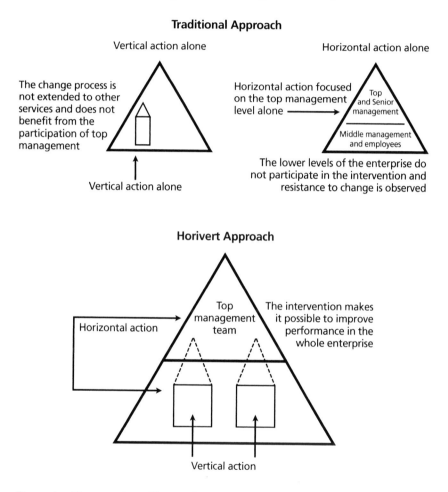

Figure 4.   Horizontal and Vertical Socio-Economic Intervention Method (HORIVENT-ISEOR Approach)

IMPLEMENTATION, INTEGRATION AND MANAGEMENT SUPPORT

Managers are often trained in specific disciplines such as accounting, marketing, finance or human resource management. Specializing in a given domain, these individuals experience different stresses and tensions from other functions of the company. A prime example is the budgetary process, which can lead to missed strategic opportunities and a lack of investment in developing organizational competencies due to the typical emphasis on reducing costs in the short term. Managers, in essence, attempt to act in a type of CEO role as they are forced to integrate different sets of logic (functional orientations) within budgetary constraints. While these individuals typically view this process as improving the implementation of the company's strategy, the usual experience of ISEOR in this scenario suggests that managers experience significant difficulties integrating the various management demands that are placed on them because they lack appropriate control tools to truly integrate economic performance in both the short term and long term with the human and social needs of the workforce. The role of the socioeconomically oriented consultant is thus to train managers in the use of such integrative tools and their implementation, often on one to one basis.

There are six principal tools used by ISEOR management consultants.

1. **Internal and external strategic planning.**   This process involves listing and classifying the strategic initiatives that the firm wishes to undertake in the medium term (3 to 5 years) as a master plan. This analysis serves as the basis for planning actions that are directed toward achieving the strategic objectives of the enterprise. A three-to-five year plan also gives management and employees a clearer idea of what is important for the development of the company and what their role will be in the overall plan. In the bakery illustration used earlier, for example, all participants were aware of the stake they have in the freshness of the products because this criterion ranked first in both the strategy of the enterprise and in customer requirements.

2. **Priority action planning.**   Emphasis is placed on continuously identifying and differentiating between high and low value-added tasks. Priority action planning (PAP), which consists of planning all the development actions to be implemented in the enterprise in each of its departments, is targeted at implementing key strategic objectives and preventing organizational dysfunctions.

3. **Table of skills.**   It is also important to train employees, enabling them to gain efficiency in their new activities. The SEAM approach

proposes a "table of skills," a visual representation of the skills of each team. Especially for small companies, each set of activities represents an important part of its intangible assets. Since upgrading this knowledge base is among the most expensive efforts any enterprise has to make to keep its competitive edge, this type of analysis helps to clarify and prioritize such skill building and development activities.

4. **Time management.** Emphasis is placed on eliminating time spent on low value added tasks and devoting more time to critical development actions and management needs. Time management tools that accurately schedule development actions can facilitate getting rid of low value-added tasks, in essence, avoiding wasting time. Time management requires: (1) self-assessment (which attempts to determine how time is allotted to different value-added activities, from day-to-day endeavors to shifts in function and strategy implementation initiatives); (2) transferring or eliminating low added value tasks by reducing executive interruptions which can hinder concentration and distract from profitable time usage; and (3) implementing concerted delegation in an effort to upgrade organizational activities and enhance empowerment at each and all levels of the company.

5. **Strategic piloting indicators.** To facilitate the measurement of the relative value created through organizational change, strategic piloting indicators can be useful. These indicators include improvement factors for immediate results as well as for the creation of potential longer-term gains. Immediate results stem mainly from a decrease in hidden costs and an increase in sales and profit margins. The creation of potential gains (such as future economic results, either probable or certain) stems from improvement actions such as the finalization of new products or an increase in skills and knowledge capital.

6. **Periodically Negotiable Activity Contract (PNAC).** This tool is a system designed to fix targets and negotiate ways to achieve them. As a negotiating tool, it should be used with the other socioeconomic management tools previously presented. The PNAC allows management to negotiate the efforts required to implement the Priority Action Planning (PAP) process successfully, as presented in Table 4. The PNAC establishes a direct dialogue on the reduction of dysfunctions and improvements actions to implement the strategy. All wage earners have their PNAC geared to a salary incentive self-financed by the drop in hidden costs and the creation of potential gains. The PNAC includes a selection of objectives linked to the priority action plan over the same period. It is based on commitments made in advance by both parties (employees and management) as

regards socioeconomic performance and serves as the cornerstone of the socioeconomic approach.

Table 4.   Illustration of a Worker's Periodically Negotiable Activity Contract

Types of objectives	Objectives	Value (out of 100%)	Target level	Means
General collective target	Reduction in delivery delays	30%	Going from an average of 80 days delivery to 60 without decreasing the quality	Improved flow of the process and setting up of computer-integrated manufacturing
Collective production target	Respect for budget by reducing waste	20%	Improvement of the margin by $100,000	Cost control managers will set indicators
Team target	Increase of productive use of equipment	30%	Increase of 500 productive hours in the six-month period	Maintenance will improve reliability of the equipment
Individual target	Improvement of skills	20%	A list of precise new tasks to be accomplished	Integrated training given by the superior

Implementation of these socioeconomic management oriented tools and techniques results in the development of practices that integrate the different areas of management and organization into a coherent, interactive whole. While the different specialized disciplines of management may have made significant advances pertaining to their own logic—which has been helpful for each department of the enterprise—this emphasis has contributed to interdepartmental drift, a "siloed" approach to organizational decisions, and resulting tensions particularly at the top of the enterprise. It is thus useful to provide a unifying perspective on integrative management if such an ideal is to be truly strengthened (see Figure 5).

Figure 5.   The SEAM Star

CONCLUSION

From a management consulting perspective, ISEOR's integrated socioeconomic management method makes two key contributions. First, when consultants are specialists in a given domain, this method broadens their perspective, facilitating their ability to take fuller account of the interactions between their specific intervention and other aspects of management and organization within a given company. Second, this approach provides consultants with a globally-oriented, system-wide performance improvement model that they can use with their clients. As the brief case examples in this chapter have hopefully indicated, by combining experience working with and intervening in organizations with an academic appreciation of research and model building, consultants can create useful intervention frameworks that can help organizations enhance the overall performance and effectiveness of their operations.

NOTES

1.   The ISEOR research center is associated with the University of Lyon 2 Lumière and E.M. LYON (France). It offers a number of executive education and graduate degrees, including a doctoral program in management science and management consulting. The courses are designed to allow participants, students, professional consultants and managers to experiment with management tools and consulting methods through hands-on experience. The programs range in duration from eight-day seminars to four-year courses. To date, more than 950 researchers and management consultants have been trained at the ISEOR center.

2.   At present, the research center involves 125 permanent researchers and doctoral students, each of them carrying out interventions in companies and organizations. Research training aimed at transforming the enterprise is the basis of the doctoral program, which relies heavily on transformative action research, also referred to as "experimental research." Participants are required to formalize the results of their experiments and compare them with other approaches and existing academic literature. Among doctoral students, professional consultants reflect on their own hypotheses, models and practices, which facilitates the improvement of their professional skills. About ten theses are defended each year. The age of the participants varies from 27 to 69. They come from many countries and the center has exchange agreements at the Ph.D. level with the University of Mexico City (UAM) and HEC Montreal, Canada. ISEOR's experience, SEAM framework, and theoretical body of information on management technology and consulting engineering are available to participants and international collaborators.

REFERENCES

Ackoff, R.L. (1997). *Transformational consulting: Changing thought patterns, not just processes.* Paper presented at the Institute of Management Consultants Meeting, Chicago.

Ackoff, R.L. (1974). *Redesigning the future.* New York: John Wiley & Sons.

Ackoff, R.L., & Emery, F. (1982). *On purposeful systems.* Seaside, CA: Intersystems Publications.

Bay, T., & MacPherson, D. (1998). *Change your attitude.* Franklin Lakes, NJ: Career Press.

Buckley, W. (Ed). (1968). *Systems research for the behavioral scientist: A sourcebook.* Chicago: Aldine Publishing Co.

Burns, J.M., & Stalker, G. (1961). *The management of innovation.* London: Tavistock.

Bryan, M., Cameron, J., & Allen, C. (1994) *The artist's way at work: Riding the dragon.* New York: William Morrow and Company, Inc.

Crozier, M. (1964). *The bureaucratic phenomenon.* Chicago: University of Chicago Press.

Dalton, M. (1959). *Men who manage.* New York: John Wiley & Sons.

Demming, W.E. (1975). On some statistical aids toward economic production. *Interfaces, 5*(4), 1-15.

Etzioni, A. (1988). *The moral dimension: Toward a new economics.* New York: Free Press.

Friedberg, E. (1980). *Actors and Systems: The politics of collective action.* Chicago: University of Chicago Press.

Gharajedaghi, J. (1999). *Systems thinking: Managing chaos & complexity, a platform for designing business architecture.* Boston: Butterworth-Heinemann.

Gharajedaghi, J. (1985). *Toward a systems theory of organizations.* Seaside, CA: Intersystems Publications.

Gummesson, E. (2000). *Qualitative methods in management research.* Thousand Oaks, CA: Sage.

Lewin, K. (1951). *Field theory in social science.* New York: Harper.

Lewin, K. (1948). *Resolving social conflicts.* New York: Harper

Osborne, D., & Gaebler, T. (1993). *Reinventing government: How the entrepreneurial spirit is transforming the public sector.* New York: Plume.

Savall, H. (1981). *Work and people: An economics evaluation of job-enrichment.* New York: Oxford University Press.

Savall, H. (1978). *A method for a socio-economic diagnosis of the enterprise.* Paper presented at the Annual Conference of CERN, IAE de Nice, France.

Savall,H. (1989). *Professeur-Consultant.* Paper published in RFG, Paris.

Savall, H., & Zardet, V. (1995). *Ingénierie stratégique du Roseau.* Paris: Economica.

Savall, H., & Zardet, V.(1989). Maîtriser les coûts et les performances cachés. Le contrat d'activité périodiquement négociable. In J-M. Doublet (ED.), *Prix Harvard l'Expansion de management stratégique* (325 pp.). Paris: Economica.

Savall, H., Zardet, V., & Bonnet, M. (2000). *Releasing the untapped potential of enterprises through socio-economic management.* Geneva: ILO publications.

CHAPTER 7

NEW DIRECTIONS IN LINKING RESEARCH

Employee Satisfaction as an Outcome or Predictor?

Kyle M. Lundby, Kristofer J. Fenlason, and Shon M. Magnan

INTRODUCTION

Significant attention has recently been focused on the benefits of linking employee, customer, and financial data (cf. Heskett, Jones, Loveman, Sasser, & Schlesinger, 1994; Rucci, Kirn, & Quinn, 1998; Wiley, 1996). *Linking*, a general term used by organizational consultants and researchers, describes the practice of statistically modeling relationships between different sources of internal (e.g., employee attitudes, productivity, turnover) and external or outcome (e.g., customer satisfaction, financial results) measures (Lundby, Fenlason, & Magnan, in press). Since this type of analysis can provide a virtual roadmap of causal relationships between key variables in organizations, it has captured the attention of a growing number of internal and external consultants and numerous companies have begun similar studies in their own organizations.

Today's linking research has its roots in earlier work conducted by Benjamin Schneider and his colleagues in the area of service climate (cf.

Schneider, 1990; Schneider & Bowen, 1985; Schneider, Holcombe, & White, 1997; Schneider, Parkington, & Buxton, 1980; Schneider, White, & Paul, 1998). Specifically, Schneider and associates published a series of articles beginning in the early 1980s that detailed their investigation of the relationship between service climate and customer attitudes in service organizations. What this work, and subsequent research expanding the domain to include productivity and financial measures (cf. Johnson, 1996; Lundby, Dobbins, & Kidder, 1995; Tornow & Wiley, 1991), has shown is that a significant relationship exists between employee attitudes and important outcome measures (e.g., customer attitudes, financial criteria). The basic tenet underlying this causal link is that employee attitudes drive employee behavior, and that customers experience these attitudes and behaviors either directly, in the case of service organizations, or indirectly through the quality of goods they purchase.

Based on this early climate research, investigators expanded the content domain to include other variables to help explain such causal links, essentially questioning "what leads to what" in organizations. The resulting "linking models," as they came to be known, were highly valued because they provided organizations with veritable roadmaps of the factors that contributed to desirable outcomes in their organizations by statistically modeling the strength and direction of relationships between specified variables.

LINKING MODELS

While this relatively new field continues to evolve, the three most widely-cited linking models are Heskett et al.'s (1994) *Service-Profit Chain*, Rucci et al.'s (1998) *Employee-Customer-Profit Chain*, and Wiley's (1996) *Linkage Research Model*. All three seek to describe the relationship between internal organizational factors and important outcomes. The specific elements identified in each model, however, are slightly different.

The important internal factors in Heskett et al.'s (1994) "Service-Profit Chain" are *service quality* (e.g., employee selection, employee rewards, tools), *employee satisfaction*, and *employee behavior* (e.g., retention, productivity). According to their model, service quality precedes employee satisfaction. Employee satisfaction, in turn, drives employee behavior. Without satisfied employees, important organizational outcomes (e.g., customer satisfaction, loyalty, revenue growth) will not be realized.

More recently, Rucci et al. (1998), in their assessment of the turnaround at Sears, also posited that employee satisfaction plays a pivotal role in the process. According to their "Employee-Customer-Profit Chain," satisfaction (attitudes about the job and the company) precedes employee behavior. Customers then evaluate employee behavior in terms of service helpfulness and merchandise value. Increases in these areas, according to the model, drive customer impressions and ultimately financial outcomes (return on assets, operating margin, and revenue growth).

Finally, Wiley's (1996) "Linkage Research Model" shows a similar chain of events. Like Heskett et al. (1994) and Rucci et al. (1998), Wiley includes employee satisfaction in his model. In addition to employee satisfaction, however, Wiley includes several other variables that he summarizes under the general heading *employee results*, such as information/knowledge, teamwork/cooperation, and employee retention. According to Wiley's model, employee results drive customer results (responsive service, product quality, overall customer satisfaction, and retention), and ultimately business performance.

Thus, while all three models differ slightly in detail, all are similar in that they map important internal organizational factors to critically important external factors (e.g., customer attitudes and financial health). Of notable importance in each model is employee satisfaction. Rucci et al. (1998), for example, found that employee satisfaction at Sears had an indirect effect on outcomes by influencing employee behavior. Similarly, Heskett et al. (1994) argued that employee satisfaction had an indirect effect on customer perceptions of service value by influencing employee productivity and retention. In Wiley's (1996) work, while employee satisfaction accompanies other "employee results," it is still considered an important precursor to customer outcomes. Together, these widely cited linking models have not only supplemented our understanding of linking relationships, they have also fueled significant interest in linking research.

Based on our experience as organizational consultants, however, we have also found that these frequently cited linking models have left many organizations with the impression that employee satisfaction itself is the "Holy Grail" of linking research. It is our contention that while employee satisfaction is indeed a critical variable, it is not necessarily the primary or sole factor that determines whether an organization will be profitable or if its customer will express satisfaction. Other key factors, ranging from employee empowerment and workgroup functioning to the nature of supervision, might exert a direct effect on customers, or alternatively, an indirect (through employee satisfaction) *and* direct influence on customers. Thus, the goal of this chapter is to replicate and extend existing linking research by (1) examining the relationship between variables that have been measured in previous linking studies, and (2) comparing different structural models to help assess the role employee satisfaction plays as an influence on customer satisfaction.

Our desire to conduct this research stems from an empirical and experiential understanding that many factors contribute to customer satisfaction and bottom-line financial well being. After reviewing the published linking research, however, many consultants and researchers appear to be left with the impression that all efforts should be focused on improving employee satisfaction. Increasing employee satisfaction, it is assumed, will result in greater customer satisfaction and profitability. While we do not deny the importance of employee satisfaction, we believe that other variables may directly affect customer satisfaction and should also be considered in linking models.

STUDY DESIGN AND METHODOLOGY

The study focuses primarily on the fit and comparison of two models representing the relationships that employee satisfaction may have in the linking process. In the first paradigm, consistent with the aforementioned linking models (Heskett et al., 1994; Rucci et al., 1998; Wiley, 1996), employee satisfaction will be treated as *the* mediator of the relationship between other organizational variables (e.g., supervisor-subordinate relationships, empowerment, work group) and customer satisfaction. In the second model, employee satisfaction is treated both as a direct influence on customer satisfaction *and* as mediator of the relationship between organizational variables and the outcome of customer satisfaction. These models will be compared and contrasted using various fit indices and Chi-square difference tests to determine which model best fits the data in question. A third model will also be compared and contrasted to provide a test of whether the data might fit a model in which employee satisfaction has no effect on customer satisfaction. By comparing these models, we hope to clarify the relationship between employee, customer, and financial measures.

Sample

During 1999, data were collected from employees and customers of a large full-service bank. In general, banks have been a favorite of linking researchers because they are typically comprised of multiple identical units (e.g., branches) from which employee, customer, and financial data are easily collected. This particular bank was selected for the present study because of its relatively large number of branches, which allowed the researchers to analyze the data using structural equations modeling (SEM). Employees completed their surveys on location and returned them directly to the researchers in prepaid postage envelopes. Customer surveys were completed at home and also returned to the researchers in prepaid postage envelopes. Employees and customers were assured that their responses would remain anonymous and confidential.

Of the 3,887 employee surveys that were delivered to branches, 1,837 were completed and returned for a 47% response rate. Based on our experience as consultants, this is a reasonable response rate for an employee opinion survey. Analysis of the demographic makeup of this sample reveals that most employees were Caucasian (73%) females (87%) ranging in age from 31 to 40 (29%) or 41 to 50 (24%). Of the 66,845 customer surveys that were delivered, 11,074 were completed and returned for a 17% customer response rate. While significantly lower than the employee response rate, based on our experience, this is a reasonable response rate for a customer opinion survey. Analysis of the demographic makeup of this sample reveals that customers tended to be Caucasian (78%) females (56%) ranging in age from 34 to 53 (34%).

Measures

Branch employees completed four measures, each of which is discussed in detail below. Branch customers completed one measure that assessed their perceptions of service quality. Responses to the employee and customer survey items were made using a five-point (strongly agree to strongly disagree) Likert scale.

Supervision

Supervision was measured with four items. Sample items include, "*My manager is committed to my long-term training and development needs*," and "*My supervisor treats me with dignity and respect.*" Internal consistency between the items was good (Cronbach's Alpha = .89).

Empowerment

Empowerment was measured by three items. Sample items include, "*I feel encouraged to come up with new and better ways of doing things*," and "*I have the authority to make decisions that enable me to provide good customer service.*" Internal consistency reliability for these items was deemed acceptable (Cronbach's Alpha = .76).

Workgroup Functioning

Workgroup functioning was measured by four items. Sample items include, "*There is good communication between departments in [the organization],*" and "*When conflicts arise between work groups, they are resolved quickly and effectively.*" Internal consistency reliability was also acceptable (Cronbach's Alpha = .77).

Employee Satisfaction

Employee satisfaction was measured using a five-item satisfaction scale. Sample items include, "*Overall, I am satisfied with [the organization] as a place to work,*" and "*My work gives me a sense of personal accomplishment.*" Internal consistency across the five items was good (Cronbach's Alpha = .90).

Customer Satisfaction

Customer satisfaction with service quality was measured using a four-item scale. Sample items include, "*Overall, how satisfied are you with the service you receive from the tellers with whom you've interacted at this [the organization] in the past 12 months?*" and "*Overall, how satisfied are you with the service you received from [the organization] in the past 12 months?*" Customers completed the measure using a five-point Likert scale (ranging from extremely satisfied to not at all satisfied, and extremely likely to not at all likely). Internal consistency reliability for the customer satisfaction measure was good (Cronbach's Alpha = .91).

Statistical Justification for Aggregation

Since variables in linking models are conceptualized at the group level, responses from individual respondents were aggregated to the branch level. Consistent with previous linking research (see, Johnson, 1996; Schneider et al., 1998), two different measures of agreement were calculated to justify aggregation. First, interrater agreement was determined using James, Demaree, and Wolf's (1984) $r_{(WG)}$. This approach measures the amount of agreement among a single group of judges (e.g., employees, customers) on one single variable or multiple parallel items. Interrater agreement was assessed for each of the employee dimensions and the customer satisfaction measure. Second, James' (1982) *ICC(2)* intraclass correlation was calculated for the same measures. This index measures the degree to which branches can be reliably differentiated based on individual dimension scores (Johnson, 1996).

Interrater Agreement

Interrater agreement was computed for each branch using $r_{(WG)}$ (James et al., 1984) for the supervision, empowerment, workgroup functioning, climate for service, and employee satisfaction scales. As can be seen in Table 1, average interrater agreement for each of the measures was acceptable ($r_{(WG)}$ = .90, .83, .87, .91 and .93, respectively). Interrater agreement was also acceptable for the external customer satisfaction measure ($r_{(WG)}$ =.85). Taken together, the average $r_{(WG)}$ results suggest that there is an acceptable level of interrater agreement among employees and customers in order to justify aggregating the study variables.

Table 1.   Summary of Dimension Reliability and Agreement

Scale Label	No. of Items	Alpha	Average $r_{(WG)}$	ICC(2)
Supervision	4	.89	.90	.44
Empowerment	3	.76	83	.43
Workgroup functioning	4	.77	87	.49
Employee satisfaction	5	.90	.93	.44
Customer satisfaction	4	.91	.85	.64

Intraclass Correlation

In addition to calculating interrater agreement using $r_{(WG)}$, intraclass correlation *ICC(2)* was computed for the same measures. Bartko (1976) describes *ICC(2)* as a measure of the relative status of between and within variability using the average ratings of respondents within each unit. *ICC(2)* values are also presented in Table 1. As can be seen, the average *ICC(2)* is .49. Although this is somewhat lower than the suggested cutoff of .60 (Glick, 1985), the scores are moderate for values of *ICC(2)* (see Schneider, White, & Paul, 1998).

Based on these analyses, the average $r_{(WG)}$ values indicate that aggregating individual employee responses to the branch level is appropriate. While the *ICC(2)* values are somewhat low, they are within reasonable bounds (see Schneider et al., 1998), which further suggests that it is reasonable to aggregate both individual-level employee and customer data to the branch-level.

ANALYSIS OF THE LINKING MODELS

Structural equation modeling using LISREL 8 (Jöreskog & Sörbom, 1993) was employed to evaluate the appropriateness of different models in this study. As part of the analysis, several fit statistics were used to evaluate the models tested. The Goodness of Fit Index (GFI) measures the extent to which a proposed model better fits the data compared to no model at all. The GFI is one of the typical statistics used to assess fit because it does not explicitly depend on sample size (Jöreskog & Sörbom, 1993). GFI and other fit statistics have been developed as alternatives to the well-known problem of using Chi-square as an indicator of fit—large Chi-squares, which are typically significant, can incorrectly indicate that models should be rejected (e.g., Bentler & Bonett, 1980; Mulaik, Van Alstine, Bennett, Lind, & Stilwell, 1989). The Parsimony Goodness of Fit Index (PGFI) takes degrees of freedom into account, such that a more "clean cut" model would show higher levels of PGFI when one is concerned with using parsimony as a criterion for model selection. Larger values of GFI and PGFI indicate better fit. Finally, Steiger's (1990) Root Mean Square Error of Approximation (RMSEA) is a test of whether the model fits the data "reasonably well." According to Browne and Cudeck (1993), a RMSEA of .05 or less is indicative of close fit, and values as high as .08 are considered reasonable. The Expected Cross-Validation Index (ECVI; Browne & Cudeck, 1989) is a measure of the discrepancy between the fitted covariance matrix in the data analyzed and the expected covariance matrix that would be obtained in another sample of equal size (Jöreskog & Sörbom, 1993). It decreases only when a more complex model substantially reduces the estimate of discrepancy, and increases if needless paths are hypothesized. Therefore, when comparing nested models (i.e., all variables are included in each model), the most appropriate model is the one at which ECVI is at a minimum. A comparative analysis of different models also requires a Chi-square difference test that can be used to examine whether one model fits the data better than another.

Fit is examined for each model and the models are then compared to each other to determine which best fits the data. All latent variables are included in each model, but relationships are not hypothesized for all latent variables in all models (i.e., path coefficients equal to zero). As noted above, each of these models is a nested model, and the only difference between models is the addition and/or subtraction of paths.

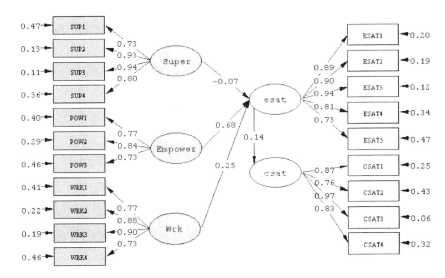

Figure 1.   Model 1: Employee satisfaction as the sole direct influence on customer satisfaction.

Model 1 (see Figure 1) treats employee satisfaction as the sole (direct) influence on Customer Satisfaction with direct paths from Supervision, Empowerment and Work Group to Employee Satisfaction. Fit statistics (Table 2) indicate a good fit to the data (χ^2 with 163 df = 220.40, p = .0018, RMSEA = .043, GFI = .90, PGFI = .70). An examination of the path coefficients in the standardized model reveals the strongest relationships in Model 1 to be between Employee Satisfaction and Empowerment (.68) and Work Group (.25). The relationship between Employee Satisfaction and Customer Satisfaction is somewhat weaker (.14). Finally, the relationship between Supervisor and Employee satisfaction is negative and much weaker (–.07).

Table 2.   Fit Statistics for Tested Models

Model	Df	χ^2	RMSEA	ECVI	GFI	PGFI
Model 1	163	220.40	.043	1.62	.90	.70
Model 2	160	210.31	.040	1.60	.90	.69
Model 3	161	215.11	.042	1.61	.90	.69

Note. N = 195. RMSEA = Root Mean Square Error of Approximation; ECVI = Expected Cross Validation Index; GFI = Goodness of Fit Index; PGFI = Parsimony Goodness of Fit Index.
χ^2 difference between Model 1 and Model 2 = 10.09, p = .018, at df = 3
χ^2 difference between Model 3 and Model 2 = 4.80, p = .028, at df = 1

Model 2 (Figure 2) adds direct paths from Supervision, Empowerment and Work Group to Customer Satisfaction. Again, the indices show a good fit of the model to the data (χ^2 with 160 df = 210.31, p = .0047, RMSEA = .040, GFI = .90, PGFI = .69). An examination of the standardized path coefficients reveals positive and moderate relationships between all latent variables except for three pairs (Work Group to Customer Satisfaction = –.03, Supervision to Employee Satisfaction = –.07 and Empowerment to Customer Satisfaction = –.41).

A comparison of the models (see Table 2 for all fit statistics) reveals that while Model 1 is a good fit to the data, Model 2 actually appears to fit better. While the PGFI for Model 1 is slightly better (indicating it is nominally a more parsimonious model), the χ^2 difference test between the models (Model 1 → Model 2) shows a significant decrease in χ^2 (χ^2 difference with 3 df = 10.09, p < .018). In addition, both the RMSEA and ECVI indices decreased which indicate a better fit and show that Model 2 represents an improvement over Model 1.

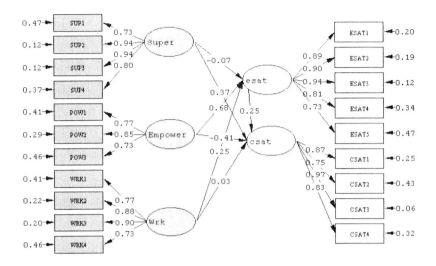

Figure 2.   Model 2: Organizational variables with direct and indirect influences on customer satisfaction.

Finally, when Model 3 is compared to Model 2, the fit statistics and the change in Chi square indicate that Model 2 is a better fit to the data than Model 3 (see Figure 3). Fit statistics show an *increase* in Chi square (χ^2 difference with 1 df = 4.80, $p < .028$), and increases in RMSEA and ECVI. Taken together, these data suggest that Model 2 has the best overall fit to the data.

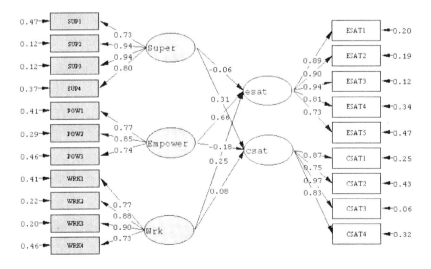

Figure 3.   Model 3: Employee satisfaction with no direct influence on customer satisfaction.

LINKING MODELS, ORGANIZATIONAL RESEARCH AND CONSULTING

The results in this study support previous empirical and conceptual work about the relationship between employee and customer satisfaction. Specifically, Model 1 shows the direct effect of employee satisfaction on customer satisfaction. As seen in Model 3, however, other organizational variables besides employee satisfaction can also have a meaningful *direct* effect on customer satisfaction as well. These two positions can be accommodated within a model that incorporates both direct and indirect influences (Model 2). Therefore, this study provides encouraging evidence that, while employee satisfaction is a critical variable to include in linking models, it should not necessarily be considered the only variable of interest that influences the outcome of customer satisfaction.

This investigation shows that there could be more than one linking model with acceptable fit to the data. A comparison of the three nested models shows that while all three models fit the data reasonably well, Model 2 fits the data better than the less complex model (Model 1) which only incorporates workplace influences on customer satisfaction through employee satisfaction. While comparisons with the third model show that we cannot completely dispense with the notion of employee satisfaction influencing customer satisfaction, linking researchers would be well advised to consider alternative models and not simply end investigations by choosing a model with all organizational variable paths leading to employee satisfaction.

These results also demonstrate the complexity of the relationships between variables that make up linking models. For organizational consultants interested in improving customer satisfaction, simply focusing one's efforts on improving employee satisfaction may *not* be the most effective strategy. An examination of Model 2, for example, clearly shows there are multiple direct and indirect (through employee satisfaction) influences of several organizational variables on customer satisfaction. In addition, these effects may not be symmetrical (affecting both employee and customer satisfaction) and may indeed have different directions of influence on a given outcome variable. Supervision, for instance, is only weakly related to employee satisfaction and more strongly related to customer satisfaction, while the opposite is true for the work group variable. In addition, while empowerment has a moderate relationship with both outcome variables, the direction of the relationship is positive for employee satisfaction and negative for customer satisfaction.

It follows that organizational interventions based on such complex results will have to be carefully considered and crafted. It is important that consultants place these analyses in their broader organizational context.

For instance, while it may be an organizational imperative (perhaps driven by company values) to empower employees, these actions *may* exert a detrimental effect on customer satisfaction, as suggested by the negative relationship between empowerment and customer satisfaction. This finding raises some intriguing practice questions. Do we counsel our clients to eliminate actions that are empowering in an effort to improve customer satisfaction? Clearly this could have a detrimental effect on employee satisfaction. Or, should we delve deeper into the data, questioning relationships more fully (e.g., do empowered employees provide poorer service?, do satisfied customers somehow make employees feel less empowered?, is there an alternative explanation?) and following up with action planning to seek a compromise approach that builds complementary actions to improve both employee and customer satisfaction? As practical interventions are crafted to specifically target ways to affect customer satisfaction, testing well-reasoned alternative models will be an integral part of evaluating and discovering new "high pay off" actions. Arguably, the more powerful intervention would be to identify actions or factors that directly or indirectly affect customer satisfaction *and* employee satisfaction.

Implications

Given these results, there are several implications for practitioners who wish to successfully counsel and guide clients through linking work. As this study demonstrates, the picture of linking relationships is more complex than simply focusing only on increasing employee satisfaction. Yet, with complex results comes a challenge of how best to present these insights to clients so that they are comprehensible and comprehensive without being unwieldy. Use of simplified path diagrams that indicate the strength and direction of relationships (e.g., using the width of arrows to indicate relative strength of relationships) is one way of capturing complex dynamics with a minimum of technical jargon. It is also a safe bet that "previewing" the results with a knowledgeable insider and then debriefing the presentation (e.g., were your 3–5 main points understood?) will help ensure that you are effectively getting your point across without undue detail.

A methodological implication is that practitioners may need to add more tools to their toolbox. Given that there are many potential influences on both employee and customer satisfaction, it is necessary to use more sophisticated methods that can accommodate this level of complexity. In this study, structural equations modeling (LISREL) was used to examine both the form (structure) of several models and the strength of the relationships within the models. With the advent of much friendlier software, this method has become much more accessible. However, as with any tool, its proper use assumes a working knowledge of the requirements and assumptions of the procedure (e.g., the need for typically large sample sizes, choosing an estimation method, having familiarity with fit statistics).

A practice implication is that while linking research may indeed point the way to potential interventions, this does not necessarily mean that interventions should be implemented uniformly in all the business units. Linking research typically involves looking at relationships for the whole organization or entire collections of groups. In order to conduct linking data analysis, researchers need to have a sufficient number of data points and, because information must all be aggregated to the same level, there must typically be a large number of the highest-level unit (e.g., in this study bank branches or other units that are similar in function). It should be kept in mind that interventions based on these findings can be applied across the board and will be likely to yield an average improvement for the entire organization. In reality there will still be differences between units, and savvy consultants can build in a measurement step to assess which units might need (or not need) such interventions. For instance, if a strong supervisor relationship is found to positively influence customer satisfaction, it would be desirable to improve this relationship. Some organizational units, however, may already have highly functional and productive supervisor relationships. It can be argued that, for these units, the intervention might be modified or eliminated if supervisor scores reach a sufficient threshold. Conversely, concentrating interventions on organizational units where scores are relatively lower on supervisor scores is likely to have a bigger pay off than in units that are already functioning at a high level.

Because each organization is unique and given that there may be a multitude of factors that can be measured, researchers should be prepared to lay out a model testing and modification plan. Determining which model presents both a good fit to the data and shows sufficiently large effects may take a while.

Finally, attention must also be paid to the practical aspects of action planning based upon the model data. While the data may point to several areas or issues that could be addressed, it is likely that some are easier or more quickly addressed than others. For instance, changing work group dynamics is likely to be a more complex and longer-term change than changing some aspect of the work environment (e.g., improving tools or resources). Quickly implementing changes where one can helps to build a sense of momentum and change. This engages employees and can give them a sense of involvement and ownership in shaping their workplace. This sort of involvement and buy-in can be particularly helpful to build early on, especially if other interventions may take longer to show visible effects.

Limitations and Directions for Future Research

Inevitably, real-world research has limitations that should be acknowledged and addressed as researchers move forward in refining their models and practice. One potential limitation of this study is the narrow focus on a financial services institution. Generalizing these results to other service or non-service organizations would be premature. However, given the current interest in linking research and the value of its information, finding a willing organization should not be overly difficult.

This study also focused only on one sub-segment of the employee population—direct service providers. Recently, Lundby, Fenlason, and Magnan (2000) demonstrated that linking relationships may be different for different employee groups within the same organization. They showed that the strength of linking relationships among the same set of variables were different for service and non-service employees within the same organization. This suggests that linking models may also exhibit more or less fit depending on how the sample is drawn within the very same organization. Again, this demonstrates the complex nature of linking relationships, and of linking research in general.

Finally, this study should be considered a limited test, given the various other variables that could impinge on employee and customer satisfaction. The study captured and included three organizational variables that are commonly found in workplace research—supervision, work group functioning and empowerment. These three variables, of course, do not completely describe the rich and complex relationship between employee workplace experiences and employee and customer satisfaction. Future investigations should certainly seek to include a broader range of variables. Schneider and colleagues extensive work in the area of *climate for service* (cf. Schneider, 1990; Schneider & Bowen, 1985; Schneider, Holcombe, & White, 1997; Schneider, Parkington, & Buxton, 1980; Schneider, White, & Paul, 1998), for example, suggests that this is another potential variable to consider.

As with most practice issues, organizational consultants engaged in linking research find themselves in a dynamic balancing act. Ensuring methodological rigor is always a challenge in "real-world" research as is communicating the richness of the data in a concise manner that will be accepted in the client organization. Certainly, wherever possible, we seek to find simple yet compelling models to describe the relationships between organizational variables and outcomes. It is hoped that this paper will assist consultants maintain this balance in their continuing efforts to help clients make the most of their organizational resources in an increasingly competitive business environment.

REFERENCES

Bartko, J.J. (1976). On various intraclass correlation reliability coefficients. *Psychological Bulletin, 83,* 762–765.

Bentler, P.M., & Bonett, D.G. (1980) Significance tests and goodness of fit in the analysis of covariance structures. *Psychological Bulletin, 88,* 588–606.

Browne, M.W., & Cudeck, R. (1993). Alternative ways of assessing model fit. In K.A. Bollen & J.S. Long (Eds.), *Testing structural equation models* (pp. 136–162). Newbury Park, CA: Sage.

Browne, M.W., & Cudeck, R. (1989). Single sample cross-validation indices for covariance structures. *Multivariate Behavioral Research, 24,* 445–455.

Glick, W.H. (1985). Conceptualizing and measuring organizational and psychological climate: Pitfalls in multilevel research. *Academy of Management Review, 10,* 601–616.

Heskett, J.L., Jones, T.O., Loveman, G.W., Sasser, W.E., & Schlesinger, L.A. (1994). Putting the service-profit chain to work. *Harvard Business Review, 72*(2), 164–174.

James, L.R. (1982). Aggregation bias in estimates of perceptual agreement. *Journal of Applied Psychology, 67,* 219–229.

James, L.R., Demaree, R.G., & Wolf, G. (1984). Estimating within-group interrater reliability with and without response bias. *Journal of Applied Psychology, 69,* 85–98.

Johnson, J. (1996). Linking employee perceptions of service climate to customer satisfaction. *Personnel Psychology, 49,* 831–851.

Jöreskog, K.G., & Sörbom, D. (1993). *LISREL 8: Structural equation modeling with the SIMPLIS command language.* Hillsdale, NJ: Lawrence Erlbaum Associates.

Lundby, K.M., Dobbins, G.H., & Kidder, P. (1995). *Climate for service and productivity in high and low volume jobs: Further evidence for a redefinition of service.* Paper presented at the Tenth Annual Conference of the Society for Industrial and Organizational Psychology, Orlando, FL.

Lundby, K.M., Fenlason, K., & Magnan, S. (In press). Linking employee and customer data to business performance—difficult but not impossible: some lessons from the field. *Consulting Psychology Journal: Practice and Research.*

Mulaik, S., James, L., Van Alstine, J., Bennett, N., Lind, S., & Stilwell, C. (1989). Evaluation of goodness-of-fit indices for structural equation models. *Psychological Bulletin, 105,* 430–455.

Rucci, A.J., Kirn, S.P., & Quinn, R.T. (1998). The employee-customer-profit chain at Sears. *Harvard Business Review, 76*(1), 82–97.

Schneider, B. (1990). The climate for service: Application of the construct. In Schneider, B. (Ed.), *Organizational climate and culture* (pp. 383–412). San Francisco: Jossey-Bass.

Schneider, B., & Bowen, D. (1985). Employee and customer perceptions of service in banks: Replication and extension. *Journal of Applied Psychology, 70,* 423–433.

Schneider, B., Holcombe, K.M., & White, S.S. (1997). Lessons learned about service quality: What it is, how to manage it, and how to become a service quality organization. *Consulting Psychology Journal: Practice and Research, 49,* 35–40.

Schneider, B., Parkington, J.J., & Buxton, V.M. (1980). Employee and customer perceptions of service in banks. *Administrative Science Quarterly, 25*, 252–267.

Schneider, B., White, S.S., & Paul, M.C. (1998). Linking service climate and customer perceptions of service quality: Test of a causal model. *Journal of Applied Psychology, 83*, 150–163.

Steiger, J.H. (1990). Structural model evaluation and modification: An interval estimation approach. *Multivariate Behavioral Research, 25*, 173–180.

Tornow, W., & Wiley, J.W. (1991). Service quality and management practices: A look at employee attitudes, customer satisfaction, and bottom-line consequences. *Human Resource Planning, 14*, 105–116.

Wiley, J.W. (1996). Linking survey data to the bottom line. In A.I. Kraut (Ed.), *Organizational surveys: Tools for assessment and change* (pp. 330–359). San Francisco: Jossey-Bass.

PART III

REFLECTIONS ON MANAGEMENT CONSULTING

CHAPTER 8

CHANGE IN HUMAN SYSTEMS

From Planned Change to Guided Changing[1]

Kenneth W. Kerber

INTRODUCTION

It is commonplace for leaders of organizations to speak passionately about the necessity of change. Indeed, the growing mantra today is that organizations must change or die. Due to the inherent difficulties in the change process, however, an oft-repeated reality is that many organizations change *and* die nonetheless (Abrahamson, 2000). The pace of business in the twenty-first century thus requires a more effective framework for understanding and guiding organizational change—one that is based on an image of organizations as living systems rather than machines (Morgan, 1997; Webber, 1999).

Change management has become a popular approach for mitigating the disruptive, and sometimes deadly, impact of organizational change. Many large consulting firms have developed extensive change management practices within their organizations (Worren, Ruddle, & Moore, 1999). A recent search on the Internet at *TrainSeek.com* revealed 36 online courses, 53 instructor-led seminars, 228 books, and 296 videos about change management. And change management courses and curricula are being added to more and more MBA programs in the hopes of enhancing the ability of future leaders to implement change.

One major reason for the popularity of change management is the all too frequent experience that poorly handled organizational change results in significant productivity losses and the failure of major business initiatives. With respect to mergers and acquisitions, for example, a 1996 study of 125 companies by Coopers & Lybrand found that 66% of the mergers were financially unsuccessful due to factors such as poor planning and communication, lack of follow-through, and the slow pace of integration (Smye, 1999). Similarly, a 1994 survey of CIOs by Deloitte & Touche (1994) identified significant obstacles to the success of business process reengineering initiatives including resistance to change, limitations of existing systems, lack of executive consensus, and the absence of a senior management champion. In the case of business partnerships, a 1993 study of 49 strategic alliances by McKinsey & Company indicated that 66% ran into serious trouble within the first two years (Bleeke & Ernst, 1993). A Conference Board survey of CEOs (Troy, 1994) identified several factors as most likely to contribute to the failure of strategic alliances, including drastic changes in the environment, different company cultures, poor leadership, overestimation of the market, and a poor integration process. Overall, Beer and Nohria (2000) suggest that about 70% of all organizational change initiatives fail.

These and other experiences with organizational change have helped to identify many of the key factors that determine the effectiveness of planned change (Beckhard & Pritchard, 1992; Kotter, 1996; LaMarsh, 1995). Yet, although planned change is an important capability in today's organizations, it usually results in significant reductions in productivity and failures to achieve stated business objectives. While several recent publications (e.g., Abrahamson, 2000; Beer & Nohria, 2000; Gladwell, 2000; Weick, 2000) describe new approaches that are intended to increase the chances of successful change, the most effective approach to addressing the challenges associated with planned change may be to enhance the ability of organizations to guide *continuous* change. Enhancing the ability to guide continuous change requires an expanded understanding of change in human systems.

APPROACHES TO ORGANIZATIONAL CHANGE

Based on my experience in several computer and computer networking companies over the past 15 years, there appear to be three interrelated approaches to organizational change: (1) imposed change, (2) planned change, and (3) guided changing.

Method 1: Imposed Change

As its name implies, imposed change is driven from the top of the organization, with relatively little consideration for how the change is implemented from a human perspective. Leaders announce the change, and then managers and employees throughout the organization cope with the now well known and expected human reactions—denial, anger and hostility, bargaining, sadness, and loss among those directly affected by the change; relief and guilt, grief and anger, uncertainty, and distrust among those not directly affected.

The prototypical example of imposed change was the frequent downsizing in many large organizations during the 1980s. Many participants and implementers of these organizational changes undoubtedly acknowledged that early downsizing efforts left much to be desired from the perspective of human change. Managers often were ill prepared to deal with the strong emotional reactions of people who were told that their jobs were eliminated. Previously trusted employees were escorted to their offices to pack their personal belongings and then were escorted off the premises, resulting in strong negative reactions from participants and observers alike. Emotional reactions from employees who kept their jobs were often unanticipated and were addressed with little more than brief announcements about the need to cut expenses or streamline operations. It was not unusual for the productivity loss among surviving workers to be significant and prolonged and, once again, managers often were unprepared to address the needs of disoriented, disengaged, and disenchanted employees (Woodward & Buchholz, 1987).

Repeated experience with downsizing taught many organizations and managers that better preparation and improved implementation of imposed change can reduce the negative reactions of affected employees as well as survivors. When a decision by 3Com Corporation to exit several markets in the late 1990s resulted in the elimination of several hundred jobs, the planning and preparation that went into the notification and renewal process was much more extensive and better informed than in the 1980s. Managers were given information, tools, and training about (1) notifying employees that their positions were being permanently eliminated while attempting to maintain employees' self-esteem, and (2) helping remaining employees to deal with the emotional impact of the downsizing and refocusing them on the most critical work of the company. Training sessions, often including role-playing activities, prepared managers to conduct notification meetings as effectively as possible. Guiding principles included treating all employees with trust, dignity, and respect, acting with a sense of urgency, openly communicating information about the organizational changes, and making every reasonable effort to assist employees to find new job opportunities, both inside and outside the company. Managers were informed about the typical range of emotional responses exhibited by employees during notification meetings, were given suggestions about how to respond, and were even provided with scripted statements to prepare them for different situations. In a similar way, managers were informed about the most common reactions of employees who keep their jobs, about how to identify typical reactions, and about strategies for encouraging employees to move forward through their own individual change process. Managers also were provided with guidance about moving ahead with their work groups, such as being visible, providing consistent information, telling the truth, meeting with their work group, and being specific about work assignments.

In summary, even the best examples of Method 1 approaches to change consist largely of coping, after the fact, with emotional reactions to changes over which employees have no control and little ability to influence. Some change management programs and interventions continue to focus simply on coping with human reactions to imposed change. However, the painful experiences associated with this method also resulted in more proactive approaches to the creation and management of change.

Method 2: Planned Change

Much like imposed change, the impetus for planned change often has its source at the top of the organization. However, planned change makes extensive use of specific actions, identified through research and experience, that mitigate the typical productivity losses associated with imposed change and that increase the chances of achieving the intended business objectives.

Planned change implicitly assumes that organizations are characterized by inertia and that change is infrequent and intentional, an occasional divergence from equilibrium, driven by external factors. In essence, the assumption is that the need for change represents a failure of the organization to adapt to a changing environment (Weick & Quinn, 1999). Underlying most planned change efforts is the Lewinian three-stage process of unfreezing, changing, and refreezing (Weick, 2000). Planned change thus involves unfreezing or releasing the organization from its current patterns, transitioning the resulting, more malleable, organization over time from its current patterns to more adaptive ones, and then refreezing the organization into a new set of patterns by weaving them into the fabric of the organization.

Considered to be one of the founders of organizational development, Richard Beckhard developed a simple, but powerful model to assess the feasibility of achieving planned change (Beckhard & Pritchard, 1992). According to Beckhard, change depends on the extent to which:

$$(A + B + D) > X$$

where

A = the level of dissatisfaction with the status quo
B = the desirability of the proposed change or vision for the future
D = the practicality of achieving the change or vision
X = the perceived cost or "price" of changing.

Factors A, B, and D must outweigh the perceived cost if change is to occur. If X includes costs that are unacceptable under any circumstances (e.g., slipping product schedules, losing key people from the organization, failing to achieve the organization's financial model, etc.), then change will be impossible.

Based on experience using these four factors to define and initiate change, the following is a more detailed description of Beckhard's critical change variables.

Dissatisfaction with the Status Quo

Change requires that there be a gap, perceived or real, between the current situation and where people want to be, leading to dissatisfaction with the status quo. The biggest obstacle to change often is a history of success that engenders satisfaction with the current situation and, occasionally, arrogance about the need to continue learning and changing. Human change requires intellectually *and* emotionally compelling reasons why the status quo is unacceptable.

Desirable Vision for Change

For change to occur, it is important to define the future state that we are trying to achieve in ways that tap into what people value. Why do we want to change? What will it look like when the change is implemented? How will we know that we are on the right track? Is the change in line with the overall goals of the company and my own personal goals? Is the proposed future a desirable and exciting place to be? How will the change benefit the company, my work group, and me?

Clear, Practical Process for Change

What steps will we take to achieve our vision? Can those steps be carried out with minimal risk and disruption? Is the change feasible? How do we get started? The path to the future does not need to be complete nor fully paved, but the initial steps should be clear and unobstructed.

Perceived Cost of Change

What will it cost the people who are being asked to change in money, time, resources, and personal discomfort? For example, if working on the current change will affect the timely completion of other deliverables, is that cost acceptable or too high to be tolerated by the organization? On the other hand, what costs might be incurred if the planned change does *not* happen? For example, if the change is critical to the success and satisfaction of key people in the organization, what is the cost of losing those people from the company because the change is not successfully implemented? Despite the fact that planned change is a significant business investment, organizations often do not look carefully at the cost side of the equation.

Although Beckhard identified four of the most critical factors associated with effective planned change, experience has shown that other factors are important, as well. Based on research and application in a wide variety of organizations, for example, Kotter (1996) and LaMarsh (1995) describe several additional factors that increase the chances of successful planned change.

A Guiding Coalition

A guiding coalition is a group of people who encourage and model change in the preferred direction. The initial guiding coalition typically consists of innovators who desire significant change. If successful, this group later includes early adopters who show others how to "take the leap." The change becomes institutionalized when the majority of people who need to change follow in the footsteps of the innovators and early adopters. At times, however, people embrace the *ideal* of change as long as they do not have to change themselves; it is thus important that people in the guiding coalition take the lead in changing their own beliefs and behaviors.

Communication about the Change Vision and Process

The vision and steps to achieve the vision needs to be effectively communicated to all stakeholders. Key information about the change effort must be communicated to the sponsors and the guiding coalition on a regular basis. Presentations and other materials, such as brochures, posters and Web sites, are critical tools for communicating about the change to all stakeholders. Of course, for planned change to be effective, key stakeholders must also have the opportunity to express their hopes, concerns, and suggestions about the change vision and process. One-way communication is characteristic of imposed change; effective planned change provides opportunities for stakeholders to influence the outcomes and steps for achieving change.

Education and Training

Appropriate and timely education and training provide all stakeholders with needed information and skills to work in the new situation. Well-designed educational experiences can also energize people about the change vision and get them started with changes in their part of the organization.

Short-term Wins

Early successes encourage people to use new processes and create new habits. They are the small changes that create momentum for the overall change.

Rewards and Recognition

Formal and informal rewards and recognition can be used to support change among all stakeholders by rewarding and recognizing movement in the desired direction. Special awards can be used to publicly acknowledge significant change and to further communicate the change vision under positive circumstances. An implicit, but often not very subtle, assumption underlying the need for such rewards and recognition is that people resist change and, therefore, require incentives to make the change more palatable.

Sponsorship

Organizational change requires support from the people who have authority over the resources necessary to make the change happen. Sponsors understand why the change is necessary and important, show public and private support for the change, provide the resources necessary to make the change happen, and review progress regularly. Lip service, even passionate lip service, is insufficient.

Skilled Change Agents

The people who operate as dedicated implementers of change must understand the vision for change and the change process, know what is required of good sponsors and negotiate for that sponsorship, and listen and learn from the people who are being asked to change the way they work.

History and Cultural "Rules"

It is also important to understand and deal with written and/or unwritten cultural rules that either support or block the change, as well as with people's good and bad experiences with past change efforts.

Attention to these critical factors is especially valuable when designing and tracking major organizational change efforts. In the late 1990s, 3Com Corporation initiated a corporate-wide effort to improve the software development capabilities of the organization through software process improvement. The first step was to identify the nature of the required changes. An assessment of sixteen past and current software development projects suggested that the current development environment at the company could be improved. An established and tested framework for software process improvement, developed outside the company, promised a future that included increased project schedule and cost predictability, defects reduced by 90%, and costs as well as completion time cut in half. Initial steps for implementing best practices in software development were identified, and the costs relative to the overall engineering budget were calculated, suggesting that a moderate investment could achieve a high return in terms of quality, time-to-market, cost, and customer satisfaction.

The next step was to organize the project in greater detail. The scope of the initiative was defined to cover all software engineering groups at the company, and key milestones with target dates were established. A small, full-time team of change agents, with appropriate expertise in software process improvement, training delivery, and communication, was created to implement the initiative. Their goal was to make the process improvement journey by the company as simple and easy as possible for the engineering organizations and project teams who would be changing their software development methods.

Simultaneously with these first two major steps, the overall leader of the initiative recruited several key senior management sponsors, as well as other sponsors at various levels throughout the company. In addition, coaches were identified, recruited, and trained within each software engineering group to guide their respective organizations through the process improvement efforts. Meanwhile, the full-time team operated as a service organization providing start-up as well as ongoing consultation, training, and personalized help to the coaches, engineering groups, and key product development projects.

To sustain the change initiative over time, a number of ongoing processes were created. A regularly updated Intranet Website for the project communicated the change vision and process, identified key people and their roles, provided tools and templates for implementing software process improvements, and updated the corporate community about progress. A training schedule was created and publicized so that people throughout the organization could develop key process and software development skills. Metrics were established for tracking and reporting progress to sponsors and to the project team and coaches. And successes were identified and publicized on the Web site as well as in public forums through awards to software development teams who achieved significant process improvement milestones and improved business results.

The full-time project team and the coaches from each engineering organization met quarterly to create specific plans, evaluate software development tools, receive training on key software development processes, coordinate with other initiatives at the company, and review progress. Progress reviews included checking not only on the achievement of process improvement milestones and bottom-line business results but also on the key factors associated with successful planned change. Several months into the project, a simple 24-item questionnaire was completed by the members of the full time project team and by the coaches. Respondents were asked to evaluate each of the twelve factors associated with successful planned change, described earlier, on two rating scales: (1) the importance of each element of successful change to achieving the goals of the software process improvement initiative; and (2) the effectiveness of the efforts to use each element of change to achieve the goals of the initiative. Each factor was rated twice using 11-point scales ranging from 0, unimportant or poor effectiveness, to 10, very important or excellent effectiveness. The questionnaire also included a brief description of each change factor.

Figure 1 shows the average importance and effectiveness ratings of the twelve change-related factors for this initiative, as well as the gap between the two ratings. Given that this is not a psychometrically validated questionnaire, specific ratings are less important than the conversation and action planning that was generated as a result of completing the questionnaire and reviewing the results. In this instance, the team and coaches concluded that: (1) while the engineering organizations, overall, were dissatisfied with the status quo, they were not clear about the vision and initial steps for changing their software development processes, nor were they

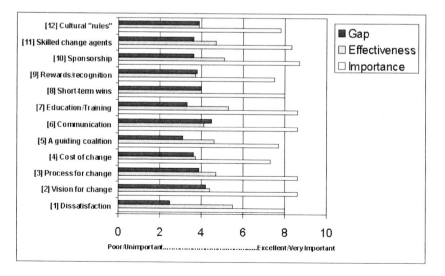

Figure 1.   Software process improvement change factors.

clear about the resources required for this effort; (2) the team and the coaches needed to increase their communication about the initiative so that everyone in software engineering understood what the future would look like when the targeted software process improvements were in place, how they could get started with making those improvements in their own organization, and what resources would be required; and (3) while sponsorship was strong at the top levels of the company and interest in making process improvements also was strong among software development engineers, the middle management of the company was much more wary of the value of the initiative. Actions were taken to address each of these issues. Subsequent administrations of the same questionnaire obviously would yield different results, different conversations, and different actions depending on the most crucial change issues at different phases of the project. Such ongoing evaluation of the key factors associated with planned change is a characteristic of effective Method 2 approaches.

In summary, although Method 2 approaches to change typically deal with projects that are started and sponsored at the top of the organization, careful consideration is given to the factors that have been shown to affect successful change. Rather than simply announcing a major change and coping with the emotional reactions of people who are affected, Method 2 approaches encourage people to participate in the form and impact of the changes by defining how to achieve them and by helping to create the resulting shifts that occur in the organization. While the emotional reactions that characterize Method 1 are typically those associated with loss, Method 2 reactions often are characterized by resistance due to insufficient knowledge about the change and/or not being willing or able to change (Galpin, 1996). Communication, training, and performance management are key factors in helping people move forward through each of these types of resistance (Galpin & Herndon, 2000). In the end, Method 2 approaches to change often reduce the decline and shorten the period over which productivity losses occur, but the well-known negative impact of planned change on productivity is not eliminated, even among the most well managed change initiatives.

Method 3: Guided Changing

As noted earlier, planned change implicitly assumes that organizations experience significant inertia and that senior management must intentionally create internal change to ensure that their companies keep pace with changes in the external environment. Yet, for those who work inside organizations and who carefully observe what happens, it is quite common for changes to arise from all levels of the organization, for people to make small and large changes in their work based on successes and failures, and for changes initiated by one person or one department to spread to other parts of the company (Weick, 2000). The ideal of continuous change appears to be a natural part of human organizations.

Continuous change assumes that organizations are self-organizing and that change is a pattern of endless modifications in the way work is done, a constant evolution of work processes, driven by the instability of the internal and external environment coupled with alert reactions to current circumstances (Weick & Quinn, 1999). In contrast with the unfreeze transition, the refreeze process that implicitly or explicitly underlies virtually all of the popular models of change management, Weick and Quinn (1999) suggest that continuous change follows a different three-stage process: freeze, rebalance, unfreeze. More specifically, continuous change involves freezing or pausing the action in an organization, at least figuratively, so that sequences and patterns can be identified. Based on the resulting clearer understanding of what is happening, patterns can be rebalanced, reinterpreted, relabeled, or resequenced to eliminate obstacles and blockages to the changes that have emerged. At this point, the pause button is released, unfreezing the action and, once again, resuming the learning and improvisation that characterize so much of human behavior in organizations. In strong contrast to both imposed and planned change which are initiated by intention, continuous change largely involves redirecting what is already happening. Also, whereas imposed and planned change typically have a clearly defined end state or vision for the future, continuous change often proceeds without a specific end state in mind.

What are the critical elements that influence the effectiveness of continuous change? Over the past several years, leadership development efforts at 3Com Corporation have focused on the generative spiral[2] (see Figure 2) as a framework for understanding and guiding continuous change in a complex business environment. The term "generative" is meant to imply a number of important characteristics of the continuous change process. A generative process is:

- Energizing: the process creates excitement among the people who use it.
- Self-improving: the process gets better naturally, as it is used.
- Self-sustaining: the process continues to be used because of its high and expanding value to the organization.
- Innovation spawning: the process encourages creativity and the formulation of new ideas and approaches.
- Simple: the process achieves the elegant simplicity that underlies the surface complexity of the work environment.

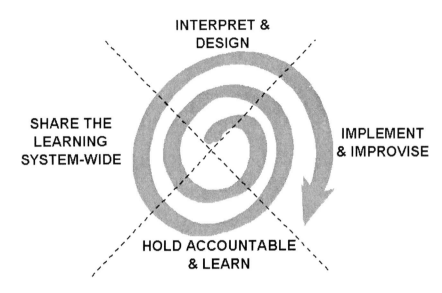

Figure 2.   The generative spiral.

According to this framework, four sub-processes are essential to creating a generative change process.

Interpret and Design

This sub-process involves two major components: (1) observation of the current environment along with identification of emerging changes; and (2) exploration of how to intervene in the organization, whether by means of a slight redirection of the action or a more substantial attempt to shift what is already underway. Interpretation and design involves freezing the action, making sense of what's already happening, and redirecting emergent changes to achieve a more powerful effect. Interpretation and design questions include the following: Have we identified and do we understand the changes that are already happening in the organization? What forces in the environment and among the members of the organization are encouraging changes to emerge? What is the level of synergy among interdependent changes and initiatives? How might we redirect those changes and initiatives to greater business advantage? What are the intended outcomes and the impact of the intervention on different stakeholders?

Implement and Improvise

Implementation and improvisation involve unfreezing the action and unleashing an intervention, whether small or large, and making adjustments along the way based on emerging circumstances. The assumption is that we cannot control change but only guide the process of changing, not just in the external business environment but inside the organization, as well. Improvisation occurs to the extent that the creation and the execution of an action converge in time (Moorman & Miner, 1998); it is a process for dealing with largely unpredictable, fast moving, and messy businesses in which control and long-term predictions are impossible (Brown & Eisenhardt, 1997; Crossan, Lane, White, & Klus, 1996; Lowe, 2000). Implementation and improvisation questions include: What is the quality of our observation and listening to people in all parts of the organization affected by our intervention? What is the quality of feedback that we receive through quantitative metrics and more subjective impressions? How willing are people to adjust their actions in the moment? What are the consequences of taking risks and failing in the organization? How long does it take for decision-makers, at all levels of the organization, to get clear feedback on the full consequences of their choices?

Hold Accountable and Learn

Implementation of an intervention and improvisation in response to new circumstances will result in learning about our actions, the organization, and the changes that are underway. The third sub-process in the generative spiral involves people holding themselves accountable to meet commitments, even as those commitments shift in response to new circumstances. Accountability typically involves meetings where people answer for achieving their objectives. However, when the view of organizations includes emergent change as a major component, the focus of accountability meetings is not blame for unachieved objectives, but rather learning about experiments with intervention and improvisation. Some questions at this point in the generative spiral include: Is the truthfulness and integrity of communication strengthened by accountability meetings? Are failures to meet commitments seen as important sources of learning and breakthrough ideas? Do accountability meetings encourage appropriate risk-taking and entrepreneurial activity? What is the quality of decision-making during this phase? How are the relationships among people in the organization affected by accountability meetings?

Share the Learning System Wide

Learning in organizations routinely happens at the individual level, and quite often teams review their experiences after a major project to generate learning at the team level. Unfortunately, team learning often remains within the team that generated it and is not shared with the rest of the organization. Sharing the learning system wide involves transforming experience into strengthened or new *organizational* capabilities, not just team or individual capabilities. Wheatley and Kellner-Rogers (1998) point out that to strengthen a complex, living system, it is important to connect it to more of itself; in other words, solutions will be discovered within the system if more and better connections are created among different parts of the system. Systemic learning encourages the entire organization to engage in resolving its challenges. Some questions at this phase include: Are people rewarded for learning, not just for knowing how to do it "right" the first time? How thoroughly are breakdowns and breakthroughs examined for learning? Do failures to achieve expectations result in lasting breakthroughs to new levels of performance, not just incremental improvements? How quickly is learning propagated throughout the organization? Are external sources and practices consulted to stimulate new ideas?

The generative spiral can be applied to address major organizational challenges that require significant changes in how a company does business. As an illustration of the power of this process, several years ago, 3Com Corporation was faced with creating a strategic planning process that would involve product divisions from a number of different acquired companies. 3Com's customers expected integrated networking solutions, not just an array of strong, individual products from separate divisions. Internally, the company needed to make more efficient use of its resources by prioritizing and funding product development projects across all product divisions in order to share expertise across divisional boundaries and avoid duplication of effort. Previous attempts to package products from different divisions as an integrated solution and to coordinate product development activities across internal organizational boundaries sometimes met with success; however, current planning and decision-making processes made this more difficult and more dependent on individual heroics than was desirable.

The first step in creating a more effective strategic planning process was to charter a process design team made up of general managers, engineering leaders, marketing directors, and finance people from across the divisions who would ultimately use the redesigned process. The team also included an external expert who brought knowledge of best practices in strategic planning and an internal organization development consultant who contributed specialized expertise about change in human systems. The majority of the team was, therefore, intimately familiar with existing efforts to make better strategic decisions at the company, but the team also included people who could bring a fresh perspective to the design process.

The design team began its efforts by examining the external and internal environment of the company to determine what was needed from a customer perspective in the computer networking industry as well as what processes were emerging inside the company to respond to those needs. The team discovered that customers needed simple, reliable, easy-to-use packaged solutions for specific types of networking requirements; yet 3Com's heritage as a combination of product start-ups joined through numerous acquisitions made the creation of these packaged solutions much more difficult than necessary and much more expensive than the company could afford. Drawing on internal experience and external best practices, the design team began to create and document a process for making strategic decisions.

Two early and important decisions by the design team and its sponsors were critical to making this initiative an example of guided changing rather than imposed or planned change. First, the design team realized that it would be impossible to create the "perfect" strategic planning process; instead, the goal from the start was to design, at best, a 70% effective process that would be refined and improved indefinitely over time through experience. Second, simultaneous with the creation of the design team, two business planning teams that focused on specific customer markets were created. The planning teams were made up of people from product design, supply chain, marketing, sales, customer service, and finance. As a result, the design of the 70% strategic planning process was informed by the simultaneous implementation of new approaches as well as adjustments made to address real customer needs and real decisions about the allocation of company resources. Design and implementation, improvisation and interpretation proceeded *simultaneously* and influenced each other non-linearly so that the resulting strategic planning process was both a function of best practices in strategic planning as well as emerging changes in the real-time business environment at 3Com.

The two business planning teams faced some daunting challenges. Not only were they charged with creating compelling business plans for their target markets, but they were also tasked with helping to create a strategic planning process that increased in value over time, in essence changing the way 3Com made key business decisions and allocated its resources! While the teams were chosen because of their business expertise in their respective target markets, they were also provided with tools, training, and the support of the design team and their sponsors from among the leadership of the company. Although there was a frequent exchange of ideas between the design team and the two business planning teams as they did their respective work, the business planning teams also held specific accountability and learning debriefs as they neared the completion of their efforts. These debriefing sessions were designed to achieve a positive sense of learning from the initial efforts at a new approach to planning and to influence the design of the overall strategic planning process. Among other findings, the design team learned that, to be successful, the business planning teams required a significant time commitment from relatively senior employees, were highly dependent on the functionally focused organizations such as the product design centers, and needed tangible support through allocation and coordination of scarce resources. These and other more detailed observations were shared with the larger organization at

3Com through presentations and conversations, but also were communicated via the company's Intranet.

Almost simultaneously with the creation of the overall design team and the two business planning teams, a Website for the new strategic planning process was created on 3Com's corporate Intranet. The Website was designed to: (1) communicate key elements of the new strategic planning process; (2) communicate the output of the process in the form of key strategic decisions and business plans for specific markets; and (3) share learning from the process company wide. The Intranet Website was accessible to every employee at the company and included the ability not only to read about the process and its results, but also the ability to ask questions and comment about the decisions being made and about the process of getting to those decisions. To accomplish this, the Website included the ability to post and download documents, as well as to contribute to threaded conversations about all aspects of strategic planning. In this way, it was possible to share and generate new learning throughout the company.

Thus, the first "pass" through the generative spiral for this strategic planning project included: (1) interpretation and process design by the overall design team; (2) implementation and improvisation by the two business planning teams; (3) accountability and learning debriefs; and (4) individual, team, and system wide learning through the use of the company Intranet. These activities, for the most part, occurred simultaneously, with each influencing the others in a nonlinear fashion. The second "pass" through the generative spiral included a reconfigured design team made up of both new and old members who focused on implementing the 70% process, the creation of four new business planning teams targeted at specific markets, a cross-divisional strategy meeting designed to review and make decisions about the balance of investments in the company's portfolio of customer solutions, the expansion of the strategic planning Web site to include more opportunities for interactive learning, and plans for a strategic planning learning event with participants from all divisions touched by the new process.

This strategic planning example points out that the generative spiral is:

- Iterative.
- Requires a significant commitment of resources for interpretation and design, accountability, and systemic learning, as well as for implementation.
- Avoids the pitfalls of repeating the same actions while hoping for different results as well as analyzing and designing but never taking action.
- Raises consciousness about the possibility of significant, not just incremental, improvements.
- Integrates planned and continuous change into one framework.

My experience with the generative spiral in the context of several process design projects (specifically, the strategic planning process described above, but also the design of a talent review process as well as an acquisition integration process) is that people quickly understand and appreciate the value of the four activities in the generative spiral, largely because this framework is very action-oriented. The goal is not to create the "perfect" process first time out, but to create an acceptable process that is refined over time through direct experience, improvisation, and learning. That being said, it is also clear that accountability and systemic learning are *not* typically built into most processes—people must be reminded frequently about why these activities are important and not optional. In a fast-paced organization where people already have more to do than there is time, it is very easy to accept the flaws of the process as originally designed and not take the time to make incremental improvements, not to mention significant breakthroughs.

It is also very challenging for people to balance the desire for a stable process with the ability to change. If improvisation is acceptable at every turn, then there *is* no established process; but if the process is followed rigidly regardless of the circumstances, then it will become less and less useful over time, eventually requiring the organization to impose changes on a useless or unused process. The key to resolving this issue appears to be (1) creating, documenting, and communicating an approved process, (2) diligently learning from improvisations and their resulting impact, and (3) changing the documented process based on an accumulation of effective improvisations and breakthrough ideas.

One final observation about the generative spiral is that it applies simultaneously at multiple levels. For example, it can be used to create and refine the overall design of a company's strategic planning process, but it can also be used to create and refine specific meetings that are part of the overall process. Once the concept of guided changing is embedded in people's thinking, the opportunities for application are numerous.

In summary, guided changing represents a significant shift in thinking and application from the previously described approaches to imposed and planned change. Imposed and planned change typically assume that change is painful, drains people's energy, and is resisted due to a wide variety of situational factors (e.g., threat of the loss of position power, altered social relationships, previous exposure to failed change efforts) and personality characteristics (e.g., risk-taking, conservatism, closed-mindedness). In contrast, guided changing assumes that change emerges naturally from within human systems that are driven by the instability of the environment to constantly improve the way work gets done. Method 3 approaches to change suggest that, in a very real sense, organizations must get out the way of people's natural tendency to change and, instead, guide the process in ways that allow improvisation and learning to affect the broader organization more quickly and efficiently.

PLANNED CHANGE AND GUIDED CHANGING

Central to an understanding of human change is control. People initiate significant changes in their own lives all the time and often view those changes quite favorably (e.g., getting married, studying for a degree, changing employers). Driven by the excitement of new possibilities, self-initiated change frequently stimulates bursts of creativity and productivity. It is imposed change, change over which a person has little or no control, that most often results in negative emotional reactions and declines in productivity. In fact, the perception of control is so powerful, research has shown that the belief that a person is in control of a situation has positive effects whether or not the perception is either true or acted upon (Langer, 1983).

It appears that part of the success of Method 2 approaches to change is the result of giving people some control over imposed change by encouraging them to participate in the form and impact of the changes. As Wheatley & Kellner-Rogers (1998) point out, people have a strong need to participate in change and only support what they help to create. Rather than delivering changes to an organization, people need to be involved in their creation, and that means engaging the whole system, over time. Perhaps the primary reason that 70% of change efforts fail is that they typically occur in reaction to issues outside the system rather than emerging from within the system. Change that leads to increases rather than declines in productivity must come from within.

If giving some control over the course of an imposed change mitigates the negative consequences associated with change, why not encourage people to initiate and experiment with change as they see fit? Method 3 approaches to change give people the opportunity to create continuous change in response to altered circumstances, as well as in the attempt to achieve breakthroughs to new levels of performance, before a crisis demands that change must be imposed. In other words, Method 3 approaches include control over decisions about whether or not to initiate change, as well as decisions about the manner in which change is to be implemented. The resulting changes that are initiated not only include the incremental changes associated with continuous improvement methods (Choi, 1995) but also encompass transformational, breakthrough changes as well.

When Planned Change? When Guided Changing?

During times when the pace of change in the business environment appears to be increasing rapidly, the ideal organization is one that is capable of continuous adaptation (Weick & Quinn, 1999). Both planned change and guided changing are necessary to achieve this ideal. For example, the coordination necessary at a large company typically requires that many information technology systems be used corporate-wide. Changes in technology can make systems obsolete nearly overnight, often requiring that a new system be "imposed" on the organization over the objections of people who are quite comfortable with the capabilities of the current system. At the same time, most managers encourage ongoing changes in how information systems are used to better serve internal and external customers, and the first indications that a new system is needed often come from people in the front lines of the organization.

Weick (2000) suggests that planned change is most appropriate when: (1) it is important to capture people's attention and focus it in one direction; (2) a cover is needed for changes that are peripheral to the planned change vision; (3) the change is aligned with the distribution of power in the organization; (4) it is important to convey the impression of a rational program to key stakeholders; (5) an informed choice must be made among different implementation options; and (6) it is important to extend the change throughout the organization easily by making it very explicit and focused. He suggests that continuous change is most appropriate when: (1) sensitivity to local differences is important; (2) real-time experimentation and learning is needed; (3) it is important to satisfy needs for autonomy, control, and expression; (4) fast implementation is necessary; (5) concern is high about the changes unraveling; and (6) when the goal is to exploit existing tacit knowledge.

My own experience suggests that planned change is most appropriate for:

- Small-scale changes that are acceptable to the people involved.
- One-time events or projects (e.g., a switch to a new system that is likely to be in place for some time with only minor modifications).
- Changes where the future state is predictable and known (e.g., based on well documented and widely known experience or research).

Guided changing, in contrast, is most appropriate for:

- Large scale changes where those involved differ strongly in their perception of the value and effectiveness of the change.
- Ongoing processes that naturally iterate (e.g., yearly strategic planning, performance management, or succession planning).
- Changes where the future state is unknown and unpredictable (e.g., e-commerce or e-learning).

Human Reactions to Planned Change and Guided Changing

Many of our ideas about change have been influenced by experience with mechanical and electronic systems that respond without consciousness to our attempts at control. Change that involves living, conscious human beings must address people's emotional reactions to change. According to Brent Filson (1996), "*Emotion* and *motivation* come from the same Latin roots meaning 'to move.' Motivate people to move, to take action, by engaging their emotions." Emotion is *not* something to be eliminated from the process of change. Change in human systems is about movement; therefore, change *requires* emotion.

When it comes to planned change, it appears that human emotions often get in the way of successful movement. Feelings of comfort and satisfaction with the status quo hamper planned change because people see no reasons to think or behave differently. Feelings of sadness, grief, and anger about changes that have been imposed can lead to significant declines in productivity and delays in effective implementation. Therefore, with respect to human emotions, the primary challenge associated with planned change is to make the vision for change so attractive and exciting that people are drawn toward the new future despite the emotional costs of leaving the past behind. In addition, rewards and recognition for movement in the desired direction can generate the positive emotions required for additional change. So, in the case of planned change, we must acknowledge the paradox that people both love it and hate it, and we must learn to work with both reactions.

When it comes to guided changing, the situation is quite different. The potential exists to replace the passive-aggressive resistance and open hostility that so often accompany planned change with the creativity, hope, and inspiration associated with participating in the creation of new possibilities through continuous change. At first, fear of mistakes may limit attempts at improvisation and experimentation with continuous change, and this fear must be eliminated and replaced with the positive emotions typically associated with learning and improvement. However, once the habit of changing is created, the real challenge may be emotional burnout. Research (Bargh & Chartrand, 1999) has shown that most of people's everyday life is determined not by deliberate choices but by mental processes that operate outside of conscious awareness. The conscious self plays a causal role in guiding behavior only 5% or so of the time (Baumeister & Sommer, 1997). This appears to be an energy saving mechanism, given that consciously and willfully regulating one's behavior, evaluations, and decisions requires considerable effort. In fact, it appears that human mental systems operate to drive frequent and consistent conscious choices out of conscious awareness both to save energy as well as to create behavioral reactions within fractions of a second—a highly adaptive mechanism especially in dangerous environments. If this analysis is correct, continuous change represents a significant energy drain and may lead to all the symptoms of emotional burnout. The ability of organizations to adapt continuously may come face-to-face with the limits of the human capacity for conscious choice.

Support for Guided Changing in Organizations

If we could increase the support for guided changing inside an organization, it might reduce the need for major imposed and planned changes. It would be less likely that the organization would fail to adapt to a changing environment and, as a result, fewer sudden externally driven changes would be required. In addition, creating new breakthrough opportunities by choice from within the organization would bring excitement to major changes, much like the energy in a start-up company. In general, the people who must change would initiate required changes from within the organization. But how can this be accomplished? Increasing continuous change will require shifts in our beliefs about change as well as shifts in our behavior.

At a conceptual level, we must think about organizations as living systems, rather than as machines, with life's change process reflecting the way that change actually occurs in organizations (Wheatley & Kellner-Rogers, 1998). If we view organizations as living systems, then we realize that people (1) need to be involved in the creation of organizational changes, (2) always react to changes, never simply obey directives, and (3) need to be creatively involved in how their work gets done by altering, reinterpreting, and adding to other people's ideas. If we ignore or attempt to stop these processes, people become discouraged and little organizational change occurs, unless it is imposed. We must also alter our view that organizations are characterized by inertia and that organizational change is infrequent and driven only by external forces (Weick, 2000). These assumptions are implicit to most, if not all, of the popular approaches to change management, and are based on organizational structures and systems that suppress people's natural tendency to improvise and learn. These assumptions blind us to the frequent changes that emerge and spread through organizations based on people's reactions to changing circumstances as well as their desire to achieve dramatically higher levels of performance. Continuous change is present in our organizations *right now*, but our beliefs and frameworks for thinking about change have blinded us to this reality, and our systems and processes create obstacles for what is already happening.

At a more pragmatic level, we must encourage rational experimentation as well as intuitive improvisation, tightly coupled with accountability and systemic learning, if we are to encourage continuous change. We must be flexible to plan for that which is predictable, but also to experiment with and react in the moment to that which is unpredictable (Crossan et al., 1996; Stacey, 1992). In addition, we must change the way we solve problems to include the principles of breakthrough thinking (Nadler & Hibino, 1990). This process includes recognizing that (1) no solution is final and that solving one problem inevitably leads to others, (2) those who will use a solution should be intimately and continuously involved in its development, and (3) the only way to preserve the usefulness of a solution is to build in and monitor a program of continuous change.

Ultimately, the greatest challenge to building support for guided changing may be the unwillingness of leaders to let go of tight management control and embrace a messy, dynamic process that involves the entire organization. Rather than assuming that the intelligence of the enterprise resides in a relatively small number of people at the top, leaders must become more willing to trust the intelligence of the system.

CONCLUSION

The pace of business in the twenty-first century requires an expanded framework for understanding and facilitating organizational change—one that is based on a view of organizations as living systems. Effectively planned change is capable of achieving major improvements in business results when compared with imposed change. However, as valuable as planned change may be, it is not sufficient in today's world. The nature of business has shifted. Change is pervasive, the only constant. Guided changing is intended to tap into the inherent capacity of people to learn and change and, simultaneously, to create organizations that take advantage of this capacity, rather than blocking its contribution to business success. We must shift our thinking about organizational change and find ways to effectively guide the changes that emerge within today's organizations.

Our approaches to change in human systems must therefore be expanded to include both planned change and guided changing. As Table 1 suggests, this will require a number of shifts in our beliefs and actions.

Change is a crucial component of organizational survival and success. People at all levels of the organization must remain vigilant for changes required by shifts in technology, markets, customer needs, and the competition, and must proactively guide changing by experimenting with innovations that emerge from within the system. Guided changing is especially appropriate in the case of iterative processes where learning as a result of adjustments to changing circumstances can enhance the capabilities of the entire organization. When everyone adapts continuously, bringing involve-

Table 1.   From Planned Change to Guided Changing

From:	*To Include:*
• People resist change	• People initiate changing
• React to external changes	• Experiment proactively
• Organizational change is a discrete event	• Changing is a continuous organizational process
• Change is disruptive to established work processes	• Changing is a natural part of all work processes
• Responsibility for change resides largely with management	• Changing is everyone's responsibility
• Implement change imposed from above	• Initiate changing from within
• Change is painful and drains people's energy	• Changing leads to bursts of creativity and productivity
• Unfreeze, change, refreeze	• Freeze, adjust, unfreeze
• Implement the plan	• Improvise along the way
• Cope with change	• Thrive on changing
• Linear	• Systemic
• Mechanistic	• Ecological
• **PLANNED CHANGE**	• **GUIDED CHANGING**

ment and excitement to the change process, the typical productivity losses associated with change may be eliminated and replaced with the energy of an organization fully alive. At the same time, no amount of vigilance will unerringly prevent sudden and surprising changes in the environment that require planned change. When integrated with strong project management and an understanding of the factors that influence successful change in human systems, planned change is a critical supplement to guided changing. The key is to find an appropriate balance of both approaches, using, as fully as possible, the innovative and creative talents of all organizational members.

NOTES

1.   The author thanks Paul Draper, Suzanne Graves, Jeanenne LaMarsh, Rob Adams McKean, Stephen Meyer, Royce Singleton, Jr., and Bill Veltrop for their comments about earlier versions of this article.

2.   Bill Veltrop introduced the idea of the generative spiral, which then evolved over time through our joint work on specific change initiatives. The author is responsible for the version of the generative spiral described here.

REFERENCES

Abrahamson, E. (2000, July-August). Change without pain. *Harvard Business Review,* pp. 75–79.

Bargh, J.A., & Chartrand, T.L. (1999). The unbearable automaticity of being. *American Psychologist, 54*(7), 462–479.

Baumeister, R.F., & Sommer, K.L. (1997). Consciousness, free choice, and automaticity. In R.S. Wyer, Jr. (Ed.), *Advances in social cognition* (pp. 75–81). Mahwah, NJ: Erlbaum.

Beckhard, R., & Pritchard, W. (1992). *Changing the essence: The art of creating and leading fundamental change in organizations.* San Francisco: Jossey-Bass.

Beer, M., & Nohria, N. (2000). Cracking the code of change. *Harvard Business Review, 78*(3), 133–141.

Bleeke, J., & Ernst, D. (Eds.). (1993). *Collaborating to compete: Using strategic alliances and acquisitions in the global marketplace.* New York: John Wiley & Sons.

Brown, S.L., & Eisenhardt, K.M. (1997). The art of continuous change: Linking complexity theory and time-paced evolution in relentlessly shifting organizations. *Administrative Science Quarterly, 42,* 1–34.

Choi, T. (1995). Conceptualizing continuous improvement: Implications for organizational change. *Omega, International Journal of Management Science, 23,* 607–624.

Crossan, M.M., Lane, H.W., White, R.E., & Klus, L. (1996, Spring). The improvising organization: Where planning meets opportunity. *Organizational Dynamics,* pp. 20–34.

Deloitte & Touche. (1994). *Leading trends in information services: Information Technology Consulting Services sixth annual survey of North American CIOs.* New York: Deloitte & Touche.

Filson, B. (1996). *Authority is a poor excuse for leadership: 325 maxims for action leadership.* Williamstown, MA: Williamstown Publishing Company.

Galpin, T.J. (1996). *The human side of change: A practical guide to organization redesign.* San Francisco: Jossey-Bass.

Galpin, T.J., & Herndon, M. (2000). *The complete guide to mergers and acquisitions: Process tools to support M&A integration at every level.* San Francisco: Jossey-Bass.

Gladwell, M. (2000). *The tipping point: How little things can make a big difference.* Boston: Little, Brown and Company.

Kotter, J.P. (1996). *Leading change.* Boston: Harvard Business School Press.

LaMarsh, J. (1995). *Changing the way we change: Gaining control of major operational change.* Reading, MA: Addison-Wesley.

Langer, E.J. (1983). *The psychology of control.* Beverly Hills, CA: Sage.

Lowe, R. (2000). *Improvisation, Inc.: Harnessing spontaneity to engage people and groups.* San Francisco: Jossey-Bass/Pfeiffer.

Moorman, C., & Miner, A.S. (1998). Organizational improvisation and organizational memory. *Academy of Management Review, 23*(4), 698–720.

Morgan, G. (1997). *Images of organization.* Thousand Oaks, CA: Sage.

Nadler, G., & Hibino, S. (1990). *Breakthrough thinking: Why we must change the way we solve problems, and the seven principles to achieve this.* Rocklin, CA: Prima Publishing & Communications.

Smye, M. (1999). *Managing the human risks of mergers.* Philadelphia: Right Management Consultants.

Stacey, R. D. (1992). *Managing the unknowable: Strategic boundaries between order and chaos in organizations.* San Francisco: Jossey-Bass.

Troy, K. (1994). *Change management: Strategic alliances.* New York: The Conference Board.

Webber, A.M. (1999, May). Learning for a change. *Fast Company,* pp. 178–188.

Weick, K.E. (2000). Emergent change as a universal in organizations. In M. Beer & N. Nohria (Eds.), *Breaking the code of change* (pp. 223–241). Boston: Harvard Business School Press.

Weick, K.E., & Quinn, R.E. (1999). Organizational change and development. In J.T. Spence, J.M. Darley, & D.J. Foss (Eds.), *Annual review of psychology* (pp. 361–386). Palo Alto, CA: Annual Reviews.

Wheatley, M.J., & Kellner-Rogers, M. (1998). *Bringing life to organizational change.* Provo, UT: The Berkana Institute.

Woodward, H., & Buchholz, S. (1987). *After-shock: Helping people through corporate change.* New York: John Wiley & Sons.

Worren, N.A.M., Ruddle, K., & Moore, K. (1999). From organizational development to change management: The emergence of a new profession. *The Journal of Applied Behavioral Science, 35*(3), 273–286.

CHAPTER 9

TRANSFORMING CONSULTING KNOWLEDGE INTO BUSINESS FADS

Bertrand Venard

INTRODUCTION

Management fashions have become a common aspect of contemporary business life. Use of the term "fashion" implies looking at various managerial innovations as mystification, a process that, in essence, mixes different prescriptions with elements of futility and irrationality. The widespread dissemination of business process reengineering (BPR)—literally throughout the industrial world—is a good example. Even if the idea of fashion leads us to think that any given management concept will be temporary—as evidenced by the waning popularity of BPR—there are always different fashions on the company "stage" at any point in time.

Consultants, as one group of such fashion setters (Abrahamson, 1991, 1996), are at least partially responsible for this situation. From the initial invention of ideas and concepts through their expansion and ultimate decline, consultants are involved in the spread and the practice of management fashions. While many of these fashions do enhance management thought, an underlying danger is when these concepts are simplified and utilized without full and proper diagnosis, as they are typically offered to enterprises as "universal," "scientific," and "efficient" means of improving organizational performance. In fact, more than partially to blame for this situation, cynics might even suggest that consultants are responsible for complete business mystification, the final objective of which is sell more and more consulting assignments.

EXAMINING BUSINESS FADS

The basic purpose of this chapter is to examine how a process of knowledge accumulation is transformed into business fads. In exploring this research question, the study combines documentary and action research. The available literature on management consulting, of which a considerable body now exists, was content analyzed. The author also worked for two large management consulting firms during 1992 and 1993, in essence serving as a participant observer in the role of Senior Management Consultant. Written information from both consulting firms was collected and analyzed, including strategic plans, corporate communication documentation, internal training documents, internal consulting files, and various reports written by consultants in the firms. Throughout this period, field observations (based on case study protocols, Berry, 1995; Eisenhardt, 1989) were structured in a systematic manner, notes and minutes of meetings were kept, and face-to-face and telephone conversations were recorded (see Van Maanen's Field Notes, 1998).

The initial approach was inductive, focusing on identifying research themes and generating hypotheses. Data sources, categorization of respondents, collection and analysis of the data, and the formulation, improvement and testing of hypotheses were also re-evaluated throughout the study period. The process of moving from induction to theory building was circular rather than linear. The author relied on both a theoretical and practical approach to analysis, reflecting on a number of key concepts— including business fads and management fashion life cycles or knowledge—while examining the field data and content analyzing the literature. Even though a guiding aim was to establish a concomitant relationship between data collection and analysis (Glaser & Strauss, 1967), the fact that the author was engaged in participative research did create difficulties in trying to remain objective while engaging in immediate analysis. This dynamic raises the specter of "death by data asphyxiation" (Pettigrew, 1973) juxtaposed with what might be thought of as "death by participative action." In essence, the proximity of the research subject made remaining objective difficult on occasions. Yet, while triangulation through multiple data sources provides some substantive control (Miles & Huberman, 1984), it can also create an overabundance of data.

The most natural approach to this quandary—triangulation as control versus triangulation as data overload—is to emphasize significant points, in particular critical points of context (Dyer & Wilkins, 1991) while summarizing the data (Van Maanen, 1988). Another simple approach to enhancing objectivity is to let sufficient time pass between the field phase (1992/1993) and the explanation of the results, allowing greater perspective on the basic objective of the research. A third approach also used in this study was to make intermediary presentations of this research as a way of generating scientific debate and discussion.

The Field Context

During the time spent in the consulting business in a middle-management position, the author participated in a wide range of company activities, ranging from meetings with prospective clients and drawing up proposals, to engaging in training seminars and collecting data from clients, to writing up intermediary and final reports and giving oral presentations to clients, as well as updating consulting methodology and participating in internal company meetings. The two consulting firms examined during the 1992–93 field work are among the world's top twenty largest audit and consultancy groups, and are located in more than one hundred countries.

During the study period, Company A, which was originally created in the United States, employed a team of 200 management consultants (out of a total of 1,600 audit staff) in Paris and three other large French cities. One part of the business activities in the Paris office targeted not only France but also Africa and the ex-communist countries in Europe. Consulting missions concerned strategy, organization, and company finance and information systems, with particular focus on the banking, insurance, energy and public administration sectors. The company was also going through a crisis during this period, which had led to a drop in the volume of business and a reduction in force with certain consultants being made "redundant."

Company B, which was originally created in Europe, had already been through several periods of restructuring which included radical changes to the management team (certain partners were made redundant) and the consultant team (approximately 150 in total). During the study period, the company was in a growth phase following the arrival of partners from its American and European offices to "consolidate the practice." Business was essentially concentrated on missions within France, but for certain large international clients there was cooperation with other offices around the world. Consulting assignments concerned organization, marketing, finance, and information systems across many different economic sectors.

In order to improve the efficiency of its sales network, the author was responsible for setting up a consulting methodology for Company B. This methodology consisted of: the consulting context, problems to be solved, resolution strategy, examples of successful missions, listings of consultants and their curriculum vitae, and testimonials from satisfied clients. Overall, this approach attempted to capitalize on the knowledge gained through the successful completion of different assignments. On a more operational level, it also served as a sales tool (documents and computerized presentations) and a guide to drawing up proposals and carrying out missions. Thus, participant observation in both consulting firms was informed by a high level of active involvement in the consulting process, an important dimension of this study since much of the work that has been done in this area is completely theoretical (cf. Abrahamson, 1991; Huczynski, 1993; Kieser, 1997).

The Literature on Consulting

An analysis of the consulting literature can easily leave the reader confused, largely because assessments typically range from anecdotal pieces to in-depth analysis. Viney (1992), in his short satirical work, for example, compares the job of a consultant to that of confidence tricksters—self-declared experts in a domain that they themselves have invented. As Viney notes, these individuals insist on pointing out to their clients that they can do better than anyone else, even without the benefit of several years of hard-won experiences. In contrast to such fierce criticism, other observers literally place consultants on a pedestal. Sarvary (1999), for example, presents consultants as "technology brokers" (a term which he borrows from Hargadon & Sutton, 1996). According to Sarvary (1999, p. 98), these individuals have such a command of knowledge management that they are capable of making "highly customized and context-dependent" recommendations, even in the process of retail consulting, an example of which is Ernst and Young's "Ernie" product which is an internet-based consulting service (providing advice via internet to solve current problems).

In contrast to such anecdotal assessments, serious research on consulting does exist. This chapter will limit itself to the body of work that critically examines the role of consultants in creating and disseminating management fashion. One seminal contribution that attempts to explain how this unfolds is by Abrahamson (1991, 1996, p. 257), who focuses on the "relatively transitory collection of beliefs, disseminated by management fashion setters, that a management technique leads rational management progress." While the importance of consultants in managerial life may be open to debate, an underlying question that these observations raise concerns the consultant's *real* role, between being vectors of knowledge (Abrahamson, 1991) and creators of business fads (Abrahamson, 1996; Midler, 1993). Thus, the potential of the manipulative character of consultants' strategies in developing tactics in order to be seen as economic gurus and attain their financial objectives—despite potentially disastrous failures associated with some consultancy assignments (Micklethwhait & Woodridge, 1996)—must be addressed. Critics suggest that an underlying reason why knowledge is manipulated in this manner is to ensure that as many assignments as possible can be sold (by creating a stereotyped consulting tool/product which appears to be unique) at as low a cost as possible (by simplifying the needs of the client). As Keiser (1998, p. 11) notes, "creation and transfer of knowledge is not the ultimate goal of consultancies. Profit is." These dynamics suggest an industrialization of consulting activities, where attempts are made to standardize services (i.e., standardization of consulting tools) and what is being offered to the client (i.e., standardization of client needs by a process of making the problem fit the existing methodology). Such industrialization is made even easier for consultants because clients often find it difficult to evaluate the real quality of the consulting service offered (Clark, 1995; Venard, 1995).

Given the characteristics of this type of consulting relationship, consultants attempt to provide a standardized service while at the same time making the client think that they are receiving a tailor-made solution. The dichotomy between what is done compared to what is said in the consulting business, thus, creates a situation where the consultant's role can be described as manipulative. Clark (1995, p. 118), for example, describes the consultant performance as "exercises in persuasive communication." This manipulation, which is far from being constant and homogenous, follows the life cycle of a management fashion from its creation to its decline. While there is a body of research that underscores the influence of the client in the consulting relationship in general and in the emergence of management fashions in particular (e.g., McGivern, 1983; Sturdy, 1997), the author has not found any research that illustrates the importance of a consultant's perception and understanding of client needs in creating business fads.

Management Fashion Life Cycles

The analysis of the morphology of a management fashion suggests a three-stage process. In the first phase, *invention*, the fundamental logic is the creation of a specific consulting tool. It is the period of movement from intuition, described by Weick (1995, p. 25) as "a preconscious recognition of the pattern and/or possibilities inherent in a personal stream of experience," to interpretation (Crossan, Lane, & White, 1999). The creation of a new, highly intangible service like consulting emerges from an elaboration of a presentation based on unconscious ideas and/or consultants' experiences. The arguments are centered on the new or totally innovative character of the service (Rogers, 1995) as well as the context, the crucial problem, and the solution. Broader economic, political, social and technological contexts may also be used to present a situation where profound change and the resulting crisis require a "necessary revolution." In this phase, the formulation of the context can be imprecise and may reflect such generalizations as the need to deal with the "appearance of new competitors," the "appearance of new products," or the "difficulties in winning new markets or clients."

The problem that needs to be resolved is also described during this first phase. The overriding importance of the problem demands a solution, which is described in a way that reflects the business fad. The business fad is then presented as a solution—based on an "analysis" of the situation.

The structure of the presentation itself (context, problem, solution, and application) should not lead one to believe that the concepts described by the "management fashion setters" are easily understood or clearly defined. In reality, the concepts used by consultants are most often very general and very vague (Kieser, 1997). A young consultant from Company A, for example, informed us that:

> what we sell the client is the rigor and reliability of the Anglo-Saxon culture, which is based on the audit approach. In reality, our company is anarchic with methods that are far from clear. For example, what I have just jotted down on this sheet of paper is supposed to correspond to a specific methodology.

In addition, the terms used in the presentation are typically outrageous. In the case of Company A, clients and prospects received documents which contained such terms as "revolution," "optimization," "best practices of leading firms," and "world class principles." Similarly, presentation of the methodology applied by Company B noted that the approach would enable clients to "devise and set up *new approaches* in order to generate *exceptional performance.*" These terms and phrasing leave little room for debate. The resulting business fad is thus an oversimplification of reality, literally excluding all contingent factors that might limit its use.

In the second phase, the fad moves from invention to *innovation* as the concept finds a market. The notion of incremental innovation, borrowed from work on the industrial economy (Nelson & Winter, 1982), helps to underline the progressive character of the stabilization of the presentation of business fads. The fad and its presentation gradually benefit from different minor innovations. The business fad thus follows a technological trajectory, as defined by Dosi (1984), an uncertain trajectory between invention (the creative phase) and innovation (the sales phase). The fad follows this trajectory while benefitting from the interactions between the creators of the fad and the potential users who may improve it. The trajectory is uncertain, however, because the fad must not only be created at the "right" time but it must capture the "right" audience as well. In some cases, certain methods remain at an intermediary level (Midler, 1993), for example a doctoral thesis that attempts to put forward a new paradigm but which is only read by a handful of people before disappearing into oblivion.

The lack of clarity concerning the content of the fad allows for an appropriation of the concepts, not only by the fashion setters and the followers but also by the actors (Kieser, 1997). Well aware of the evolutionary nature of the presentation of the fad, for example, all the partners of Company B obliged their consultants to use the term "project" in all documents given to clients before validation of and agreement on the final assignment. According to one partner, this was a clear signal that "nothing is certain, we are still in a learning phase ... in case of mistakes, we can point out to the client that it is only a project."

Gradually, the presentation of the fad moves from something vague and ambiguous to a more peremptory formulation, which affirms its potential. The tone of the presentation will be one of clear affirmation of the convincing results of the fad and the feasibility of setting it up (Abrahamson, 1996). In Company B, for example, the consultants were called upon to create a particular method similar to Business Process Reengineering (BPR). This involved the creation of an acronym to designate the company's reputedly exclusive method—the *BXX Method* (copyright of Company B) and the company logo was printed on every page—and a mix of French and English words were used to form a particular jargon.

This *diffusion* phase is where the fad moves from being the domain of those who initiated it in the first phase to being recognized by a much larger public. The people concerned, apart from the creators, are management experts (teachers and consultants), executive managers and the general public. In those cases where the fad becomes a success, it is diffused on a massive scale as it moves from the domain of experts to that of the general public. Different media will have an influence on this diffusion phase. For example, books, newspapers, television, conferences and training programs gradually popularize the fad. What follows is the creation of a market for the fad, a market complete with sellers (consultants) and buyers (company managers, journalists, teachers and researchers). The monetary exchanges that take place have the effect of reinforcing the credibility and the effectiveness of the fad. Schein's (1988) work, which suggests that the consulting process is similar to the relationship between a psychiatrist and patient, helps to explain why the belief often emerges that the higher the value of the transaction, the better the quality of the advice.

The role played by the employees of companies who accept business fads should also be examined. At first, it would appear that clients of business fads adopt a passive attitude in relation to the diffusion of the fads. Indeed, Starbuck (1992) suggests that the act of consulting an external expert implies an inadequacy in the client's own understanding. However, further research work has led to justifiable criticism of this limited vision of the role of the client in the consulting relationship (Clark & Salaman, 1996), and certain authors have even talked of a limited or partial point of view (Sturdy, 1996, 1997). Sturdy (1997, p. 393), for example, points to "the interactive nature of the process and the extent to which 'popular' ideas are actually taken and applied by managers." Clients, in fact, play a highly active part in the acceptance of fads (Fincham, 1999), but do act under certain constraints.

Indeed, the integration of a business fad into companies is facilitated by the complexity of situations, the lack of individual resources available, and the organizational context of the acceptation of the fad.

Organizational members work in complex situations and are constantly called upon to make judgments and choices. However, they typically work with information that is incomplete and not always reliable, and with little time to make decisions. Therefore, employees often base their decisions on a synopsis of reality. For example, the adoption of a business fad like Business Process Reengineering (BPR) corresponds to choosing a synopsis in the face of a reality, reflecting the wish to rapidly and significantly reduce time and costs. The choice of a BPR method leads to time saved, as decisions are made as rapidly as possible (a recognized solution must be selected without really comparing it to other alternatives) and easily justified in terms of choices made in relation to other alternatives (valorization in the social body of a recognized solution).

Organizational decision-makers also often find themselves faced with limitations in terms of personal resources, especially given the important nature of the decisions, individual capacity for analysis, values and personal goals, all of which raise create implication in the adoption of the fad. Finally, the organizational context of the decision to adopt a fad itself structures the final adoption decision. In essence, the consulting firm's client organization removes a part of each employee's autonomy of decision and substitutes a decision process at the level of the organization itself.

In the third phase, the business fad ultimately disappears in terms of a management fashion. The first option in this case is that of generalized adoption, as the fad becomes a norm for organizations (Gill & Whittle, 1990; Midler, 1993). Another option is that of the resounding failure of the method. Companies reject the business fad because the results turn out to be unprofitable. The third option is that of replacement (Midler, 1993). The operators turn their attention to another method that is possibly more suitable or more recent. As an illustration, the author set up a method in Company B, based on an incremental process, which implied that the method in question was progressively improved. Each new version replaced the old. The process of replacement in this particular case was permanent. Thus, the problem, which justified the use of a management fad, either disappears or is solved definitively. The solution to the problem, which has disappeared, is therefore no longer justified.

It is perhaps in this last phase that it is possible to better identify the diversity of the roles of the different operators in relation to the business fad. In addition to the fashion setters and followers, there are also observers, whether they are facilitators or opponents. As suggested earlier, fashion setters produce "collective beliefs" (Abrahamson, 1996, p. 265) and the followers transform these ideas into business fads (Kieser, 1997). In the case discussed above, the fashion setters were the consultants and the clients were the followers. Thus, diffusion, the ensuing mass adoption and the final rejection of the business fad do not only depend on the consultant and client. Other operators must be identified. While observers/facilitators are not active in the creation of the business fad, they do contribute to its diffusion through communicating positive information, which is passed on to them by the fashion setters, to a larger public. In the case of rejection in the third phase, the observers will adopt a negative attitude in their communication. This devalorization will consequently accelerate the process of rejection. This role is often played by journalists—whose job, by nature, is to inform. Their desire to attract readers often pushes them toward valorization or devalorization, simplifying the information that is available to the larger public. To be read, and, perhaps even more important, to be listened to, for journalists, means putting economic information into a simplistic form that is short and sensational.

Apart from journalists, public authorities also serve as observers. Their objective of political, economic, and social efficiency pushes them to adopt a language favoring managerial efficacy. Without necessarily being able to appreciate the quality of the arguments put forth by the fashion setters, the public authorities play a role in relaying information. In France, for example, the Chambers of Commerce, the regional headquarters of the Treasury, and the regional economic departments counties and towns all have a role in disseminating information in the economic world. In certain cases in France, these authorities even grant financial aid to companies in order to realize consultancy missions. Finally, the academic world contributes to spreading information on management fashions. Academics are often tempted to adopt a language that valorizes a certain management fashion, especially if it is perceived to be in the mainstream from the point of view of the world of consultants or management scientists. Management scientists, however, typically find it difficult to have their point of view on business fads heard in the first phase of the life cycle. In fact, in order to produce a scientific analysis, a latent period is required to distance oneself from a management practice. It is therefore in Phases 2 and 3 that researchers, with longitudinal analyses, are able to better judge the management reality.

SUPPOSITIONS BETWEEN LEARNING AND MYSTIFICATION

As has already been emphasized, the author was assigned the task of creating a consultancy methodology, whose underlying objective was to become a management fashion for Company B. The objective of this methodology was to improve the organization of clients' sales networks. Company B had numerous assignments in this area, and the basic intent was to try to capitalize on the accumulated knowledge across these different missions. The partners felt a need to set up a particular methodology, which would simplify prospection (presentation to clients), the realization of consultancy proposals, and the subsequent realization of the missions themselves. The consultancy methodology was intended to serve as a concrete aspect of accumulated knowledge for commercial ends.

In creating this methodology, the author integrated his own personal consulting experiences with a study of the files created by consultants during different assignments in France and abroad, and interviews with the consultants. Construction of this methodology was iterative, going back frequently to the consultants for their reaction and additional input as a way of refining the final methodology. Finally, the approach was tested and continuously improved on while being used in actual consulting assignments.

During the initial analysis, the methodology provided an opportunity to both generate new ideas within Company B and assess those ideas with clients during "test missions." We were, in fact, in a typical organizational learning situation in which various members of an organization are involved in elaborating or implementing new competencies (Huber, 1990).

During subsequent analyses of the methodology, we noticed that the learning process, which was apparently genuine, transformed into a business fad. While the structure of the methodology was based on real knowledge, its development was based on the suppositions of Company B and its clients. These hypotheses, which were really strong beliefs, were then used to construct the advice given by the consultancy firm concerning what method to adopt. The choice of each word, each experience and each application of the methodology was guided by this set of hypotheses. For example, an internal training seminar organized to improve the quality of consulting assignments included, as a preliminary exercise, a long analysis of "client requirements." In addition to the importance of capitalizing on company knowledge, the object of the methodology was to sell consulting missions. As a result, the framing of client demand assumed a primary role in structuring the methodology, which ultimately took the form of an exhaustive sales pitch.

As a way of presenting the impact of these hypotheses, a systematic link can be made between initial supposition and the subsequent emergence of the business fad.

First Supposition

"The client has not succeeded in resolving the problem himself; he wants to be reassured." This supposition exerts a major influence on the movement from knowledge to mystification as the consultant transforms intuition, imitation and sometimes innovation into a real consulting product. Whatever the status of the added value of the consulting product, which can range from a vague idea to a literal copy of an existing approach, the consultant must make the client believe that the consultancy method is completely coherent. The resulting mixture of intuition, imitation and innovation provides the foundation for the transformation of the consulting product into a business fad. Consulting firms typically use an acronym to name their methodology, highlighting the fact that the methodology, which is owned by them, is original. Subsequent efforts to reassure clients depend on the presentation of the methodology and the creation of high-quality interpersonal relationships with the client. As a young consultant remarked: "For a partner, the most important criteria in evaluation of performance is your relationship with the client."

Second Supposition

"The client asks for tried and tested methodology." The methodology presented to the client must be seen as valid and perfectly adapted to the client's needs—despite the fact that this may not be the case. This presentation typically introduces the methodology as part of the *fixed* knowledge—rather than *emergent* knowledge—of the consultancy firm. In this case, the consulting firm essentially hides the reality that incremental improvements occur in the application of the methodology. Every consulting assignment, of course, goes through a series of progressions during which consultants rely on stereotypes in their analysis of the problem and the solution (as a way of carrying out the mission more quickly). Each assignment, however, also presents opportunities to enrich the experience of the consultants involved, which can eventually be transmitted to other consultants through iterative, marginal improvements in the methodology.

Third Supposition

"The client wants a tailored assignment adapted to his needs." In this instance, the consultant adapts the client's demand to a prepackaged solution. In Company B, for example, a partner explained, "consulting is putting various demands into pre-made boxes." This approach, however, is not how the proposal and the assignment are presented to the client. In an assignment proposal, one often finds a description of client needs, the specific economic and competitive context of the client, the presentation of expert consultants with experience in the sector, and the problems of the client. All these elements are intended to make clients think that the proposal was customized for their organizations. As an internal training document from Company A stipulated, "Above all, the clients want to talk to a consultant who understands their business." A senior consultant of Company A also drew attention to the fact that, "The client must have the feeling that we are thinking only of him, by making him think that what we do is tailored to his needs." The proposal is thus accompanied by specific terms used by the client (e.g., the name of the customer's firm, the logo, technical terms used in the company, particular jargon). As a way of simplifying this adaptation process, both Company A and Company B held meetings with competitors of their prospects, in order to obtain information on the context and the importance of the problem to be resolved. Another approach is to adapt the graphic presentation of the methodology. The basic method used in the two consulting firms was used was quite standard in its graphic form, with different oblong shapes corresponding to different stages and arrows showing the links. For each client, the standard presentation was adapted slightly using the client's own terms. The indiscriminate use of this approach is reflected by an incident in one of these firms when a page of a service proposal was supplemented with another client's logo. Fortunately, the person responsible had changed the document's form (but not all of its content). Quality control is thus very strict in large consulting firms with two checks, carried out by a senior consultant and by a partner (Venard 1995) after the work has been completed by the consultant.

Fourth Supposition

"An important advantage of consultants is their objectivity." Consultants attempt to emphasize the objective value their consulting firm brings to the client, including a clear methodology and the experience of the consultants on the project. Consultants are supposed to be objective as they are not members of the client organization, with no inherent prejudice against any manager or employee or any particular solution. In principle, consultants can make recommendations that are not influenced by vested interests or organizational politics. Moreover in practice, consulting assignments are often augmented by a pilot committee of members from different levels of the client organization. The role of such committees is to provide information, to validate the different stages of the mission, and to communicate them internally. The fact that the pilot committee is heterogeneous is intended as a guarantee of the relative objectivity if its work. The objectivity of the mission is further induced by the methodology itself, the quality of the method of problem resolution. A critical analysis of the problem permits the formulation of appropriate recommendations to the client, recommendations that are based on what is presumed to be best for the client and not influenced by the particular interests of any group of employees. Thus the approach used by both Company A and Company B in all consulting assignments was essentially the same—an "objective" analysis of the current situation followed by the creation of the "ideal" solution (which, in practice, was constructed by exploiting the experience of the consultants and the wishes of the client management). The fact that the consultants often have significant experience in advising their clients means they can easily identify the differences pointed out earlier, leading to the suggestion that their recommendations flow "naturally" from their analyses (the term "naturally," for example was frequently repeated by a partner of Company B).

By communicating and emphasizing these three elements—added value, a clear methodology, and experience—the consultant attempts to illustrate his or her objectivity to the client. In reality, this objectivity is present in discourse as well as in action. In fact, consultants, aware of the importance of objectivity for the client, try to rationalize the presentation of their diagnosis and recommendations. With respect to the content of their presentation itself, consultants are encouraged to play on a kind of mythical rationality with the client by including tangible facts, numbers and statistical analyses in their proposals and reports. As one partner told us during a mission, "Clients love figures in reports, add as many as you can." During different assignments, the same partner asked for succinct studies on small numbers of unrepresentative samples (for example, telephone conversations with ten clients to establish the level of customer satisfaction concerning the sales network) to lend credence to our conclusions. This small, non-representative sample did not stop the partner from communicating "superb statistics," much to the satisfaction of the client. Similarly, in selling a proposal to a client, a partner of one of the consulting firms argued that his firm's methodology showed that: "Fifty percent of firms do not know the profitability of their products and services, and 60% of client accounts are not profitable." While the partner was uncompromising on the importance of having the client accept the firm's methodology, there was lingering uncertainty about its real value. In reality, the numbers provided the client seemed completely arbitrary and it was never possible to establish where they came from.

Fifth Supposition

"The client has to be dependent on the consulting firm." The critical description of the consultancy relationship must not omit the fact that consultants give advice, which is sometimes useful for the clients. Therefore, a learning phenomenon exists, a process that is centered on ideas and new practices, which circulate with the help of consultants. As a partner of Company A stated, when faced with the author's skeptical reaction that he could formulate a strategy for a sector better than the client,

> All you have to do is listen to the employees (of the client). They often have good ideas, but no one listens to them. It's up to us to present their ideas in a better way.

As this quote illustrates, consultants often capture the insights across different segments of the client organization, ranging from the executive management level, to operational and technical management, through employees at headquarters and in the field.

The learning process, however, is deliberately limited by the consulting firm. Bloomfield and Danielli (1995), for example, showed the role of the consultant as a network builder with the objective of making himself indispensable. The consultant gives much information to reassure the client but not enough so that the client would be capable of doing the assignment without the consultant. This lack of details implies that the methodology looks like an "empty tool box." The client is provided with various reports, but never with the consulting file that contains much more information and detail.

An underlying intent of such dependency is to make the client buy other missions, which is why so many final reports contain options for other service proposals. These options are often posed in the form of questions or comments, which pepper the final report with comments like "the stock management policy needs checking" or "it seems that there is room for improvement in the management of foreign exchange risk." An internal training document at Company A, for example, noted that, "the measure of customer satisfaction is in getting repeat business." In extreme cases, there can be a final supplementary part of the report entitled something like "Follow up to the Study," with a subtitle like "Paths of complementary investigation." Faced with questions about the superficial nature of the "options for new missions," a young manager from Company A lamented, "the partner decides how to reach his financial objectives."

CONCLUSION

Based upon the author's experiences in two large consultancy firms, this chapter has attempted to illustrate how consultant suppositions about their clients can transform a process of learning into a management fashion, which itself could be transformed into a business fad during its life cycle. Some consultants, of course, are quite aware of their role as fashion setters. Driven by the goal of making money, these consultants may present their clients with a mixture of real innovation, new knowledge and business fads. The line between knowledge building and dissemination and abject mystification, however, can easily be crossed during the consulting process. A major reason why this line is crossed can be traced to the different suppositions about client requirements discussed in this chapter. Driven by the dual goals of respecting the client's needs and making money, the consultant may inadvertently become a fad setter instead of a knowledge broker.

The desire to sell consulting services is a powerful incentive, one that can easily shape and influence how a consulting firm approaches business opportunities. In Company A, for example, a partner, whose volume of business was in steep decline, was particularly unscrupulous. In response to questions about the pointlessness of a consulting assignment and doubts concerning the project's recommendations, he replied, "as long as they don't notice anything, we earn money." (At the time of this quote, the client was committed to spending 1.250 million francs in consultancy fees with Company A over a 6-month period. The client subsequently lost hundreds of millions of francs on a venture that the partner had recommended.)

The objective of this chapter, however, is not to question the legitimacy or integrity of consultants and their advice. Many professionals in consultancy do remarkable work. In Company B, the author participated in many consulting assignments whose results were highly successful and very much appreciated by clients. Yet, a question that lingers concerns the extent to which consultants themselves should be blamed for weaknesses within the consulting process. Both the consultant *and* the client share responsibility for managing the underlying relationships in any consulting engagement. Yet, clients are often obsessed with the question of *how* to change the organization and less with the critical questions of *why* and *what* to change. This orientation contributes to the enhancement of management fashion—the quick fix—and the resulting mystification of managerial "innovations."

One of the key elements to manage this relationship is for the consultant and the client to keep in mind the necessity of the knowledge creation process, from the vantage point of both the client organization and the consulting firm. Some tactics which contribute to such understanding include being mutually involved in the consulting process (e.g., in data finding), clients having the access to the consultant 's internal information concerning the assignment, jointly controlling the consultancy process itself (not only the final report), spreading the resulting knowledge among various employees in the client organization, and, in case of selection of the same consulting company for multiple assignments, selecting the team of consultants who have developed knowledge about the client and its environment. Clients, of course, also need to benefit from consultants in their role as true agents of change—consultants who bring a level of objectivity and legitimacy to the consulting assignment—focusing on problem solving and the knowledge creation process rather than the creation of management fashion and fads.

REFERENCES

Abrahamson, E. (1991). Managerial fads and fashion: The diffusion and rejection of innovations. *Academy of Management Review, 16*(3), 586–612.

Abrahamson, E. (1996). Management fashion. *Academy of Management Review, 21*(1), 254–285

Berry, M. (1995). Research and the practice of management: A French view. *Organization Science, 6*(1), 104–116.

Bloomfield, B., & Danielli, D. (1995). The role of management consultants in the development of information technology: The indissoluble nature of sociopolitical and technical skills. *Journal of Management Studies, 32*(1), 23–46.

Clark, T. (1995). *Managing consultants: Consultancy as the management of impressions.* Milton Keynes: Open University Press.

Clark, T., & Salaman, G. (1996). Telling tales: Management consultancy as the art of story telling. In D. Grant & C. Oswick (Eds), *Metaphor and organizations* (pp. 166–184). London: Sage.

Crossan, M.M., Lane, H.W., & White, R. (1999). An organizational learning framework: From intuition to institution. *Academy of Management Review, 24*(3), 522–537.

Dosi, G. (1984). *Technical change and industrial transformation.* London: Macmillan.

Dyer, W.G., & Wilkins, A.L. (1991). Better stories, not better constructs, to generate better theory: A rejoinder to Eisenhardt. *Academy of Management Review, 16*(3), 613–619.

Eisenhardt, K.M. (1989). Building theories from case study research. *Academy of management review, 14,* 532–550.

Faust, M. (1999). *The increasing contribution of management consultancies to management knowledge.* Paper presented at the Conference EGOS, Warwick, UK.

Fincham, R. (1999). The consultant-client relationship: Critical perspectives on the management of organizational change. *Journal of Management Studies, 36*(3), 335–351.

Gill, J., & Whittle, S. (1990). Management by panacea: Accounting for transience. *Journal of Management Studies, 30*(2), 281–295.

Glaser, B., & Strauss, A. (1967). *The discovery of grounded theory: Strategies for qualitative research.* New York: Aldine de Gruyter.

Hargadon, A., & Sutton, R.I. (1996). Technology brokering and innovation: Evidence from a product design firm. *Academy of Management Proceedings,* pp. 229–233.

Huber, G.P. (1990). A theory of the effects of advanced information technologies. *Academy of Management Review, 15*(1), 47–72.

Huczynski, A.A. (1993). *Management gurus: What makes them and how to become one.* London: Routledge.

Kieser, A. (1997). Rhetoric and myth in management fashion. *Organization, 4*(1), 49–76.

Kieser, A. (1998). *How management science, consultancies and business companies (do not) learn from each other: Applying concepts of learning to different types of organizations and to interorganizational learning.* Germany: Mannheim, Universität of Mannheim.

McGivern, C. (1983). Some facets of the relationship between consultants and clients in organizations. *Journal of Management Studies, 20*(3), 367–386.

Micklethwait, J., & Wooldridge, A. (1996). *The witchdoctors: Making sense of management gurus.* London: Heinedmann.

Midler, C. (1993). Les modes managériales. France: Paris, Annales des Mines, *Gérer et Comprendre.*

Miles, M.B., & Huberman, A. M. (1984). *Qualitative data analysis.* Beverly Hill, CA: Sage.

Nelson, R., & Winter, S. (1982). *An evolutionary theory of economic change.* Cambridge, MA: Harvard University Press.

Pettigrew, A. (1973). *The politics of organizational decision making.* London: Tavistock.

Rogers, E.M. (1995). *Diffusion of innovation.* New York: Free Press.

Sarvary, M. (1999). Knowledge management and competition in the consulting industry. *California management review, 41*(2), 95–107.

Schein, E.A. (1988). *Process consultation: Its role in organization development.* Reading, MA: Addison-Wesley.

Starbuck, W.H. (1992). Learning by knowledge intensive firms. *Journal of Management Studies, 29*(4), 713–740.

Sturdy, A. (1996). Managing consultants: Consultancy as the management of impressions. *Journal of Management Studies, 33*(4), 563–565.

Sturdy, A. (1997). The consultancy process: An insecure process? *Journal of Management Studies, 34*(3), 389–412.

Van Maanen, J. (1988). *Tales of the field: On writing ethnography*. Chicago: The University of Chicago Press.

Venard, B. (1995). Les maîtres d'industrie: Un point de vue sur le métier de consultant. Paris, France: Annales des Mines, *Gérer et Comprendre*, pp. 19–30.

Viney, N. (1992). *Bluff your way in consulting*. Horsham: Ravette Books.

Weick, K. (1995). *Sense making in organizations*. London: Sage.

CHAPTER 10

ARE WE PRODUCING INFORMATION AGE CONSULTANTS?

Reflections on U.S. Business Schools' Course Offerings

Susan M. Adams and Alberto Zanzi

INTRODUCTION

The Information Age is transforming every industry. Products and services are described and evaluated online, and virtually anything and everything can be purchased on the Internet. Company websites not only serve as outlets for sales but are increasingly being used for public relations endeavors, and the reputation of a company seems to be increasingly impacted by the look and functionality of its website. Productivity tools, ranging from a greater use of e-mail to far-reaching ERP (enterprise resource planning) systems, are streamlining business operations and connecting people across the globe. Information technology is also revolutionizing business-to-business initiatives, literally reconstructing the multitude of ways in which companies interact with each other.

Since consultants work with the myriad of industries affected by such Information Age changes, it seems logical to expect changes in the consulting industry in general and what is expected from consultants in particular. Yet, while preparing consultants for Information Age work is a challenge faced by business schools, little is known about the nature of the preparation provided by today's B-schools. What *are* schools offering and what *should* they be offering? Examining the current state of school offerings can provide us with a glimpse of the adequacy of current programs as well as point toward adjustments that B-schools should consider in preparing their students for Information Age consulting.

THE CHANGING CONSULTING ENVIRONMENT

Management consulting, both as a profession and as a business, is expanding rapidly throughout the world. In the United States, the consolidation of the industry into large multibillion dollar firms (e.g., Andersen Consulting revenues for 1999 exceeded $7.5B) and the disappearance of smaller regional firms are clear indications of the maturing of the consulting industry. According to WetFeet.com (2000), four of the five top firms by consulting revenues are units of pre-existing public audit firms: Andersen Consulting (now Accenture), Cap Gemini, Coopers & Lybrand (now PricewaterhouseCoopers) and Deloitte Consulting, each with more than 20,000 consultants and all with revenues in excess of $4B. Initially, the growth of these firms was generated by IT intervention projects for potential Y2K problems and the implementation of massive software solutions such as SAP. In fact, the six largest consultancies have become more tools deployment firms rather than traditional consultancies (Greiner, 2001). Now they are covering a wide range of consulting areas, to the point of infringing into strategic consulting, previously the exclusive domain of "boutique" firms such as McKinsey, Bain and BCG. This group represents the "low" end of the strategic consulting market characterized by high volume and relatively low revenues per consultant (typically in the $100 to 200K range). At the "high" end, the more traditional strategic consulting firms generate revenues per consultant in excess of $500,000 (Dehni, 1999). Yet, despite these changes, niche consulting is also growing. As outsourcing continues to grow, for example, consultants are taking roles in advising and even managing the relationship between firms and their outsourcing partners (Motamedi, 2001).

The environment of management consulting is shifting largely due to global competition, the migration from manufacturing to service industries, and the impact of the Internet (Werther & Harris, 2001). This Information Age environmental shift has changed the nature of consulting from primarily strategic direction of standardized operations to a variety of services that include strategic direction for complex, global firms to the implementation of business tools for managing the complexities of mass customization across the globe. The shift into IT consulting opened the door to a wider range and larger volume of consulting positions that can no longer be filled by the few elite schools. This means that more B-schools need to be preparing students for consulting to cover the widening range of positions and needs now characterizing the consulting industry.

Starting salaries reflect the levels of entry to consulting and the explosive expansion of U.S.-based consulting firms, both domestically and internationally. There is a high demand for junior and senior level professionals. More than one third of the Harvard Business School MBA graduating class is expected to join top consulting firms, with starting salaries of $140,000 plus signing bonuses and other fringe benefits. The high volume firms at the other end of the spectrum are actively recruiting at the undergraduate level, even among non-business majors, with starting salaries in the $40–$50,000 range (Dehni, 1999). These attractive starting salaries indicate the tight labor market for consultants and the need to entice top talent, yet little is known about how (and even whether) B-schools are adequately preparing students for management consulting roles.

The high number of students entering the consulting profession directly after graduation and the need of the consulting firms to make them "billable" as soon as possible thus pose a key question: how adequately are university curricula preparing students, even at the most rudimentary level, for the consulting profession? The purpose of this chapter is twofold: (1) to explore the course offerings of ranked American business schools in the specific topical area of management consulting, and (2) to evaluate the adequacy of these offerings for preparing graduates to participate in the field of management consulting. The initial phase of this exploratory study focused on current course offerings. The second phase extended this analysis by reviewing current offerings and comparing those offerings to industry needs.

AN EXAMINATION OF COURSE OFFERINGS

The primary objective of our initial exploratory study was to identify what U.S. business schools are currently offering in the way of courses for students interested in a career in management consulting. This focus includes formal academic management consulting courses at the graduate and undergraduate level and also other courses with partial content related to management consulting. A secondary objective was to identify the specific content of these management consulting courses to determine the nature of preparation being offered.

Study Design and Method

The sample included the top ranked U.S. business schools aggregated from listings in the *Princeton Review, Business Week,* and *U.S. News & World Report* for their 1999-2001 reviews (see Appendix 1 for the listing). The compiled listing of the top three tiers of business schools yielded a target sample of 93 schools. This approach was used for two primary reasons. First, consultancy firms tend to recruit at the top business schools so it was important to ensure that these schools were represented in the sample. Second, since determining B-school rankings is subject to variation, the compiled listing was used to capture as many high quality programs as possible.

Complete data from 68 schools were collected. Of these 68 schools, only 27 (40%) offered any management consulting courses. Qualitative analysis was conducted using the course descriptions from the 27 schools with identifiable management consulting courses. Information from individual universities was collected from the individual school websites, catalogues, and related websites that collect such information (e.g., www.collegesource.org). The available data were analyzed for management consulting course offerings—at the undergraduate and graduate level—either fully dedicated to or with partial content centered on management consulting. Courses were also content analyzed to detect commonalities in topics and methodology. Since we did not have any preconceived notions concerning course content, our focus was truly exploratory, attempting to ascertain the availability and nature of such course offerings.

Findings

Overall, the academic course offerings in management consulting were found to be extremely limited. As noted above, of the 68 schools from which data were available, only 27 (40%) offered any courses in management consulting: 24 had full-length courses dedicated to management consulting, three had courses with partial management consulting content, and one school offered both partial and full-length courses.

The schools offering full-content courses were limited to approximately 35% of the schools examined. Most offered only one course (17 schools, 25% of the sample), but five schools offered two courses (7%). Only two schools (Boston College and Emory University) offered three courses (4%). Courses (either full or partial content) were concentrated at the graduate level in 23 schools (34%) and at the undergraduate level in only five programs (7%). None of the schools offered a mix of graduate and undergraduate courses.

There was no evidence in the sample of any degree or major in management consulting—either at the graduate or undergraduate level—though some B-schools offered a concentration in management consulting as an individualized or customized field of study (e.g., George Washington University). Thunderbird lists a specialization option in management consulting as part of its Master of International Management, but course descriptions were unavailable and, consequently, not a part of the final sample.

A content analysis of the description of the courses offered indicated three major topic areas. Consulting skills and techniques was the most common content, present in 22 schools (32%), and industry trends in consulting were covered in 8 schools (12%). Management consulting courses required a field project in 12 schools (18%). Six of the schools (9%) in the sample specifically mentioned preparation for internal consultants. Table 1 presents a summary of topic area content in the courses offered.

Table 1.   Research Summary on Management Consulting Course Offerings from the Compiled Listing of the Top 93 Ranked U.S. Business Schools

School	Undergrad	Grad	Full*	Part**	Content Areas Trends	Project	Skills
American	0	1	1	0	0	1	0
Arizona State U	1	0	1	1	0	0	1
Babson College	0	1	0	3	0	0	1
Baylor U.	0	1	0	1	0	0	1
Boston College	0	1	3	0	1	0	1
Boston U	0	1	1	0	0	1	1
Carnegie Mellon	0	1	1	0	1	0	1
Case Western U	0	1	0	1	0	0	1
Claremont U.	0	1	2	0	0	1	1
Columbia U.	0	1	1	0	0	1	1
Cornell U	0	1	1	0	1	0	1
Emory U	0	1	3	0	1	1	1
George Washington	0	1	1	0	0	1	1
Georgetown U	1	0	1	0	0	0	1
MIT Sloan	0	1	1	0	0	1	1
NYU Stern	1	0	2	0	0	0	1
Notre Dame	0	1	1	0	1	0	1
Northeastern	0	1	2	0	0	1	1
U Cal, Berkeley	1	0	2	0	1	0	0

Table 1.   Research Summary on Management Consulting Course Offerings from the Compiled Listing of the Top 93 Ranked U.S. Business Schools (Cont.)

School	Undergrad	Grad	Full*	Part**	Content Areas		
					Trends	Project	Skills
U Cal Irvine	0	1	1	0	1	0	1
U of Chicago	0	1	1	0	0	0	1
U of Pennsylvania	1	0	1	0	0	1	1
U of Rochester	0	1	1	0	0	0	1
U of SC, Marshall	0	1	2	0	0	1	0
Wake Forest U	0	1	1	0	0	1	0
Washington U	0	1	1	0	1	0	1
William and Mary	0	1	1	0	0	1	0
Totals	5	22	33	6	8	12	22
% of total sample (68)					12	18	32

Notes: * Full courses offered specifically on Management Consulting
** Only a portion of the course covers Management Consulting topics

Comparative Analysis

The second phase of the study was dedicated to answering the "so what" question by conducting a comparative analysis of available offerings with the needs of those who seek education in the field of management consulting. In those B-schools where consulting-oriented courses are available, emphasis is placed on basic consulting skills development, field experiences, and information about the consulting industry. The actual value of these different foci will depend on the experience base and background of the students in question. For the purpose of this research, we identified five categories of potential student segments: Raw Recruits, Junior Consultants, Expert Contributors, Accidental Entrants, and Managing Consultants.

The categories of students were based on career paths into and within management consulting. Individuals already in the field of management consulting can be classified as junior or managing level (Dehni, 1999; Upton & Steinman, 1996; WetFeet.com, 2000). The early developmental roles of analyst and associate used in most consulting firms for new hires are categorized as *Junior Consultants. Managing Consultants* are those individuals with three years or more of experience and on the track to partner. This category would include the "in charge" consultants who oversee the daily work of the project. The distinguishing mark of a Managing Consultant for the purposes of this analysis would be taking the supervisory/lead role in a project. Many of the newer firms are using the titles of Practice Manager and Business Development Manager to describe what we classify as Managing Consultants.

Students just entering the field of management consulting may or may not have relevant experience. Those who have little or no work experience are classified as *Raw Recruits*. Experienced managers entering the consulting industry may or may not have some consulting experience. Those who have technical or managerial work experience but limited or no consulting experience are classified as *Expert Contributors*. Experienced managers with some consulting experience are classified as *Accidental Entrants*. As the following discussion will indicate, the academic needs of the five categories of students differ and are satisfied only on a limited basis by existing course offerings (see Table 2).

Table 2.   Need for Course Content by Student Category

	Industry Trends	Field Projects	Skills Training
Raw Recruits	High	High	High
Experienced Managers			
• Expert Contributors	High	Moderate-High	Moderate-High
• Accidental Entrants	High	Low	Moderate
Junior Consultants	Low	Low	Moderate-High
Managing Consultants	Low	Low	High

In general, those students with little or no consulting experience have a higher need for field projects to understand the nuances associated with client management, teamwork, and other aspects of consulting not easily taught in the classroom. Those who are not familiar with the industry and practice of consulting would benefit from a fuller understanding of the lifestyle that is driven by client expectations, recruitment practices, career paths, the consulting process itself, and the strategic position of the client as it relates to the consulting business. Figure 1 depicts the job requirements of consultants at the junior and managing level. Raw Recruits and Expert Contributors will most likely enter at the junior level while Accidental Entrants may qualify for entry at the Managing Consultant level. The life of a Junior Consultant is primarily data collection and analysis with some diagnosing and reporting. While these individuals typically need to work in teams with clients to accomplish their assignments, the actual client management and team supervision are handled by the Managing Consultant, the person "in charge" who oversees the project (Upton & Steinman, 1996). Project selling and long-term client relationships are handled at the partner level (or Business Development Manager), which

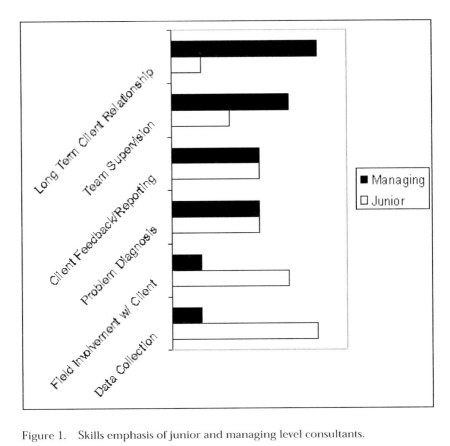

Figure 1.   Skills emphasis of junior and managing level consultants.

we have included in the Managing Consultant category. The different categories of students thus have different educational needs based on their daily task demands.

Firms that provide extensive training often prefer Raw Recruits. Raw Recruits are hired for their potential and lower salary expectations (Dehni, 1999; WetFeet.com, 2000). These individuals need to learn about the consulting industry and its business practices. Industry information should include knowledge about typical career paths and the lifestyle of consultants. Since the consulting field needs to change on an ongoing basis to address Information Age concerns, courses should be updating industry information and sharing those insights with students on a regular basis. Personal assessments to determine fit with industry expectations and types of consulting are examples of the type of information that might be included. An understanding of what recruiters value in candidates might be demonstrated in mock case interviews exercises. Since Raw Recruits need to develop basic skills such as data gathering and analysis, client management, confident communication, and teamwork capabilities, courses for these students should include extensive skills training and field projects to provide practice in realistic situations. Class exercises should be used to practice client feedback and presentations. Raw Recruits have a high need for knowledge about industry trends, field projects, and skills training to prepare for Information Age consulting.

Experienced managers have more varied needs due to their diverse backgrounds and the rationale for their entry into the field. Some enter management consulting because they have developed expertise in a specific area such as IT, finance, operations management, or macroeconomics from their work experience. In a recent Information Age shift, Ph.D.'s in a wide variety of fields and JDs are being sought to fill demand for credible specialized expertise such technical product development advice or the tax and legal implications of corporate decisions (WetFeet.com, 2000; Leonhardt, 2000). Consulting firms find such individuals—who we refer to as Expert Contributors—attractive due to the depth of their knowledge and ability to provide tangible services. Additionally, their deeper level of education provides evidence of credibility for the consulting firm. These individuals have a high need to understand industry trends and the consulting profession so they are prepared to manage a new career path. They have a moderate to high need for field projects and skills training, depending on the extent that their previous jobs entailed teamwork and interaction with senior-level executives. In their previous roles, Expert Contributors usually performed their work autonomously and may not have needed to interact directly with organizational leaders, so basic skills such as teamwork and developing client relationships become important learning issues.

Other experienced managers, in contrast, simply stumble onto the notion of management consulting because they were involved in company projects as internal consultants or performed some consulting work on the side that they enjoyed. While these individuals have been exposed to the complexities of consulting from their organizational experience, they, like Expert Contributors and Raw Recruits, may know little about the consulting industry and, perhaps more important, the consulting process itself. They are likely to stumble through projects rather than employ deliberate consulting methodologies because they have not been trained in consulting techniques. These individuals—who we refer to as Accidental Entrants—have a high need for industry trends knowledge, a low need for field projects, and a moderate need for skills training. They have had enough field experience to understand the major issues involved in consulting but have not had the exposure to potential solutions they could receive from some skills training. An interesting observation from several unscientific polls of academic audiences provides anecdotal evidence that most acade-micians who engage in consulting began as Accidental Entrants.

Junior Consultants are fairly new employees of consulting firms, so they are directly involved in the consulting industry and have sufficient experi-ence to begin identifying their strengths and weaknesses. They have a low need for industry trends knowledge and field projects, but a moderate to high need for more skills training to develop their weaknesses.

Finally, Managing Consultants are embarking on a new phase in their consulting careers. They are beginning or will begin to supervise teams and find clients. Therefore, they have a high need for advanced skills training that they may have dismissed as irrelevant in earlier training and a relatively low need for industry trends knowledge and field projects. As an example of advanced skills, a Managing Consultant needs to learn to cultivate client rela-tionships for repeat business and referrals. In earlier stages of consulting, the focus is more on completing the job rather than building relationships.

B-SCHOOL TRAINING AND MANAGEMENT CONSULTING

The findings of this exploratory study suggest that business schools in the United States currently play a marginal role in preparing students for a career in management consulting. The academic courses that are offered are limited in number and isolated in the curriculum, with no degree or major offered. It appears that based on the information generated in our research the developmental needs of consultants are not being addressed through course offerings. As summarized in Table 3, while most B-schools that offered management consulting courses provided skills training, few provided actual field experiences and fewer still provided industry knowledge.

Table 3.   Comparative Analysis of Student Needs and Course Con-tent Availability

	Undergrad	Graduate	Industry Trends	Field Projects	Skills Training
Raw Recruits	NM	Available	NM	SA	Available
Exp. Managers					
• Expert Contributors	NP	Available	NM	SA	Available
• Accidental Entrants	NP	Available	NM	NP	Available
Junior Consultants	NP	Available	NP	NP	Available
Managing Consultants	NP	Available	NP	NP	Available

Notes: NM—Need more offerings; offerings extremely limited
SA—(Somewhat Available)—Can be found, though offerings limited
Available—Likely to be available where consulting courses are offered
NP—Not a priority, need fairly well satisfied

Comparing the needs of students to the available course content provides some indications of where management consulting preparation falls short. Few institutions have offerings that cater to the specific needs of any of the five identified markets of students. Courses are mainly at the graduate level and only in very few schools are they clustered to offer sufficiently broad coverage of the field needed by these different student market segments. Especially since Raw Recruits are increasingly being sought from the undergraduate ranks (Dehni, 1999), there is a definite need for more undergraduate training in consulting skills and expertise. The explosion of tools-oriented consulting can be served by undergraduate programs that provide technical training and by young MBAs with technical knowledge (Werther & Harris, 2001). Recent graduates from cutting edge B-schools are likely to have been trained on the most updated technologies. While technology expertise provides necessary credibility for consulting found largely in the past by pedigree degrees from elite B-schools, these entrants still need extensive consulting skills training and an orientation to the industry.

Raw Recruits, Expert Contributors, and Accidental Entrants are not being served by the limited availability of schools that provide industry trends knowledge. The consulting industry is associated with an intense work ethic usually dictated by client demands. Individuals entering the field of consulting are best served by realistic previews so they are ready to adapt to and deal with a consultant's lifestyle, the ambiguity associated with consulting tasks, and the political, social, and emotional concerns that clients may present. At a recent gathering of IT professionals and consultants from major firms, for example, the question of what students should know before entering the field of IT consulting was posed. Almost all the consultants agreed that despite what they tell candidates, rookie consultants still do not understand the extent of travel involved and the implications that a heavy travel schedule poses for their lives. As one consultant remarked, "Students need to be told that they won't be able to bring their dogs to work; in fact, they won't be able to have dogs if they go into IT consulting."

Raw Recruits and Expert Contributors are somewhat underserved by the availability of management consulting field experiences. As a dimension of this process, deselection can be an important decision. As a former student noted, "I am so glad I had this experience as a student consultant because I now know that I will never be happy with a career in consulting." The student took the course fully intending to seek a consulting position but learned first hand about the demands of the profession through field experience, something that was not readily apparent in course work or from reading about consulting. It should be noted that a recent study of MBA programs (Baker, 2000) found that only 40% of the schools offered field studies. This finding suggests that a significant minority of programs offer students the opportunity to participate in field studies, even if they are not specifically designed for management consulting preparation. Yet, even if 40% of B-schools offer such field experiences, a large number of students are still not offered the opportunity to experience real-time client management, an essential skill of consulting not easily replicated in the classroom. Furthermore, such field studies usually focus on understanding the application of course material rather than the process of management consulting.

In summary, course offerings are not sufficiently widespread or comprehensive enough to conclude that academia is providing the necessary preparation for management consulting in any age, much less the current Information Age environment. An underlying problem with our analysis, however, is that courses are difficult to find and to identify as related to consulting, possibly due to the lack of consistency in academia in labeling course offerings for management consulting development.

These findings have potentially profound implications for the role academia can play in fulfilling the expanding demand for graduates with sufficient consulting background to be able to quickly enter the profession, thereby appealing to consulting firms or companies seeking graduates to fill internal consulting roles. Universities, in general however, do not seem to be able or interested in preparing students for a consulting career. The "consulting universities" of the major consulting firms possibly fill this void by training graduates in a few weeks of intense seminars, by non-academic, external seminars, and more commonly by the time consuming and expensive practice of "on the job training" (Upton & Steinman, 1996; WetFeet.com, 2000). This last alternative, in particular, has generated substantial "rumblings" from the client side that accuses consulting firms of training newly minted, "green" MBAs at the clients' expense. These factors can only be partially mitigated by a strong orientation toward consulting skills and techniques present in the content of the academic courses currently offered. Much more attention should be given to providing industry knowledge and realistic behavioral expectations through field projects as a total package for consulting preparation.

Universities are also ignoring the potential markets represented by Junior and Managing Consultants. It is more likely that training programs provided directly by employers service these groups, but this is an untested notion. Given the schedule that most consultants keep, however, schools would need to provide courses that cater to them specifically. Saturday classes with supplemental online work such as "chat room" debates could be an attractive option. Any attempt to appeal to current consultants might be construed by some as a radical suggestion, since most schools are not overtly acknowledging the field with current offerings. Schools that are already offering consulting-oriented classes, however, are likely to have the infrastructure such as faculty expertise and weekend classes to welcome current consultants as students. The challenge lies in convincing schools that they can offer more than the consulting firms' internal training programs. We believe that B-schools can offer a cross-pollenization experience not possible in internal programs. The academic approach of critical and impartial examination in contrast to stringent, socialized training from internal consulting firm programs can provide a broader view of the industry and its practices which, in turn, could lead to more innovation in the consulting industry.

A corollary consideration is the lack of academic status of management consulting as a discipline. Not being in the academic mainstream with rigorous research, publications, or teaching credentials generates a circular, self-perpetuating problem of no status, no recognition—no recognition, no status. Much more work needs to be accomplished to further the understanding of how to best develop consultants as a first step in attracting attention for curriculum development. Currently, faculty have little data about what is needed for developing consultants making it difficult to lobby for the addition of consulting classes. A deeper, more troubling issue is trying to increase the value of those who do research concerning consulting. They have little power in institutions to expand course offerings or to attract funding for further research if their work is not valued. The expansion of consulting as a major industry that B-schools serve may help in this effort but academia has a record of slow change.

This assessment, of course, is based on a limited study. The sample size should definitely be expanded to several hundred schools, including lower-tier and international universities. Content analysis of the courses offered should also be expanded to an examination of syllabi, rather than course descriptions, for a more accurate evaluation. Moreover, this exploratory study did not include non-credit bearing activities such as consulting clubs and career services training. There is anecdotal evidence that consulting clubs are a growing phenomenon. The clubs provide field projects, speakers from consultancies, and networking events that often impart a resume boost as well as realistic job and career previews and related information that can help students make informed decisions about entering consulting. Another emerging trend is to house consulting courses in various disciplines other than general business or management. The University of Texas at Dallas and Bentley College, for example, provide IT consulting courses that are grounded in disciplines other than management and in MS programs rather than in the venerable MBA. This trend may increase as the expected demand for specialized consultants increases. Such courses were not examined and should be considered in future study.

FINAL CONTEMPLATIONS

This reflection on the current state of management consulting education reveals an image of days gone past. Gone are the days where consulting was the exclusive privy of the elite ivies. Gone are the days where the boundary of management consulting was limited to advice about organizational strategy or financial management to senior-level managers. In the past, when consulting was not a consideration for students from schools below the top handful of elite programs, courses in consulting were not needed. The demand for consulting skills, however, has increased and the nature of consulting itself has changed. Add to this mix the changing backgrounds and needs of consulting candidates as captured by the different types discussed in this chapter. In the past, a pedigree, poise, energy, and trainability were the key criteria for entry (O'Shea & Madigan, 1997). Essentially, courses needed to provide the basic skills that would promote confidence and poise. Schools that have had extensive consulting recruitment have cultures that provide industry knowledge from alumni and career service units that are familiar with the consulting recruiters. Moreover, the top schools generally have students with more years of work experience and higher levels of management experience upon entering school. Thus, a narrower range of experiences had been necessary in courses for traditional consulting skills. The current Information Age shift, however, is toward valuing functional or technical expertise as well as the traditional values with a strategy emphasis. Current course offerings, therefore, should focus on more aspects of consulting in broader contexts for a wider variety of students.

Unfortunately, current course offerings do not appear to reflect the evolving nature of management consulting. The future of management consulting is interdisciplinary, still covering strategy but also focusing on such activities such as the deployment of IT tools and liaison services across different levels of an organization as well as across different organizations. Courses need to reflect the variety of consulting engagements available to the field. Students need to understand where they fit in the blossoming industry of management consulting if they will be able to effectively market their services and manage their careers. They need to understand the dynamics of consulting as they relate to the context of managing an organization in a competitive environment. Courses in consulting within functional disciplines may miss the big picture of management required for successful use of technical tools, so there is also a continued need for general management consulting courses for students with a "tools" orientation.

While Raw Recruits, Expert Contributors, and Accidental Entrants have different educational needs, they appear to be treated as homogeneous groups. B-school courses and programs should reflect greater tailoring to their specific needs. Comprehensive well-conceived curricula rather than the occasional course or clustering of available management courses would better serve the constituency of aspiring consultants. If advanced skills development and senior-level consulting issues are included in the curriculum, a new market that includes practicing Junior and Managing Consultants could be attracted to B-Schools for consulting education. Their curricula needs would also include career management since multiple job changes and self-management of careers are increasingly the norm (Arthur & Rousseau, 1996; Hall, 1996). It is not unusual for consultants to move into firms to implement changes they suggested as consultants (Upton & Steinman, 1997). During the recent dot-com boom and bust, for example, we saw consultants move from consulting to managing start-ups and back to consulting (Bennett, 2001). We suggest viewing consulting as one of the career options individuals may choose at various times through their career journeys. Those with cutting-edge technical expertise or pedigrees may enter consulting earlier in life. Others may develop industry or disciplinary experience first, entering the consulting field through projects they have been working on. All of these individuals need adequate preparation to succeed as consultants and to provide service that their client organizations require.

Are we producing Information Age consultants? Probably not. This reflection serves as a challenge to B-schools of the need to provide a better fit between the changing consulting industry demands and the changing nature of student needs to meet those demands. It is time for academia to be more sensitive to the changing needs and demands of the market.

REFERENCES

Arthur, M.B., & Rousseau, D.M. (Eds.). (1996). *The boundaryless career: A new employment principle for a new organizational era.* New York: Oxford University Press.

Baker, H.K. (2000). *Executive summary—MBA Field Study Survey.* Washington, DC: Kogod School of Business, American University.

Bennett, J. (2001, April 24). Consultancies cash in on e-commerce experience. *Wall Street Journal,* p. B13.

Dehni, J. (Ed.). (1999). *The Harvard Business School guide to careers in management consulting: 2000 edition.* Cambridge, MA: Harvard Business School.

Greiner, L. (2001, March 30). *Does management consulting have a future?* Keynote address at the Knowledge and Value Development in Management Consulting Conference, Lyon, France.

Hall, D.T. (1996). *The career is dead—long live the career: A relational approach to careers.* San Francisco: Jossey-Bass.

Leonhardt, D. (2000, October 1). A matter of degree? Not for consultants. *New York Times,* sec. 3, p. 1.

Motamedi, K. (2001, March 31). *Closing comments and reflections.* Comments at the Knowledge and Value Development in Management Consulting Conference, Lyon, France.

O'Shea, J., & Madigan, C. (1997). *Dangerous company: The consulting powerhouses and the businesses they save and ruin.* New York: Random House.

Upton, D., & Steinman, C. (1996). *Deloitte & Touche Consulting Group.* Boston: Harvard Business School Press.

Werther Jr., W.B., & Harris, M.E. (2001, March 31). *The future of management consulting: Drivers and responses.* Paper presented at the Knowledge and Value Development in Management Consulting Conference, Lyon, France.

WetFeet.com (2000). *Careers in management consulting.* San Francisco: WetFeet.com.

APPENDIX 1

Compiled Listing of Top 93 U.S. Business Schools (alphabetical order)

American University: Kogod College of Business Administration
Arizona State University: College of Business
Babson College: F. W. Olin Graduate School of Business
Baylor University: Hankamer School of Business
Boston College: The Carroll School of Management
Boston University: School of Management
Brigham Young University: Marriott School of Management
Carnegie Mellon: H. John Heinz III School of Public Policy and Management
Case Western Reserve University: Weatherhead School of Management
Claremont Graduate University: The Peter F. Drucker School of Management
Clark Atlanta University: School of Business Administration
College of William and Mary: Graduate School of Business
Columbia University: Columbia Business School
Cornell University: Johnson Graduate School of Management
CUNY Baruch College: Zicklin School of Business
Dartmouth College: The Amos Tuck School of Business Administration
Duke University: The Fuqua School of Business
Emory University: Goizueta Business School
Fordham University: Graduate School of Business Administration
George Washington University: School of Business and Public Management
Georgetown University: School of Business
Georgia Institute of Technology: DuPree School of Management
Harvard University: Graduate School of Business Administration
Hofstra University: Frank G. Zarb School of Business
Howard University: School of Business
Illinois Institute of Technology: Stuart Graduate School of Business
Indiana University: Kelly School of Business
Loyola University, Chicago: Graduate School of Business

Massachusetts Institute of Technology: Sloan School of Management
Michigan State University: Eli Broad Graduate School of Management
New York University: Leonard N. Stern School of Business
Northeastern University: Graduate School of Business Administration
Northwestern University: J. L. Kellogg Graduate School of Management
Ohio State University: Fisher College of Business
Penn State University: Mary Jean and Frank P. Smeal College of Business Administration
Pepperdine University: The George L. Graziadio School of Business and Management
Purdue University: Krannert Graduate School of Management
Rice University: Jesse H. Jones Graduate School of Management
Rutgers University: School of Business
Southern Methodist University: Cox School of Business
Stanford University: Stanford Graduate School of Business
State University of New York: Buffalo: School of Management
Syracuse University: School of Management
Texas A & M University: College of Business Administration
Texas Christian University: M. J. Neeley School of Business
Thunderbird University: American Graduate School of International Management
Tulane University: A. B. Freeman School of Business
University of Alabama: Manderson Graduate School of Business
University of Baltimore: Merrick School of Business
University of California, Berkeley: Haas School of Business
University of California, Davis: Graduate School of Management
University of California, Irvine: Graduate School of Management
University of California, Los Angeles: The Anderson School at UCLA
University of Chicago: Graduate School of Business
University of Colorado at Boulder: Graduate School of Business Administration
University of Connecticut: School of Business Administration
University of Delaware: College of Business and Economics
University of Denver: Daniels College of Business
University of Florida: College of Business Administration
University of Georgia: Terry College of Business, Graduate School of Business Administration
University of Illinois at Urbana-Champaign: College of Commerce and Business Administration
University of Iowa: Iowa School of Management
University of Kansas: School of Business
University of Kentucky: Carol Martin Gatton College of Business and Economics
University of Maryland: Robert H. Smith School of Business
University of Massachusetts at Amherst: Isenberg School of Management
University of Miami: School of Business Administration
University of Michigan: University of Michigan Business School
University of Minnesota: Curtis L. Carson School of Management
University of North Carolina at Chapel Hill: Kenan-Flagler Business School
University of Notre Dame: College of Business Administration
University of Pennsylvania: The Wharton School Graduate Division

University of Pittsburgh: Katz Graduate School of Business
University of Rhode Island: College of Business Administration
University of Rochester: William E. Simon Graduate School of Business Administration
University of San Francisco: McLaren School of Business
University of South Carolina: Darla Moore School of Business
University of Southern California: Marshall School of Business
University of Southern Indiana: School of Business
University of Tennessee at Chattanooga: College of Business
University of Tennessee at Knoxville: College of Business Administration
University of Texas at Arlington: College of Business Administration
University of Texas at Austin: Graduate School of Business
University of Virginia: Darden Graduate School of Business Administration
University of Virginia: McIntire School of Commerce
University of Washington: Graduate School of Business Administration
University of Wisconsin, La Crosse: College of Business Administration
University of Wisconsin, Madison: Business School
University of Wyoming: College of Business
Vanderbilt University: Owen Graduate School of Management
Wake Forest University: Babcock Graduate School of Management
Washington University: John M. Olin School of Business
Yale University: Yale School of Management

CONTRIBUTORS

Susan M. Adams, Director of Field-Based Learning and associate professor of management at Bentley College, has a Ph.D. in management from Georgia Institute of Technology. Her research interests, corporate positions, and consulting focus on individual and organizational development involved with anticipating and coping with changing environments.

Marc Bonnet is Professor of Management at the University of Lumiere Lyon 2 and deputy manager of the ISEOR Research Center. His current research and consulting interests focus on change management and management consulting through socioeconomic management.

Anthony F. Buono, series editor, has a joint appointment as Professor of Management and Sociology at Bentley College. He holds a Ph.D. in Industrial and Organizational Sociology from Boston College. His current research and consulting interests focus on organizational change and interorganizational alliances, with an emphasis on mergers, acquisitions, strategic partnerships and firm-stakeholder relations.

Kristofer J. Fenlason is manager of research and assessment within 3M's HR Measurement Systems group where he manages the organizational survey research group. He consults with internal clients on a variety of survey and assessment issues. Kris received his M.A. and Ph.D. in Industrial/Organizational Psychology from Central Michigan University.

Kenneth W. Kerber, Director of Training & Development at 3Com Corporation, has a Ph.D. in Personality Psychology from the University of Illinois at Champaign-Urbana. His work includes managing a worldwide team of human resource development professionals and consulting with management on such issues as leadership development, strategic planning, organizational design, merger integration, team development, and change.

Kari Lilja is Professor in Organization and Management at the Helsinki School of Economics and Business Administration, where he also earned his Ph.D. His current research interest is cross-national comparative study of economic actors in the context of globalizing corporations. His publications cover topics such as workplace industrial relations, resource-based strategies, and managerial work in forest-industry corporations and the dynamics of change of the Finnish business system.

Kyle M. Lundby is a senior research consultant for Questar where he works with clients and conducts research in the areas of employee, customer, and 360-degree feedback. He is an adjunct faculty member at Augsburg College and serves on several SIOP committees. Kyle's Ph.D. in Industrial/Organizational Psychology is from the University of Tennessee.

Shon M. Magnan is a senior research consultant for Questar's market research division. His recent research includes customer value analysis, tying customer loyalty measures to client business results, and the relationships between employee and customer satisfaction through linking models. Shon is a doctoral candidate in Sociology at the University of Minnesota.

Rickie Moore is Professor of Management and Entrepreneurship at E.M.LYON and an associate researcher at the ISEOR research center. Moore's specialization includes performance measurement and organizational effectiveness. His current research interests include comparative (American and European) approaches to management consulting.

Aaron J. Nurick is Professor of Management and Psychology at Bentley College. He received his Ph.D. in Organizational Psychology from the University of Tennessee. His current research and consulting interests include interpersonal relations, emotional intelligence, and diversity issues in organizations.

Flemming Poulfelt is Professor of Management in the Department of Management, Politics & Philosophy and Director of the LOK Research Center at the Copenhagen Business School in Denmark, from where he earned his Ph.D. His current research and consulting interests focus on managing knowledge-intensive firms, knowledge management, strategic management and management consulting.

Henri Savall is Professor of Management at the University of Lumiere Lyon 2. He is the founder and manager of the ISEOR Research Center since its creation in 1976. He has created and experimented the socioeconomic approach to management through transformative action research and intervention within a broad array of organizations. Dr. Savall is also the director of a doctoral program in management consulting and socioeconomic management.

Matthew Semadeni is a doctoral student in strategy at Texas A&M University. Prior to his doctoral studies, he worked as a consultant engaged in technology and process consulting. His current research interests include competition among top consulting firms, the use of consultants as professional scapegoats, and the use of consultants in new ventures.

Hans Thamhain is Professor of Management at Bentley College. His industrial experience includes twenty years of high-technology management positions with GTE/Verizon, General Electric, Westinghouse and ITT. Dr. Thamhain holds a PhD from Syracuse University, as well as MBA, MSEE and BSEE degrees. Well known for his research on project management and team leadership, he the recipient of the IEEE *Engineering Manager of the Year 2000 Award* and a Certified Project Management Professional, PMP.

Bertrand Venard is Professor of Management at ESSCA, a major French Graduate School of Management. He has a Doctorate in Management from the University of Paris Dauphine. Professor Venard has held various research positions at the Ecole Polytechnique in France, and the University of Cambridge and the London Business School in the UK. His current research interests are in organizational theory and services management, especially focusing on consulting, insurance, and tourism.

Kate Walsh is an assistant professor of management in the School of Hotel Administration at Cornell University. She received her Ph.D. from Boston College. Her research interests include examining intra and network-based organizational relationships, specifically those in the services industries. Currently, she is focusing on the role of organizational identity in service delivery.

Alberto Zanzi is an associate professor at Suffolk University Sawyer School of Management. He has a Ph.D. in Organizational Behavior from the University of Southern California and has been a practicing consultant for several years. His current areas of research include international business restructuring, managing family business, and political aspects of organizations.

Veronique Zardet is Professor of Management at the University of Lumiere Lyon 2 and co-manager of the ISEOR Research Center. She has co-authored books on socioeconomic management and change management, as well as many articles on hidden costs and performance in organizations.